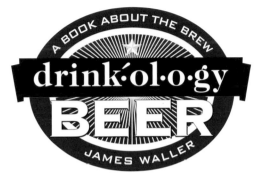

A BOOK ABOUT THE BREW

drink·ol·o·gy

BEER

JAMES WALLER

with contributions by
TONY MOORE

Editorial consulting by
DANIELLE CASAVANT

Illustrations by
GLENN WOLFF

stewart, tabori & chang

NEW YORK

For Mary O'Connor and Fritz Kenemer

Published in 2011 by Stewart, Tabori & Chang
An imprint of ABRAMS

Text copyright © 2011 by Thumb Print New York, Inc., with the
exceptions of the essays "Pent-Up Demand" and "Home Run,"
which are © 2011 by Tony Moore.

Illustrations copyright © 2011 by Glenn Wolff

Library of Congress Cataloging-in-Publication Data

Waller, James, 1953–
 Drinkology beer : a book about the brew / James Waller.
     p. cm.
Summary: "An informative reference about beer styles, touring breweries,
beer festivals, beer-cocktail recipes, and recipes for dishes made with
beer"— Provided by publisher.
 ISBN 978-1-58479-851-4 (hardback)
 1. Beer. 2. Brewing. 3. Cooking (Beer) 4. Cookbooks. I. Title.
 TP577.W246 2011
 663'.42—dc22

                                 2011008521

Editor: Kate Norment
Designer: Jay Anning, Thumb Print
Copy Editor: Ana Deboo
Production Manager: Ankur Ghosh

The text of this book was composed in Adobe Caslon.

Printed and bound in China
10 9 8 7 6 5 4 3 2 1

Stewart, Tabori & Chang books are available at special discounts when
purchased in quantity for premiums and promotions as well as fundraising
or educational use. Special editions can also be created to specification.
For details, contact specialsales@abramsbooks.com or the address below.

ABRAMS
THE ART OF BOOKS SINCE 1949

115 West 18th Street
New York, NY 10011
www.abramsbooks.com

Contents

Preface

BEER WAS THE FIRST ALCOHOLIC BEVERAGE I EVER DRANK. IN the German-American household in which I spent my formative years—I lived with my grandmother, two unmarried uncles, my divorced mother, and my little brother—beer flowed like the River Rhine. Children were occasionally allowed to sip from an adult's glass—mostly, I think, for the adults' diversion. Like most (though not all) children, I hated the stuff, and whenever I took a sip, I made my displeasure known with a scrunched-up face, a stuck-out tongue, and a loud declaration about how bad it tasted. This always made the adults laugh. (Adults are *so* easy to amuse.)

Let it be noted that, despite my dislike, I did keep trying.

The beer that flowed so endlessly and so freely in my grandmother's house was, for years and years, of a single brand: National Bohemian. "National Boh" was one of Baltimore's leading local brands; another was called American Beer. (Both brewers went out of business years ago, though the National brand has been revived by Pabst.) Just as some Americans in those days—the 1950s and early 1960s—drove only Chevrolets while others drove only Fords, Baltimoreans were divided into irreconcilable camps when it came to their city's brews: some people drank only National Boh; others drank nothing but American. When it came to beer, the drinkers in my family were committed National (Boh) leaguers.

My distaste for beer lasted only till adolescence. With puberty, a young man's body undergoes some radical alterations. Little noticed among that list of changes is a transformation of the taste buds: the previously unpalatable becomes, suddenly, tolerable—and potently desirable. By the time I was in my mid-teens, my mother had remarried, and she, my brother, and I were living in a ranch-style house in a distant suburb of Baltimore with her second husband, Rod. It will not surprise those of you who've had stepfathers to learn that Rod and I did *not* get along. Part of our trouble was ordinary Oedipal struggling, but the warfare between us was surely exacerbated by the era we were living through. My stepfather was a clean-cut, politically and religiously conservative Catholic; I was a long-haired hippie who trumpeted my atheism, carried around a paperback copy of *The Communist Manifesto,* and shouted "Sieg Heil!" whenever Rod expressed a reactionary opinion at the dinner table (which was frequently). He, in turn, referred to me as "the Animal."

"MR. BOH," THE ONE-EYED MASCOT FOR BALTIMORE'S NATIONAL BOHEMIAN BEER

But there were truces in the ongoing combat between Rod and me, and beer played an important role in calming the tensions. One of Rod's good qualities (in long retrospect, I do see that he had several) was his easygoing attitude toward booze. He certainly never encouraged me to get drunk, but he did sometimes invite me to have a beer with him. On those evenings, we'd crack open our cans of Miller (I think it was Miller) and settle down in the living room to watch TV together. I was flattered to be treated as the adult I so wanted to be. I especially remember the times we'd watch the sitcom *All in the Family*—a show that Rod and I equally if contradictorily enjoyed: I'd hoot at Archie Bunker's right-wing idiocies; Rod would bust his gut whenever Archie's pinko son-in-law, Mike (a.k.a. Meathead), was the butt of a joke. Peace—punctuated by laughter—briefly reigned between us.

At eighteen, I went away to college, where my relationship with intoxicants, including beer, grew more complicated. It was the early 1970s, and I and most of my college chums spent much of our time stoned, or drunk, or both. I'm not proud of my excesses, but I'm not about to be dishonest about them either. In the drink- and drug-saturated environment that was my college dorm, beer played a relatively minor role. Oh, we certainly liked to drink while smoking dope, but my friends and I generally opted for cheap, sweet wines rather than beer; when it came to pairing booze with marijuana, Mateus beat Miller, Boone's Farm beat Bud.

Still, a couple of beer-sodden memories do stand out. There was, for example, the evening following an oral exam for a philosophy course. I'd never taken such an exam before, and I was sure I'd perform disastrously. To calm my nerves, I laid in a six-pack of Budweiser, chilling it in ice I'd loaded into my dorm-room sink; it would be there, waiting for me and ready to help me drown my sorrows when the hour-long one-on-one session in my professor's office was through. (It somewhat astonishes me, now that I think about it, how very easy it was for me, a nineteen-year-old in a state where the legal drinking age was twenty-one, to get hold of a six-pack. But it was.)

Anyway, much to my surprise, the exam went well. It turned out that I *had* understood something about Kierkegaard and could even vaguely articulate what I knew. So instead of consoling me, that six-pack offered me a means of celebrating. I drank all six cans in rather rapid succession, then, reeling, went out with friends to eat at a local pizza parlor. And of course I spent the whole of the long, long night that followed throwing up.

I was, gradually, becoming acquainted with beer's various meanings: beer as a cultural marker and ensign of group identity, beer as a medium for peacemaking and fellowship (and, especially, for male bonding), and beer as a consoler and co-celebrant (a friend in whatever need one happens to be having). As time went on and I continued to drink, I grew familiar—as either participant or observer—with even more of beer's many purposes: beer as a stimulant for sexual desire and a catalyst for hooking up, beer as a spur to bad behavior, beer as an antidote to boredom, beer—icy cold beer—as one of the few genuinely satisfactory thirst-quenchers on a hot, hot summer day.

What I did *not* really learn, through all of this, was very much about beer's *taste*. Almost all the beers I drank throughout my early life were mass-produced American pilsners—Miller, Budweiser, Pabst, and the like—that were light on flavor even when they were not calorically "lite." There were occasional exceptions—but not many, since American pilsners so completely dominated the market back then. (They still do, of course, but the number of alternatives is now infinitely greater.)

And so it went. Through my mid-thirties, I continued to drink lots of beer without, however, particularly liking it. What I never realized, over those many years, was that the reason I didn't much like the taste of the beers I was drinking was because there wasn't, in fact, very much to like about their taste.

So I gave up beer drinking, more or less completely, when I was in my late thirties. I'd discovered whiskey. I'd discovered cocktails. I'd discovered wine. I'd discovered, in other words, that one could drink for both the effects *and* for the taste. Granted, I'd still have a beer occasionally—on one of those hot, hot summer days when only a crisp, cold lager will really do, or at a party where the only thing on offer besides beer was some really crappy wine.

Then, back in 2003, I was given the opportunity to write a cocktail guide. The result of my labors, *Drinkology: The Art and Science of the Cocktail,* sold surprisingly well, and my publisher invited me to follow it up with a book on wine. I began that book *(Drinkology WINE: A Guide to the Grape)* with trepidation. I liked wine, but I immediately realized that *I knew nothing about wine.* And who was I, anyhow (I asked myself), to be writing about wine in a world that already possessed a more than sufficient quantity of bona fide wine experts?

I conquered my fear (well, kinda sorta) only when I recognized that one could—*I* could—begin my research from the perspective of someone who *didn't* know anything about wine, and that the resulting book might be of some use to others who liked wine and wanted to know a little something about it but who were intimidated or simply bamboozled by most wine writing. I could, in other words, write a wine book that presupposed exactly zero knowledge of wine on the reader's part—the kind of book that I myself yearned for.

Two years ago, I proposed to my publisher that I write a book on beer. I'd become dimly aware that there was this thing going on in the culture at large—a phenomenon that was being referred to as the "craft beer movement" or the "beer renaissance." Of course, this movement/renaissance had been going on for about four decades, but, having long convinced myself that I didn't like beer and therefore wasn't interested in it, I'd paid it scant attention.

To my delight—and my fright—my publisher accepted the proposal: delight because I needed the cash; fright because I realized, going in, that I knew as little about beer as I'd known about wine when I'd begun work on my wine book. Correction: I knew *less* about beer. What's worse, I quickly discovered that beer, as a subject, is every bit as complicated as wine. Correction: It's *more* complicated. And what's even worse, I found that I was joining this movie in the middle. The world turned out to be every bit as soaked with knowledgeable beer lovers—credentialed and uncredentialed—as it is saturated with experts on wine. Perhaps worst of all, from a prospective beer-book writer's viewpoint, beer had already become "the new wine." Oh, dear Jesus. A culture of beer snobbery was spreading, like a culture of *E. coli* in a petri dish, across the agar-agar of our land. I didn't yet know that beer snobs are nicer than wine snobs, and so the intimidation I felt growing in my gut was, I began to notice, as paralyzing as the intimidation I'd experienced when setting out to write my book on wine.

There was, for me, only one possible way of overcoming that intimidation: I could admit my vast ignorance (consider it done!) and then proceed to write the book that, as someone who knew nothing about beer, I myself needed in order to begin to understand something—a little something—about the subject. And, as I went along, I could hope that my efforts would be helpful to others who are likewise interested in beer but humbled by their lack of knowledge. In this regard, part 2—which amounts to a dictionary of beer styles—is the core of this book, bringing together a diversity of basic information that I, when doing my research, felt I most sorely needed. This being a Drinkology book, it contains much that I hope you'll find engaging and fun, but part 2 amounts to a book-within-a-book that I dare think any beer neophyte will find useful.

And, finally, let me announce that I'm happy to be drinking beer again—and to have discovered, through my "diligent research," that there's lots and lots of beer out there that tastes just great.

—James Waller

ACKNOWLEDGMENTS

W HEN IT COMES TO BLESSINGS, MY BEER GLASS RUNNETH OVER. There are two people without whose assistance the making of this book would not have been possible. One is Danielle Casavant, who served—graciously, cheerfully, and always incredibly informatively—as *Drinkology Beer*'s editorial consultant. The other is Tony Moore, who contributed the book's insightful (and, I think, hilarious) sections on attending a beer festival and on home brewing. It has been nothing short of amazing to work with such intelligent, generous, and good-humored collaborators, and I can't thank either of them enough.

Next, let me express my great gratitude to Jay Anning, the book's designer, and to Glenn Wolff, the illustrator. The success of the Drinkology series is largely due to their beautiful work. I am also immensely grateful for the commitment of the Stewart, Tabori & Chang staff—especially publisher Leslie Stoker and my editor, Kate Norment—to *Drinkology Beer*'s publication. Their patience and understanding have been remarkable, and are deeply appreciated. A sincere tip of my hat goes to copy editor Ana Deboo, whose savvy fact-checking saved me from some grave errors.

Among those who supplied much-needed help at various stages of this book's creation were Mary O'Connor, Fritz Kenemer, Mary Edwardsen, Betsy Keller, Michael Ross, Amy Hughes, and Christine Sismondo—good friends all, and each deserving of a special thank-you. Rainer Sonderman provided much-needed guidance concerning the intricacies of Beer Pong. Al Sbordone has provided ongoing moral support throughout this project; thanks, Al.

Much of the early research for the book was performed at the Bobst Library of New York University; thanks go, especially, to Marvin Taylor, director of the Fales Library, which is housed in the Bobst building and which possesses an astoundingly rich collection of books and ephemera on food and foodways—including historical material on beer that I wouldn't have found elsewhere.

And, finally, let me shout out my undying gratitude (and undying love) to my life partner, companion, and soul mate, Jim O'Connor. How anyone ever manages to write a book without a steadfast spouse's steadfast support I simply do not know.

—James Waller
Lawrenceville, New Jersey
April 2011

PART 1

Basically Beer

I N THE BEGINNING WAS THE BEER.

In all probability, beer was the first beverage—besides mother's milk and, of course, plain water—that human beings ever drank. Our word *beer* probably derives, at some remove, from the Latin verb *bibere,* "to drink," which neatly illustrates the primacy of the relation between beer and human existence. For human beings, "to drink" means "to drink beer."

And it's meant that for an awfully long time.

BEER THROUGH A STRAW

Talk about a keg party. In 879 BC, Ashurnasirpal II, king of Assyria, threw a ten-day-long bash to celebrate the completion of his palace in the new Assyrian capital, Nimrud. Seventy thousand people came. (Ashurnasirpal invited only 69,574, but you've got to assume there were a certain number of crashers.) To feed the partygoers, the king did some grocery shopping—laying in a thousand cattle, a thousand calves, ten thousand sheep, fifteen thousand lambs, a thousand ducks, a thousand geese, and a multitude of other livestock, birds, and fish. To quench his guests' thirst, he placed an order for *ten thousand jars* of beer. (These were *not* small jars.) Now, Ashurnasirpal II was not really what you'd call a benign ruler. His reign was mostly marked by the merciless suppression of various revolts. But for those ten days, he was a very, very popular guy.

The city of Nimrud stood near the contemporary city of Mosul, Iraq—a spot better known, of late, for getting literally rather than figuratively bombed. But make another geographical note: this area of present-day Iraq sits nearly smack-dab in the center of the so-called Fertile Crescent. You remember the Fertile Crescent, yes? It's the scimitar-shaped swath of territory—stretching northeastward from the Nile Valley, in Egypt, and curving around through the area demarcated by the Tigris and Euphrates rivers until it reaches the Persian Gulf—that high school history textbooks tend to refer to as the "Cradle of Civilization." What those textbooks tend to leave out, however, is that the Cradle of Civilization was, in all probability, also the Birthplace of Beer. In fact, it was beer that rocked that cradle. And, by the time of Ashurnasirpal's housewarming party, it had been rocking it for several thousand years.

Beer rocked the cradle

We say that the Fertile Crescent was beer's birthplace "in all probability" because no one is really certain where beer was first made. It may even be that there was no "first" beer making—no singular beer-making event from which all subsequent beer making has descended. Instead, basic methods for making beer may have

A SUMERIAN BEER PARTY

been discovered independently at several—or even many—different locations over the course of thousands of years of prehistory.*

What we do know is that beer appears very early on in the written records of the first civilized societies—those of the Mesopotamian city-states (and, just a little later on, those of Egypt). In fact, it's fair to say that beer appears in the "record" even *before* the invention of writing. For example, a pictograph discovered at a Mesopotamian site called Tepe Gawra—and dating from around 4000 BC, hundreds of years before the first surviving written texts—depicts what scholars

---

* The theory that beer was discovered in different locales at different prehistorical times is lent credibility by the fact that many different cultures, in many places throughout the world, have created their own beerlike beverages.

are certain is a beer-drinking session. How do they know? Well, this little image shows two simplified human figures, one on either side of a large clay jar; two bent lines connect the figures' heads to the mouth of the jar. The whole setup looks almost exactly like later, historic Mesopotamian depictions of beer drinking, which show people sitting around big earthenware jars, sucking out the beer from inside these communal vessels through long *straws*.

Drinkology's mother always warned us about drinking beer through a straw—her hand-me-down theory being that you'd get drunk too quickly if you did. But, hey, Mom, the Mesopotamians drank *their* beer through straws. Originally, they used straws (made of reeds) because the straws prevented debris in the beer—the flotsam and jetsam of the brewing process—from reaching their mouths. But they continued to drink beer through straws even after they'd learned to filter it, and throughout ancient Mesopotamian history they continued to drink from communal jugs—giving such images the look of hookah parties.

We'll be mentioning various important moments in the history of beer making throughout this little book, but let us dwell on Before Christ–era brewing for a little while longer. The ancient Mesopotamians and Egyptians thought of beer as a gift from heaven (in this regard, they weren't all that different from Homer Simpson), and the Mesopotamians even had a goddess, name of Ninkasi, whose wonder-working portfolio specifically focused on gifting human beings with the divine beverage. One surviving early Sumerian text—the Sumerians being the makers of the first of the several great Mesopotamian cultures—is a hymn to Ninkasi, portraying her as setting down for humankind the step-by-step instructions for transforming barley into beer, which, in the words of the hymn, then pours out of Ninkasi's vat "like the onrush of the Tigris and Euphrates."*

What's interesting about the "Hymn to Ninkasi" isn't the hyperbole of its language. (All hymns to gods and goddesses are gushy.) It's that this song of praise isn't just a praise song; it's also a *recipe* for beer making and therefore revelatory of Sumerian brewing methods. For instance, one line of the hymn addresses Ninkasi as the one who "bakes the *bappir* in the big oven." What *bappir* is, it turns out, is a flat, hard, twice-baked loaf of bread that was used by the Mesopotamians for beer making. The Egyptians also made beer from bread that was baked specifically for brewing purposes,** and they also identified beer with a goddess (the cow-horned Hathor). This association of brewing with *female* deities is telling. Not only were ancient beer-makers often or even primarily female (as Egyptian figurines of brewers at work show), but the brewing of beer would, for millennia after its discovery, remain an activity performed mostly by women. If you've ever heard the English word *alewife* without being quite certain of its meaning, take

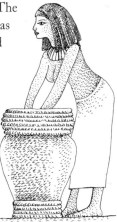

AN EGYPTIAN BEER MAKER

---

* The entire text of the "Hymn to Ninkasi," translated by Miguel Civil, can be read at www.piney.com/BabNinkasi.html.

** There's an echo of this practice in the method for making the traditional Russian low-alcohol beer called kvass, which is brewed from crumbled bread (usually rye bread; see pages 163–64).

note: an alewife is, or was, a woman responsible for brewing the beer for her community, and it's possible that alewifery—or its ancient equivalent—is actually "the oldest profession."

As old, perhaps, as the practice of human beings gathering in permanent settlements and raising their own food, which they may have done for the express purpose of *ensuring themselves an uninterrupted supply of beer*. Agriculture, of course, predates recorded history, so the reasons why people first abandoned the nomadic, hunting-and-gathering lifestyle in favor of tending crops—which required them to live together year-round in villages near their fields—remain mysterious. That said, it's clear that cereal grains—ancestral varieties of wheat, barley, and so on—were among the first plants to be domesticated. Now, cereal grains have to be cooked in some way to make their carbohydrates amenable to the human GI tract—their indigestible starches have to be converted to usable calories. One can do this by making porridge or, for a more culinarily interesting result, by baking bread or brewing beer. There's no scholarly consensus about which—bread or beer—came first. What's undeniable is that beer ranks among the first foods people made from grain. (An aside is needed here: The intoxicating *drink* we call beer is also a nutritious, carbohydrate-rich *food*—something that wasn't lost on the ancients. The Egyptian roughnecks who constructed the pyramids were, for example, sustained by the beer they received as payment for their labor.)

BECOMING HUMAN

It's been said that what *really* separates humans from other animals is—of all things—cooking. Animals (e.g., chimps, crows) use tools;

animals (e.g., gibbons, songbirds) produce sounds that, even if they don't rise to the level of language, are language-like in purpose. But we're the only creatures that don't eat all our food raw. And the ancient Mesopotamians seem to have recognized that cooked food—especially beer—is a marker dividing the human from the animal worlds.

If you happen to have read the Mesopotamian *Epic of Gilgamesh* in a college history or literature-survey class, you may recall one of the pivotal points in that ancient book's plot: the moment when the character called Enkidu becomes human. Enkidu, you may remember, has been **We cook; chimps don't** created by the gods to be a companion to Gilgamesh, the king of the Sumerian city of Uruk, whose deeds and derring-do the epic recounts. The problem is that when Enkidu is first deposited on earth, he's a "wild man"—he thinks he's an animal and spends his days in the fields and forests, romping with the local gazelles and taking his refreshment from their watering holes.

Hearing news of this strange creature's appearance in the countryside outside Uruk and wanting to capture him, Gilgamesh (who's not in on the gods' plan to provide him with a buddy) hires a practitioner of the *other* possibly oldest profession—a harlot named Shamhat—to go out from the city, set up camp in the place where Enkidu has been sighted, and entice him to hook up with her, which she dutifully does. After having great sex (for six days running), Enkidu begins to notice that he's not really a gazelle—a point underscored when his erstwhile friends the gazelles take one sniff of Enkidu's postcoital b.o. and promptly run away. In the words of the epic, Enkidu's "understanding had broadened."

But he's not yet quite fully human. For that transformation to be finalized, Enkidu—mightily hungry and thirsty after all those days in the sack—must eat human food and drink human drink. Shamhat therefore leads him off to a shepherds' encampment, conveniently located nearby, where the obliging shepherds present

FALSE AND TRUE

Before you read any further, there's something you've got to understand (if you don't already know it) about beer terminology. And this absolutely basic thing is that the word *beer*—as used in this book and as used, universally, by knowledgeable beer drinkers—is a general term covering both **ales** and **lagers**. The most fundamental distinction between styles of beer has to do with whether a particular beer is an ale or a lager—and that most basic difference involves the kind of yeast used to make it. You'll find much more info about ale yeasts versus lager yeasts on pages 21–25. For now, though, just get clear on this one thing: lager is a kind of beer, and ale is a kind of beer, too.

In other words, ale and beer are *not* two different things. If you're in the habit of thinking that they are, we beg you to break that habit right now. You are the victim of history—or, rather, you're the victim of a particular period of beer history, which stretched from the later nineteenth century until just several decades ago. During that time, a certain style of lager beer—the crisp, light-bodied, light-gold-colored style known as pilsner—grew so popular that it became synonymous with "beer" in popular parlance, which began to distinguish between "beer" (pilsner) and "ale" (not pilsner). (You can read much more about pilsner, and a bit of this history, beginning on page 151.) Brewing companies him with loaves of bread and *seven* jugs of beer. Enkidu eats the bread and is "sated." He drinks the beer and becomes "expansive" and "elated"; his face glows and he sings out with joy. Yeah, the bread's great. But the beer . . . the beer is something else. It's what makes Enkidu a *person*.

---

themselves adopted this lingo, sometimes advertising themselves as "makers of fine beers *and* ales." But the distinction is a false one.

We also want you to put out of your mind any preconceived ideas you might have about what ales and lagers are like. If you think, "Okay, I know the difference between an ale and a lager," but you *also* think, for instance, that lagers are lighter in color than ales, you're under a misconception. The words *ale* and *lager* both cover a multitude of styles. There are ales that are as light in color as pale lagers, and there are lagers that are nearly black.

And to continue with this tirade for just a few more sentences: If you happen to know that the word *lager* comes from the German *lagern,* meaning "to store," and if you also know that lagers are subjected to a period of cold storage (i.e., **lagered**) before being **released** (i.e., offered for sale and consumption), good for you. (And if you didn't know that, now you do.) But do *not* let this knowledge lead you to believe that this is an essential difference between lagers and ales. It's not. There are, in fact, several ale styles that are typically lagered before their release.

We know this is confusing. It used to confuse us. To dispel that confusion, just keep repeating to yourself, "Ales and lagers are both beers, and the difference between them has to do with the type of yeast used to make them," and you'll do just fine.

Simple Stuff?

So what *is* beer, anyway? On the very simplest level, beer is very simple stuff. It's easy to imagine how our ancient ancestors discovered beer making. And beer—all these thousands of years later—remains simple.

Sort of.

At its most basic, beer is *an alcoholic beverage made from fermented grain.* But that tidy definition is, in fact, too tidy. Human beings, you may have noticed, have a talent for making simple things complicated—and that's as true of beer as of anything else. So we'll begin our exploration of beer by expanding on that bottom-line definition. Take heed, however. As we expand the definition, things will become clearer, but they'll also become a little cloudier. That's because beer making, over brewing's long history, has changed. And there are now untold thousands of beers made in hundreds of ways that differ from one another—sometimes subtly, sometimes dramatically.

The Gang of Four

Most beer (that is, most of the beer of the past five hundred years or so) is made of just four ingredients—a kind of Gang of Four of brewing:

Grain

Water

Yeast

Hops

There. We've just expanded our original definition. So we've clarified things, right? Well, not quite, as we shall immediately see.

Nipped in the Bud

Let's look first at the first item on the ingredients list above: grain. As you already know, there are numerous varieties of the domesticated grasses we call grains. Some are widespread and familiar (wheat, rice, corn), others less so (spelt, sorghum, quinoa). Theoretically, beer might be made from any of them, but it generally isn't. Most beers are based on just one kind of grain: **barley**. And, yes, Drinkology can hear your objection. *But what about* wheat *beers and* rye *beers?* Well, here's the thing: even in beers named for other kinds of grain, barley is usually the predominant grain in the mix. Some reasons for barley's premier role are explained in the sidebar on pages 12–17. (And do note, if you haven't already, that we keep using words like "most" and "mostly" and "generally" and "usually"; that's because, when it comes to beer, there's almost always some exception to the general rule. Depending on your temperament, you'll either be fascinated or frustrated by this.)

So beer is made, first of all, from grain, and the grain from which most beers are mostly made is barley. True enough, but there's a crucial piece of information missing from the previous sentence. And that's that beer *isn't* made from barley per se; rather, it's made from barley **malt**—barley that has been processed in a particular way. You'll also find more on malt and the malting process in that sidebar on pages 12–17, but, in a nutshell, what happens is this: The barley kernels are moistened, which causes them to begin to sprout. (They are, after all, seeds, and sprouting is what they were put on earth to do.) Then, just as the little buggers are coming to life, they're bumped off—by being heated, which dries and (to a lesser or greater extent) roasts them.

Why go through the trouble of malting—of activating the barley kernels and then *de*activating them? It all has to do with what the yeasts that will ferment the beer do and do *not* like to eat. In their unmalted state, barley kernels are composed largely of starches—long, relatively complex organic compounds that yeasts find indigestible. When barley kernels begin to sprout, however, enzymes are produced that begin breaking down the starch molecules into

JOHN BARLEYCORN MUST DIE

For if you do but taste his blood,
  'Twill make your courage rise
  —"John Barleycorn" (Robert Burns version)

Many beer drinkers doubtless consider drinking beer to be a sacred experience, but the anonymous writers who penned the lyrics to the traditional English/Scottish ballad "John Barleycorn" took the idea of beer's sacredness to a whole 'nother level. The ballad, which exists in several versions (including one adapted in the eighteenth century by Scottish poet Robert Burns, lines from which are quoted above) and which was a standard of the British folk-music revival of the 1960s and '70s (recorded by Traffic, Jethro Tull, Steeleye Span, and Fairport Convention, among other groups), is a brutal allegory of the life, death, and resurrection of John Barleycorn—a Christlike personification of the barley plant. Poor John Barleycorn, a true man of sorrows, is subjected to multiple and violent ordeals by his human torturers— "wasted o'er a scorching flame," "crushed . . . between two stones," and heaved "into a darksome pit / with water to the brim"—and finally killed . . .

So that he might be reborn *as beer*. The ballad turns beer making into a kind of Passion of the Grist, and beer drinking into an Everyman's Eucharist.

simpler sugar molecules. The barley kernel's aim—if it can be said to have one—is to create an energy source that the germinating plant can readily use. The aim of the **maltster** (that's what a malt maker is called) is to jump-start that process but then to nip it in the bud, so to speak, thereby creating food for the yeast.

THE NAKED AND THE HULLED

While we're on the subject of religion: There's something about the barley–beer connection that could almost make one believe in Intelligent Design. One of the many cereal grasses domesticated by human beings, barley isn't very suitable for making bread (its kernels don't contain enough of the gluten that gives wheat breads their structure), but it is perfect for making beer. *Perfect.* Barley kernels aren't just rich in starches (the carbohydrate compounds that will be converted to sugar and ultimately to alcohol in the several stages of the beer-making process), but they're also **hulled**—enclosed in little husks, or skins, that help keep the individual grains of malted barley separate during that step in the brewing process called the *mash* (see pages 35–38), thereby aiding in the extraction of sugar from the malt. Wheat kernels, by contrast, are **"naked"** (hull-less) and therefore tend to stick to one another when wet, risking what's called a **stuck mash**, or **set mash** (in which too little sugar gets extracted from the grain to make a satisfactory beer). That's why it's extremely difficult to make a beer wholly from wheat and therefore why so-called wheat beers almost always contain a fair proportion of barley.

JOHN BARLEYCORN MUST DIE

Barley is grown in several varieties, which are distinguished by the arrangement of the kernels on the seed-head, or spike, of the barley stalk. It's important for you to know this only because you'll sometimes hear members of the beer-world cognoscenti speak of **two-row barley** (in which the kernels line up in two parallel rows) as opposed to **six-row barley** (in which the kernels are aligned in—that's right—*six* rows around the seed-head's spindle).* Both barleys are used in beer making, though European brewers and American craft-beer makers generally prefer the two-row variety, which is starchier and malts more easily.

THE PALE AND THE DARK

Which brings us, conveniently, to the topics of malting and malt. As we've indicated, raw barley can't be used to make beer—the complex starches must be converted to simpler sugars (simpler, that is, in terms of chemical structure) for fermentation to occur. And the malting process helps accomplish this. We can't, of course, know how prehistoric beer makers ever hit upon the necessity of malting their barley before brewing their beer. All we can do is be grateful that they did.

Malt making (which nowadays occurs in a building devoted to the purpose, called a **maltings**) is a three-step procedure:

First, the raw grain is **steeped**—soaked in water for a few days to bring the kernels to life. (You've probably planted seeds and then watered the soil, so you probably get the principle.)

Next, the grain is removed from its water bath and allowed to **sprout**. There are several sprouting techniques—one traditional method involves

---

* There are also *four-row* barleys, but these varieties aren't used in beer making. (Just in case you were wondering.)

spreading the moistened, germinating grain across a floor and raking it periodically to make sure the individual kernels get plenty of air and to prevent the little sprouts from becoming tangled.

And then—poor John Barleycorn!—the sprouting kernels are killed by being dried, usually in a **kiln**. (More about this part of the procedure in just a sec.)

The takeaway? The reason the little grains are brought to life is to induce them to begin producing enzymes that convert starches to sugars. They want to do this because they want to grow, and the sugars would give them the ready energy to do so. And the reason that we—John Barleycorn's merciless persecutors—murder them in such short order is because we don't want their germination to progress too far. We want, in other words, to preserve those sugars for our own purposes.

If you come to this book with any familiarity with beer making, you may know that there are many different kinds of malt, which are distinguished by their different colors (and by the flavors, subtler or stronger, that they impart to a brew). A malt's color—pale tan, bronze-ish, reddish, medium brown, or chocolaty dark—is partly determined by the temperature at which it's dried: lower kiln temperatures produce paler malts; higher temperatures, darker malts.

Knowing this, you might reasonably think, *So pale beers are made from pale malts and dark beers from dark malts, yes?* Reasonable, but wrong. In truth, pale malts predominate in the recipes of virtually all barley-based beers brewed today. They make up by far the largest proportion of grain in most beers' **grain bills**—a *grain bill* is the mix of barley malts and possibly other grains used in the making—and are therefore often referred to as **base malts**. Even an extremely dark beer like, say, Guinness Stout is *mostly* made from a pale base malt. And that's because paler malts are considerably higher in sugar content than dark-roasted malts. The easily extractable sugars in these base malts will be the primary fuel for fermentation.

Darker malts—which, by contrast, are often called **specialty malts**—contribute very low levels of fermentable sugar to the brew, and their purpose in modern brewing is mostly restricted to the contribution of signature colors and flavors to particular beer styles. (It wasn't, by the way, always this way; for a history lesson on the development of pale malt, see the entry on pale ales in part 2, pages 148–50.)

As you continue your exploration of beer, in this book and elsewhere, you're sure to encounter the names of various malts. To give you a leg up, here's a list of six important kinds—ranked in order of color from palest to darkest—and some brief notes on their characteristics and uses:

Pilsner malt. A very pale, sweet malt, pilsner malt is used in the pilsner style of lager (see pages 151–66) but also as the base malt for a wide variety of other beers.

Vienna malt. A somewhat darker malt with a toasty flavor, Vienna malt contributes an orangey-amber color to a brew. Used historically in the making of the Vienna style of lager (see page 199), it is also typically employed today in recipes for Märzen (Oktoberfest) lagers (see pages 142–44).

Munich malt. Darker than the two varieties above (but still relatively pale), Munich malt produces a sweet (sometimes caramel-like) flavor and a reddish color; it's often used in bock beers (see pages 88–92) and other darker lagers but can also play a role in dark ales such as porter (see pages 166–74).

Crystal malts (a.k.a. **caramel malts**). Crystal malts—we use the plural because they're available in a range of medium-brown colors that contribute a range of reddish to medium-brown shades to beer—are drum-roasted before being kiln-dried. This roasting caramelizes their sugars (hence the alias), rendering them unfermentable, which means that these sugars survive to sweeten the finished brew. Used in a variety of ales, crystal malts' flavor is often described as "toffeelike."

Chocolate malt. As its name implies, dark-roasted chocolate malt is (dark) chocolate brown in color—and may contribute a chocolaty or nutty taste to dark ales like porters and stouts (see pages 189–93). (Note, though, that it's made of *barley,* not cocoa.)

Black patent malt. An extremely dark—nearly black—malt used mostly to color very dark beers, black patent malt has to be employed judiciously or it might give the resulting beer a burnt flavor.

One final note about malt. When brewers use the word *malt,* they mean *malted barley.* Other grains used in brewing—wheat, rye—are sometimes malted, but *malt,* used by itself, always means barley.

More Than Medium

Next up: water. Believe it or not, people actually disagree about whether water should be listed as one of beer's ingredients. Those who say it shouldn't point out that the recipes for many foods—soup recipes, for example—don't include water in their ingredients lists even though water is essential to the foods' creation. The response to this argument by those who think water *should* appear on beer's ingredients list is, basically, WTF?

The latter faction is much more sensible. Beer, like any beverage, is mostly composed of water, but water isn't just beer's "medium." The character and quality of the water—especially its mineral content—can be critical factors in the success or otherwise of the brewing process, and they subtly influence the taste of the result. In fact, certain places—the English town of Burton-on-Trent comes immediately to mind—became famous because their water was particularly well suited for brewing certain kinds of beers. In part 2 of this book—which is devoted to specific beer styles—you'll find occasional mention of the importance of using certain kinds of water (especially "hard" or "soft" water) when making certain kinds of beer. For now, though, let's just note that the water *locally available* to a brewery is less critical nowadays than it was in centuries past, because brewers are now able to chemically alter their water to suit a particular beer style's requirements.

The Zesty Stuff

Etymology can be revealing. Case in point: the English word *yeast* is related to the ancient Greek word *zestos*, meaning "boiled." What's the connection? Well, yeast, when it finds its way into a sugary solution, causes a process that we call **fermentation**—and fermenting liquids look very much as if they're boiling. They froth and bubble and foam.

All that frothing and bubbling and foaming is the result of what one of the textbooks Drinkology consulted calls "the evolution of carbon dioxide during fermentation." Which is a polite way of saying that yeast, like every other living creature, produces certain by-products when it digests the food it eats—and, in the case of yeast, one of those is **carbon dioxide (CO_2)** gas. Yeast, in other words, is flatulent—*zestily* flatulent.

Ahem.

Of course, CO_2 isn't the only by-product of yeast's digestion. The other main by-product is alcohol, specifically **ethyl alcohol (C_2H_5OH)**—the kind of alcohol that produces an intoxicating effect when imbibed. This capacity of yeast to turn a sugary liquid into a boozy beverage has endeared it to human beings since before the beginning of recorded history. Yeast is essential to the creation of any sort of alcoholic drink—not just beer and wine, which are the more or less direct results of fermentation, but also of spirits, which are distilled from fermented liquids. (You'll find more on the use of beer in whiskey distillation on pages 182–83.)

The thing is, human beings used yeast (and loved what it did to

BUDDING YEAST

sugary liquids) for thousands of years *without having any idea what yeast actually is.* What it is, as we now know, is a single-celled microorganism, specifically a fungus, that, in the presence of a suitably sugary food source, reproduces *very rapidly,* often through a process known as **budding**, in which a "daughter" cell forms at the perimeter of a "mother" cell and then breaks away, shortly becoming the mother of its own daughters. Lots of yeast = lots of eating and digesting of sugar = fermentation.

None of this was known, however, until the nineteenth century, when the redoubtable French scientist Louis Pasteur, involved in research aimed at preventing spoilage of beer and wine, identified yeast as the living agent of fermentation. So here's the question: How could human beings have successfully used yeast for thousands of years without having any knowledge of what it actually is? The answer is pretty simple: Yeasts are *everywhere*—untold gazillions of yeast cells are swimming around in the air and are always on the lookout, so to speak, for something sweet to eat. That is, fermentation happens naturally, and human beings recognized the process and adapted and controlled it for their own purposes long, long before the development of modern biological science. There's more about yeast and its critical role in beer making in the sidebar on pages 21–28, but let us mention here that certain beers, even today, remain dependent on the activity of **wild yeasts**—those that float around in the ambient atmosphere, and that were responsible for the fermenting of beer for millennia before people learned to **cultivate** them (i.e., grow specific strains of yeast for specific purposes).

PITCH BY PITCH

Drinkology is like most people—or most drinkers, at any rate. We thank the Dear Lord above for having bestowed upon us the gift of yeast. But, frankly, we're not too terrifically interested in the whys and hows and whats and whens of yeast's miraculous transformation of barley (or whatever) into booze. Too science-y. Too boring. Too hard, when it comes right down to it, *to understand.*

To begin to grasp yeast's role in beer's creation, however, one really has no choice but to dip one's toe into that science-y stuff. Here, then—with advance apologies, to readers of a more technical persuasion, for everything we're leaving out—is what we've decided one must, at a minimum, know about yeast in beer making:

Number one: although hundreds of species of yeast have been identified and described by science (and it's estimated that there are thousands more species that remain unidentified), only a very few kinds are used to make beer. To give you their nonscientific names first, these are **ale yeasts**, **lager yeasts**, and the group sometimes referred to as **wild yeasts**.

THEY'RE THE TOP

Ale yeasts are, as you've no doubt sensibly assumed, used in the making of ales. Ale yeasts have been used in beer making since forever, although, as we've explained, people didn't know what yeast is or how it does what it does until about 150 years ago. What people *did* know was that as beer fermented, a foamy, icky, crusty-looking layer formed on the surface of the brew. And they figured out that they could skim off some of that foam, add it to the next batch they wanted to brew, and get a similar result.

This tendency of ale yeast to form a foamy mass on top of the beer as fermentation nears its end is one of its defining characteristics. It's why ale yeasts are often referred to as **top-fermenting yeasts** (or **top-cropping yeasts**). The widely used term *top fermenting* is, however, misleading. The fermentation process actually occurs *in suspension* in the brew. It's only when the ale yeast cells have eaten all the sugar they can eat that they go into a dormant state, begin to clump together—the technical term is **flocculate**—and rise to the surface.*

There are hundreds, maybe thousands, of different **strains** of ale yeast, but they all belong to a single species, whose scientific name is *Saccharomyces cerevisiae*—which Drinkology thinks is a very nice name, given that it means "sugar-eating beer maker." Interestingly, this is the very same species of yeast used in making bread, but bread-making strains of *S. cerevisiae* (baker's yeast) produce more CO_2 and much less alcohol than the beer-making strains (**brewer's yeast****) and are unsuited to brewing. We'll say more about yeast strains in a bit, but let's first take

---

* Actually, *top fermenting* is *also* a misleading descriptor of ale yeast in that some strains of ale yeast do *not* flocculate and rise to the top of the brew! But let's not go there. The intricacies of beer making are unending, and there are only so many contradictions one can be expected to hold in one's noggin at once.

** You've undoubtedly seen jars of brewer's yeast in the vitamins/supplements section of your local health-food store or pharmacy. Perhaps you've even used it as a dietary supplement yourself. Brewer's yeast is indeed *brewer's* yeast—a dried form of *S. cerevisiae.* The yeast contains some essential minerals (chromium, selenium), lots of B vitamins (except for B_{12}), and protein, and there's evidence it can be helpful in the control of diabetes and high cholesterol and that it may even have value as an adjunct in weight-loss regimens. (But note that Drinkology is not an MD and is not writing you a prescription.)

a quick glance at lager yeast, whose behavior contrasts with that of ale yeast in a defining way.

SWIM AND SINK

One of the chief differences between ale yeasts and lager yeasts—which we probably don't need to say are used in the making of lager beers—has to do with what happens to the yeast cells as fermentation nears completion. Like ale yeast cells, cells of lager yeasts float around in suspension in the fermenting brew, chowing down and having lots of kids, and then, when they've eaten their fill, they also grow dormant and begin clumping together, or flocculating. But lager yeast clumps don't rise to the top of the tank or vat—they *sink to the bottom*, which is why lager yeasts are referred to as **bottom-fermenting** or **bottom-cropping yeasts**. (Again, the term *bottom fermenting*, though widely used, is kind of inaccurate.)

Although ale yeasts have been employed in brewing for thousands of years, lager yeasts are relative newcomers on the beer-making scene. The place and time that lager yeasts were first "discovered" and used to ferment beer are obscure, but beer historians think it's probable that they first appeared in southern Germany (Bavaria) five hundred or so years ago. And people who study such things also seem to think that their appearance was a biological accident fostered by Bavarian beer-making practices. In other words, lager yeast *evolved* to adapt to the conditions in Bavarian brewhouses.

Which conditions were, in a word, *cold*. As you'll find mentioned several times throughout this book, beer making in temperate climates was, historically, usually a cool- and cold-weather activity, because brewing during the summer risked the beer's spoiling. Nevertheless, *ale* yeasts do require a certain degree of warmth to do their job; ales are generally fermented at a temperature somewhere between about 60 and 75 degrees Fahrenheit. If it gets much cooler, ale fermentation slows to a standstill. Well, what some (unknown, probably Bavarian) brewers discovered, about half a millennium ago, was that their beers *would* ferment at significantly lower temperatures than usual—in the range of 45 to 55 degrees Fahrenheit. We don't really know how this discovery took place—nobody recorded it. We surmise, however, that those hypothetical first lager brewers found that (1) this was awfully convenient for cold-weather brewing, (2) this kind of fermentation worked differently—it was slower and the yeasty gunk sank to the bottom of the tank rather than rising—and (3) the resulting beer looked and tasted different from what they were used to making and drinking. It was clearer and drier (less sweet), *and* it improved, becoming even more clear* and dry after being stored in a (cold) cellar for a period following fermentation.

Because the cold storage of beer in cellars was common practice in Bavaria, and because *lagern* is the German word meaning "to store," these new "bottom fermenting" beers eventually became known as *lagers* and the yeasts that create them as *lager yeasts.*

Or, anyhow, this is the story as Drinkology vaguely pieces it together. What we can't quite parse is the scientific stuff about lager yeasts that we've read (or *tried* to read). Some sources classify lager yeasts as belonging to a separate species from ale yeasts. (The scientific name given to this purportedly distinct species has changed over time, from *Saccharomyces carlsbergensis* to *Saccharomyces pastorianus,* although we've also seen such yeast called *Saccharomyces uvarum.* Sheesh.) Other sources,

---

* Note that *clear,* as used here, does not mean "pale," but rather "translucent." The first lagers were dark beers (there are still dark lagers today), and truly pale beers wouldn't be created until the invention of a method for making pale malt (see pages 148–49).

though, say that lager yeasts and ale yeasts belong to the same species—good old *S. cerevisiae*—although they diverge greatly in their behavior and their influence on beers' character. You will, we're afraid, have to look elsewhere for help in sorting this one out. Good luck.

THE WILD ONES

Most beers, ales and lagers alike, are fermented under rather strictly controlled conditions, with brewers using only a certain strain of yeast to ferment this or that sort of beer and taking precautions aimed at preventing other, unwanted microbes—yeasts and bacteria—from **contaminating** the brew and causing it to go sour and smell nasty. There are, however, a small number of beers (the best known of which are Belgian lambics) whose brewers demonstrate a very different attitude toward fermentation, a kind of "let the microbes fall where they may" kind of attitude. These brewers don't **pitch** their yeasts—they don't **inoculate** their brews with specific yeast strains bred to produce specific, predictable results. (Note those bolded terms, both of which denote the intentional introduction of yeast into the brew.) Instead, these seemingly renegade brewers—who are actually following extremely ancient practice—just let whatever's in the fermenting tank's environment infect their brew. And, yeah, the resulting beers are sour and a bit funky—and they like them that way. (And you might, too.)

Actually, if you read the information on lambics (pages 136–42) and sour beer (pages 185–87), you'll see that this kind of fermentation process—referred to as **spontaneous fermentation**—isn't really as devil-may-care as we've snarkily made it out to be. The environments in which traditional spontaneously fermented beers are fermented are controlled in a de facto way, insofar as the brewhouses have been in existence for a long time and the varieties of yeasts invisibly infesting those structures have been hanging around, doing their thing again and again, for centuries. These so-called wild yeasts are therefore somewhat domesticated, in the way that a cat that lives in a barn is somewhat domesticated.

The several species of wild yeasts that play the major role in the fermentation of lambic and other sour beers are sometimes called **Brett yeasts**, because they belong to a genus of yeasts called *Brettanomyces.*

A YEAST TASTE TEST

Yeast isn't merely a biomachine for converting sugar into hooch. The kind of yeast used to brew a beer also has an influence—profound or subtle—on that beer's flavor. On the most basic level, ales and lagers generally taste different because ale yeasts and lager yeasts behave differently. Lager yeasts are able to eat more of the sugar in a wort (unfermented beer) than are ale yeasts—are able, in brewers' jargon, to achieve a higher **attenuation**—which means that lagers, as a class, are drier (less sweet) than ales, as a class. And, besides being sweeter, ales are also generally more *complexly* flavored than lagers—and this distinction, too, has partly to do with the difference between the yeasts. You don't need to know the organic chemistry behind ale yeasts' production, during fermentation, of flavor compounds like **diacetyl** and various **phenols** and **esters**; suffice it to say that ale yeasts, because they ferment beer at higher temperatures than lager yeasts do, produce an array of flavor compounds that lager yeasts do not, or not in such sizable amounts.

The array of different flavors that different strains of yeast add to a beer is extremely wide, ranging from pleasant tastes like apple, butterscotch, pear, pineapple, plum, and prune to undesirable ones like paint thinner, rotten eggs, and a diversity of bitter, "medicinal" tastes. Achieving a desirable yeast-induced flavor or group of flavors for a given style of beer isn't just a function of choosing the right strain, however. The amount of yeast pitched, the temperature at which fermentation occurs, and the length of the fermentation also must enter into brewers' calculations to ensure that they end up with flavors they want rather than **off tastes** or other flavors that, though not inherently bad, are not appropriate to a given beer style.

If you have trouble imagining the differences that can result from using one strain of yeast rather than another to ferment a given style of beer, you might want to perform this taste test: Get hold of two bottles of wheat ale in the style called Hefeweizen or Hefeweiss (the two names, which in German mean "yeast wheat" and "yeast white," respectively, are synonymous; see pages 120–21)—but *make sure* that one of these is from a German brewer and the other is from an American craft brewer. The beers, when poured, are likely to look similar: golden in color, cloudy (because they're unfiltered), with fat, persistent heads. But in all likelihood the German-made beer will carry a set of "phenolic" flavors—banana, clove—that the American version will be missing. And this divergence has simply to do with the fact that German brewers use specialized "wheat yeasts" (sometimes classified as variants of *S. cerevisiae* but sometimes identified as a separate species) to make these beers, while American brewers generally don't, and instead aim for a more neutral taste that they believe American drinkers prefer.

Enough about yeast? Probably more than enough, though you might also want to know that strains of yeast differ not only in their flavoring potential (and in their degrees of flocculation and attenuation) but also, and importantly, in their tolerance for alcohol. Yeasts convert sugar to alcohol, yes, but the alcohol they make eventually kills them. But, as with people, some yeast strains hold their liquor better than others—and thus a brewer's choice about which strain to use for a given beer can be related to the strength of the beer the brewer wants to make, too. Twenty-two percent alcohol by volume in the fermenting tank stands as the outer limit of the alcohol level any brewer's yeast can survive, though the cells of most strains perish at lower levels.

In Pursuit of Hoppiness

Now we come to the last member of our Gang of Four, hops. And we're going to begin by saying something paradoxical, if not wholly contradictory: Hops are both essential to most beers' flavor, *and* they are inessential to beer making per se. To understand how this paradox can hold, you've got to understand a little about what hops do to beer and a little about their place in beer-making history.

Let's start with what hops do. Hops— which are the female flowers of a vinelike herb—help preserve beer. They contain anti-bacterial compounds that help prevent spoilage during fermentation and afterward. But they are essential to the flavor because they are also the primary "bittering" and "spicing" agent in most beers. Not only do they provide a characteristic bitterness, but they also impart a difficult-to-put-into-words taste and aroma that we indelibly associate with beer. Apart from the bitterness, hops' flavor is variously described as "piney" or "citrusy" or "grassy"—but, really, they don't quite taste like anything else. And you're unlikely to encounter that distinctive flavor elsewhere, because hops aren't used for much else *besides* making beer.

But hops are simultaneously *inessential* to beer making because one can brew without them. In fact, for thousands of years of beer-making history (and prehistory), hops weren't used. The first records of the plant's cultivation date from the eighth century AD. It's not until 1079 that we have any documentation of their being added to beer (this was in Germany), and it wasn't till the sixteenth and seventeenth centuries that their use in beer making spread beyond Germany, ultimately becoming more or less universal. Note that qualification, *more or less.* It may surprise you to learn that, even today, there are beers made without hops (see, for example, the information on gruit ales, pages 116–18). That qualification aside, however, the use of hops in beer has for the last several centuries been so nearly ubiquitous that hops (despite being inessential) are typically counted among beer's essential ingredients.

For more on hops, see the sidebar on pages 30–34. For now, though, it's important that you remember just a few things. Hops have a preservative function; they "bitter" beer, offsetting the sweetness of the malted grain and "balancing" the flavor; and they "spice" beer, providing the unique taste/aroma that, over the past several centuries, beer drinkers have come to expect from most beers.

Going to the Hop, Hop, Hop . . .

Hophead used to be slang for "heroin addict," but the word's meaning has morphed. Now, *hophead* is more likely to designate (or self-designate) somebody who's "addicted" to the bitterness, taste, and smell of hops, and who likes his (well, usually but not always *his*) beers to be as hoppy as can be. In some quarters, *hophead* has become a marker of a cocky, strutting, beer-chugging masculinity. Which is sort of odd when you consider that hops are the delicate little chartreuse-green flowers of the *female* hop plant.

Those flowers—flower *clusters,* actually—are also referred to as **strobiles**, or **umbels**, or **seed cones** (and they do look a bit like miniature pinecones). The plant they come from (Latin name *Humulus lupulus*) is a "climbing" herb. It can reach twenty-five or thirty feet in length as it stretches along the string or wire that supports its sunward climb in a typical hop garden, or **hop yard**. The hop plant is related, actually, to the *Cannabis* genus of herbs, and hops do have a mildly sedative effect (though, sorry, no mind-altering THC). And although they are very occasionally used as an ingredient in other things (e.g., some shampoos), the plant is cultivated *almost* exclusively for its flowers' use in beer.

Hops aren't all that widely grown. Their cultivation is mostly concentrated in a few areas of the world. Among others, these include the adjacent regions of Bavaria (in Germany) and Bohemia (in the Czech Republic), where hops were first used in brewing, as well as the county of Kent in southeastern England and the American states of Washington, Oregon, and Idaho. There are scores of cultivars, or varieties—some ancient, some recently introduced—and this or that variety is usually associated, at least historically, with a particular hop-growing region. The famous variety called **Fuggle** (rhymes with *bugle*), for example, is of nineteenth-century English origin; the varieties called

Cascade and **Chinook** (introduced in 1972 and 1985, respectively) are, as their names might tell you, associated with America's Pacific Northwest. If you're looking to style yourself as a beer geek, you'll want to know that several older hops varieties originating (and still grown) in Bavaria/Bohemia are often referred to as the **noble hops**, which strikes Drinkology's ear as Euro-snooty. (The noble hops are, BTW, used chiefly to enhance aroma.)

A given beer's **hop character**—the degree and quality of the hoppiness it manifests on the nose and tongue—is determined by a complex set of variables, including the variety or varieties of hops used in making it, the form of hops used, and the points in the brewing process at which they are added. (The amount used is, unsurprisingly, also important, especially in determining beer's bitterness.) Unless you intend to brew some beer of your own, however, you don't need to know too much about all these factors and their interaction, so the following synopsis is highly simplified.

Some varieties of hops are better for bittering beer (these contain higher amounts of compounds called **alpha acids**); others are better for imparting a hoppy taste and/or aroma (these have higher amounts of what are called **beta acids**); and some are "general [or dual] purpose," good for both bittering and flavoring. Unless dried, hops lose their essence very quickly after being picked, so the hops (of whatever variety) used in brewing are generally dried, not fresh. (But **fresh hops**, also called **wet hops**, *are* used to create some seasonal beers called harvest ales; see pages 119–20.)

Hops are dried in kilns in buildings called **oasts**—which we mention only because (1) *oast* is an unusual word and knowing it will improve your vocabulary, and (2) the historic oasts of England, many with

Rapunzelishly tall conical towers that served as flues for the kilns inside, are nifty-looking buildings. Nowadays, dried hops are available in several forms: as whole flowers, as "leaf" hops (piles of individual flower petals), in a liquefied form called **hops extract**, and as **pelletized hops**.

Drinkology was at first shocked to learn that many brewers—including craft brewers—use the pelletized form, in which the hops have been ground up and squashed into little lumps that resemble dry cat food (but greenish). We mean, the pellets just look so industrial and unnatural. It turns out, though, that pelletized hops aren't just easier to handle and (because they're compressed) easier to store—they also provide a more predictable result.

Bittering hops (also called **boiling hops**) are typically added at or near the beginning of the time the brew begins to boil (for information on this part of the brewing process, see pages 38–40). By contrast, flavoring hops—**finishing hops** is the brewer's term—are added late in the boil (during the last half hour), and if hops are being used

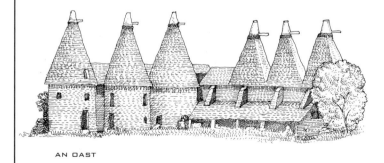

AN OAST

specifically to enhance aroma, these are added *very* late in the boil (within the last few minutes). Hops' essential oils—their flavoring compounds and aromatizing compounds—are fragile and volatile, so the amount of time that flavor/aroma hops spend in the boil must be limited lest the heat destroy those chemicals or they just evaporate away. Some beers are given an extra dose of aroma-enhancing hops later on, either during fermentation or even later, when the finished beer is maturing. This late addition is called **dry hopping**, though no one has been able to explain to Drinkology why this procedure, which involves dumping something into a liquid, is called "dry."

You might also want to know—because you're sure to encounter the term—that certain beers are made with **aged dried hops**, which impart little bitterness and no hops flavor or aroma to a brew and whose sole purpose is preservative. The "hop character" of beers employing only aged dried hops—e.g., the sour Belgian ales called lambics (see pages 136–42)—is nil.

As your experience as a beer drinker widens, you may find yourself becoming able to discriminate among the various hop varieties used in various beers. These subtleties of taste and aroma are likely to be imperceptible to most neophytes—who will probably sense only how bitter a beer is (or isn't) and how "hoppy" it tastes and smells (or doesn't). If you want to study up on hops, however, there are plenty of densely informative Web pages listing varieties of hops, their respective alpha- and beta-acid content, their flavor/aroma characteristics ("woody," "earthy," "spicy," "fruity," and so on and so on), and the differing ways they're typically employed in brewing. To get some idea of how nuanced these matters can be, have a look at the hops guides published on the BeerAdvocate.com and ratebeer.com websites.

GOING TO THE HOP, HOP, HOP . . .

Finally—and just because we find it interesting—we'll tell you something a brewery tour guide told us. The word *hop*, meaning a "party for social dancing" (as in the "sock hops" that helped define early rock-'n'-roll culture) is, according to that tour guide's telling, related to the word *hop*, meaning the hop plant. How so? Well, in the days before mechanized farming, the picking of hops was an incredibly labor-intensive enterprise, and hops growers relied on hordes of migrant laborers—whole troops of families who'd arrive at the farm in late summer or early fall, stay on for the weeks of harvest, then depart. Such workers were often working-class city folk, and their annual sojourn in the country, though it involved backbreaking work, was also a vacation from their usual urban misery, so it put them in a partying mood. They'd gather in the evenings for drinking and dancing, and these seasonal get-togethers came to be called *hops*. Drinkology hasn't, we admit, been able to independently verify this derivation. But it's a nice story, so . . . so what?

FIRST MASH, THEN BOIL, THEN . . .

If you've gotten this far, and especially if you've read the sidebars—on barley, malt, yeast, and hops—to which you've been directed, you've already learned quite a bit about how beer is made. Now it's time to put those pieces together (and to add a few more) to provide a general, simplified overview of the beer-making process. Those words *general* and *simplified* can't be stressed strongly enough, however. Brewing methods differ considerably depending on the style of beer being made (such particularities are frequently mentioned in the entries explaining various beer styles in part 2 of this book); they also differ from brewery to brewery—with large brewing operations using sophisticated equipment that's sometimes a far cry from the apparatus you might find in your local brewpub. Rather than concentrating overmuch on the technological dimensions of brewing (though some mention of technology is unavoidable), this discussion focuses on the *purpose* of each beer-making step and, along the way, introduces you to some of the beer-making terminology you're likely to encounter most frequently.

THE MASH

Before brewing can begin, the malt must be crushed. Though few if any breweries maintain their own malting operations, many do mill the grain on site. The grain isn't pulverized into meal or flour—it's *cracked*, loosening the hulls from the kernels and breaking the kernels into pieces that can be mashed more efficiently. The **mash**—the first step in the brewing process per se—is a *steeping* of the crushed grain in hot water, aimed at releasing the grain's sugars, color, and flavors and thereby creating a liquid that can be turned into beer.

Hot and wet

At commercial breweries, the crushed grain is fed into a large vessel called the **mash tun** (the unusual word *tun*, of ancient origin, is today used almost exclusively in brewing), where it is combined with hot water to make a porridge-like mixture. In that hot, wet environment, the enzymes in the malt—which, as you'll recall from the discussion on malting (pages 14–17), were produced by the germinating grain—are reactivated. As they wake up, the enzymes begin doing what Nature intended them to do: breaking down the long, complex starch molecules stored in the grain into the shorter, simpler chemical snippets called sugars. The technical term for this process is **saccharification**—or, simply put, "sugar making."

There are several different mashing techniques, with which you may want to have at least a passing familiarity. In the simplest, called an **infusion mash** (or **single infusion mash**), the mixture— itself referred to as *the mash*—is kept at a constant temperature, in the neighborhood of 150 degrees Fahrenheit. But there's a common variation on the infusion mash—one in which the temperature of the water-grain mixture is raised to a certain level, kept at that level for a certain amount of time, and then raised again, paused again, and raised again. This is known as a **step infusion mash**, and each of the temperature pauses, or plateaus, is called a **rest**. Depending on the kind of malt used, a step infusion can be more efficient than simple infusion for a biochemical reason: some of the enzymes in the malt do their best work at lower (but warm) temperatures, some at higher temperatures, so a step-by-step heating of the mash, in which the mash is allowed to "rest" at a given temperature before the heat is raised again, can produce a better result.*

Note, please, that the mash is *never* brought to a boil. Or, to put that more accurately, the *whole* mash (the *entire* water-grain mixture) is not allowed to boil, because boiling causes enzymatic activity to cease. However—and you knew there was a *however*

---

* Beer geeks, God bless them, will find this explanation incomplete, recognizing that one of the rests of a step infusion mash occurs at a temperature best suited for enzymes that break down proteins (not starches) in the grain. This destruction of proteins is desirable for most beers, since proteins can give a finished beer a cloudy or hazy appearance.

coming, because there's always a *however* coming when it comes to beer—there is a third mashing technique in which a *portion* of the mash is removed from the tun, boiled in a separate vessel, and then returned to the main mash. The boiled portion is called a **decoction**, and this kind of mash is called a **decoction mash**. And because the procedure can be done once, twice, or even three times before the mash is completed, there are **single decoction mashes**, **double decoction mashes**, and, yes, even **triple decoction mashes**. Removing part of the mash and boiling it can have several benefits, one of which is to assist in the breakdown of starches into sugars—allowing the enzymes in the main mash to do their thing more efficiently when the boiled portion is added back in. If you think about it, you'll also see that multiple decoctions have an effect that's similar, temperature-wise, to that of a step infusion. Each time a portion of the mash is boiled and then returned to the tun, the temperature of the whole mash rises.

There is always a *however*

The mash generally lasts from one to two hours, after which it's necessary to separate the solids (known as the **spent grain**) from the liquid. If you were doing something like this in your kitchen, you'd use a colander or strainer—and that, in fact, is akin to what brewers do. Except, of course, they have their own peculiar word for this straining procedure: **lautering**. Sometimes, the lautering is performed in the same vessel as the mash (in such a case, the mash tun is outfitted with a false bottom; when its slots are revealed or opened, the liquid runs through and the solids remain behind, with the settled barley husks acting as a filter to remove many smaller particulates). Sometimes, though, the mash mixture is transferred to another vessel, known as a **lauter tun**, specifically designed for this purpose. (It will, for example, have mechanical rakes that stir the grain as the liquid runs through it.) And to make sure that every bit of extracted sugar makes it into the strained liquid, the spent grain is rinsed with hot water—a procedure that brewers (who have their own peculiar words for *everything*) call **sparging**.

And, of course, there's also a word for the liquid that runs out from the lauter (or mash) tun—and it's a very important beer-making term. It's called the **wort**[*] (or, sometimes, the **sweet wort**, because it is very sweet—almost sticky sweet, in fact[**]). You might think of wort as beer-before-it's-beer.

THE BOIL

Now comes the *brewing* part of brewing: the **boil**, in which the wort is cooked. The wort is transferred to a vessel called the **brewkettle**[†] (or simply the **kettle**—or, sometimes, the **cooking tun**), where it is boiled for a period of time that, depending on the beer, may range

---

[*] Every other beer book will tell you that *wort* is pronounced "wert" (rhymes with "dirt"), and Drinkology has little doubt that that is the proper pronunciation. But we will also tell you that, listening to American home brewers and brewery tour guides, we have only ever heard it pronounced "wart" (as in that unsightly blemish you might have removed by the dermatologist). So we conclude . . . that you may pronounce the word whichever way you like.

[**] Note that, depending on the beer being brewed and the kinds of malts in the mash, not all of the sugars in the wort will be fermentable sugars. Many ales contain relatively high amounts of nonfermentable sugars—sugars that yeast can't eat. These will therefore survive fermentation, producing a sweeter, more carbohydrate-laden beer.

[†] Brewkettles as one likes to imagine them are large, gleaming copper cauldrons, and, in fact, such traditional-looking kettles are used at many microbreweries and

from 50 minutes to two hours. Cooking serves several purposes, including sterilizing the wort and concentrating it; this is also the stage during which the hops (and, in the case of some beers, other flavorings) are added. As you learned in the sidebar on hops (pages 30–34), beers are often hopped in several "installments" over the course of the boil: near the beginning (for bittering) and then again once or twice very near the boil's end (for "finishing"—flavoring and aromatizing—the brew).

At the end of the boil, the hops and other particulates in the wort are separated out, sometimes by passing the wort through a hop filter but often through a mechanical process called **whirl-pooling**, which may occur in the kettle itself or in a separate vessel designed for the purpose. Whirlpooling sends all the little pieces of unwanted stuff—collectively called the **trub**‡—spinning into the center of the vessel, where it agglomerates into a solid cone. (But note that *trub* also has another meaning, touched on in the discussion of maturation/conditioning, below.)

Trub-free, the cooked wort is almost ready to move to the fermentation tank—but first it must be cooled to fermentation

---

craft breweries. Modern versions are heated by steam that flows through a jacket enveloping an inner vessel within the kettle, allowing for a much more even boil than could be achieved through the application of direct heat and preventing the scorching—and hot-spot caramelization of sugars—that can result when a kettle is set directly above a flame. Larger brewing operations may, however, use a more elaborate apparatus, called an **external boiler**, in which the wort is pumped, again and again, through long heated tubes, called **calandria**. This technology, which Drinkology cannot pretend to understand, is employed to improve control of temperature and evaporation rates and to shorten boiling times.

‡ Pronounced either *troob* or *truhb*. Again, you decide.

temperature. Ideally, this cooling will be accomplished very quickly, the aim being to get fermentation started as soon as possible so that other microbes will have no opportunity to infect the wort before the yeast is able to begin its work. The rapid cooling is often achieved by passing the wort through a device called a **heat exchanger**. There are a number of different heat-exchange technologies, but the principle is fairly easy to grasp: hot and cold liquids are passed closely alongside one another, with the hot liquid becoming cooler and the cold liquid becoming warmer in the process.

FERMENTATION

And now the wort, having been cooled, arrives at the fermentation tank—or **fermenter**, as it's sometimes termed—where the yeast will be "pitched" and the wort will gradually, through the yeast's action, turn into beer. We've already said quite a lot about fermentation in the section on yeast and the accompanying sidebar (pages 18–20 and 21–28, respectively); let us remind you here that the wort is sometimes given an extra addition of hops (called a "dry hopping") during fermentation to boost aroma and, also, that ales and lagers are fermented at different temperatures. There's also a time differential, with ales fermenting considerably faster (about a week or perhaps a bit longer) than lagers (two or more weeks).

Fermentation tanks can be large, rectangular, metal-sided (or, more rarely, wooden) pools with open tops; these are called **open fermenters**, and the process **open fermentation**, even though the rooms enclosing them are generally sealed off as carefully as possible from the external environment. **Closed fermentation**, by contrast, occurs in—that's right—a **closed fermenter** (which is a tall, stainless-steel cylinder, sometimes having a domed cap in which the CO_2 gathers and from which it's released, as the pressure builds, through a valve). Nowadays, the latter method is much more common, largely because the risk of contamination is so much lower; still, many craft brewers of ales adhere to open fermentation, convinced that this older method contributes to the complexity of their beers' flavors.

And then, when the activity of the yeast has more or less completely ceased, and fermentation is done, you've got . . . well, you've finally got beer. Beer, that is, of a sort. At this stage, beer is referred to as **green beer**—"green" in the sense of immature. It's nearly totally flat (most of the carbon dioxide having escaped), it's cloudy, and it wouldn't taste very good if you were to drink it at this moment.

MATURATION/CONDITIONING

And speaking of this moment: this is the moment, dear reader, when Drinkology loses any hope of being able in simple and concise terms to convey to you *what happens next*. That's because the ways in which green beer may be **matured**, or **conditioned**—the terms are almost, if not quite, interchangeable—vary so greatly from brewery to brewery, beer to beer. So you'll have to accept a quick and superficial account, whose only virtue is that it's less jumbled than what you might read elsewhere.

Before the green beer is removed from the fermenting tank, the suspended solids are allowed to settle; often, this sedimentation of the **trub** is accelerated by chilling the beer to a near-freezing temperature. (Note, here, the second meaning of *trub*, which we promised you a while back; here, *trub* means the residue, including dead yeast cells, that's left over after fermentation.) Once the trub has been removed from the fermenter—or the beer has been taken off the trub by being **racked** (i.e., siphoned) into another vessel, it may undergo a **secondary fermentation**. This secondary fermentation, gentler than the first, reinvigorates the beer—and this may be the point when the beer is dry hopped (since the hullabaloo of the primary fermentation could destroy the fragile compounds that impart hops' aromas to the beer) or when fruit or other flavorings are added.

And then . . . well . . .

All that one can say *in general* is that the beer will be matured/conditioned *in some way*. It has to be allowed to sit for a time, which has the effect of clarifying the liquid (as whatever solid matter remains suspended in the brew sediments out) and of allowing flavors and aromas to develop. And it has to, somehow, get carbonated, which can happen either artificially (it is pumped into a tank and topped with a layer of CO_2 gas, which the beer absorbs) or through a natural conditioning process. To give just one example of the latter, in the case of **bottle-conditioned beers**, the beer is given a small extra dose of yeast and sugar before bottling; then the bottles are kept for a time in a warm environment to encourage in-bottle fermentation, naturally carbonating the beer.

And it's likely that the beer will undergo other treatments during the period between the end of fermentation and the time it's kegged, bottled, or canned. It will, for instance, probably be **filtered**. (Though some beers are never filtered—as is true, for example, of **cask-conditioned ales**, which are racked directly into keglike containers and allowed to develop on their own, with residual live yeast acting on residual fermentable sugars to produce, over time, a low level of carbonation.) And, depending on the beer, it might be **pasteurized** (briefly heated to stop microbial activity) to lengthen its shelf life. It might be **clarified** through the use of some **fining agent** (a substance that adheres to particulates suspended in the brew, causing them to settle—fining being a way of speeding up the sedimentation that would otherwise happen more slowly).

And so on and so on. The possibilities and permutations, if not quite infinite in number, are certainly hugely diverse, and the particular route a beer takes after fermentation has to do not only with the style of beer being made but also the proclivities of the brewer, the quality of the beer, and the size and speed of the beer-making operation.

There are, however, a couple of takeaways for you in all this. Better beers are carbonated naturally—through some secondary fermentation process—rather than through the artificial introduction of CO_2 into the finished brew. And, in general, beers are better—more complexly flavorful, that is—if they are unpasteurized and if filtration is kept to a minimum, since such interventions tend to strip away tastes and aromas.

THE BEER TOURIST

If you want to get a real, down-'n'-dirty grasp on how beer is made, the best thing you can do is probably to try your hand—and luck!—at brewing your own (see pages 302–27). Next best is to go on a tour of a commercial brewing operation—which ever-dutiful Drinkology did several times while researching this book.

A word of warning to the prospective beer tourist, however: much of what happens at a brewery is, from a visual perspective, boring. That's because what happens there mostly occurs in big, closed containers of various sizes and sorts—all usually possessed of a certain austere beauty and of a certain, usually metallic, anonymity. On a brewery tour, you'll see the mash tun, the lauter tun, fermenting tanks, conditioning tanks, etc. You'll see pipes snaking from one tank to another. You'll see dials and gauges and hoses. If the brewery employs open fermentation and if a batch of beer is being fermented while you're there, you may be permitted to look through a window (large or small) into the room where the wort in the open tank is frothing and foaming its way to becoming beer. You will *not* be allowed inside the fermentation room, basically because what you are (on the microbiological level) is a big sack of bacteria-riddled juice whose mere presence in the room might contaminate the batch.

There's one area of the brewery that may—if you get to see it—provide a greater degree of visual entertainment: the bottling area. *If* bottling is happening while you're at the brewery (smaller craft breweries don't generally bottle every day), and *if* they let you into the bottling room (which not every brewery will), it can be great fun to witness the bottling line running—all that sanitizing and filling and capping and labeling and casing of the bottles, and their crowded, push-and-shove movement as they're tracked from one station to the next along the line. Even jaded Drinkology finds it mesmerizing.

ACTOR, EMCEE, HERDSMAN

Your brewery tour guide will most probably be a young or youngish man (there must be some women who do this, but Drinkology, in our admittedly limited experience, has not encountered a female brewery tour guide). This young or youngish man will have a passion for brewing of a magnitude that only a young or youngish man could muster. He will (you'll get the feeling) have discovered the meaning of life, or a large dollop of that meaning, in beer making and beer drinking. Remind yourself that enthusiasm is a desirable trait in tour guides, and you'll be fine with this.

Some guides are, of course, more skillful than others. The best brewery guide Drinkology met while researching this book was a young/youngish man, name of Josh, who led Drinkology and a few dozen other folks (including a tour-bus contingent) on a spin through the Dogfish Head Brewery in Milton, Delaware, just a few miles inland from the resort town of Rehoboth Beach.

What set Josh apart from the general lot was his showmanship. A talented actor, emcee, and herdsman, he delivered an impeccably memorized spiel, ad-libbed amusingly, invited and responded to questions with aplomb, and managed **Visual aids** politely, rapidly, and without incident to goad this sizeable group into moving from one area of the brewery to another. Moreover, Josh was equipped with a strong and clear voice—a real asset in a brewery's acoustically challenged environment.

Kudos aside, however, the tour Josh gave was very similar in structure and content to the other brewery tours Drinkology has taken. The guide inevitably begins with a history of the brewery, then moves on to brief explanations of the several stages in the brewing process as he (or perhaps she?) guides the group from one area to the next. Almost invariably, the guide will, early in the tour, produce visual aids: jars filled with barley malt (of several varieties and shades of roasted darkness) and with hops pellets for the tour group to pass around and examine.

As you go along, various pieces of equipment (tanks, mostly) get pointed at, named, and explained. Cautions about watching your step—and instructions to put on, and then to remove, safety goggles—are delivered. And the guide will typically punctuate the patter by reminding the guidees that a beer-tasting awaits them at the tour's end—as if this promise were the only thing that might make the tour itself endurable. Which is a sentiment that, after several such tours, Drinkology has a certain sympathy with.

A FEW FIELD NOTES

Some breweries are sparkling neat and spanking clean, others less so. One rural brewery we went to had a cat that resided—very contentedly, it seemed—in the bottling room, which made Drinkology a little nervous about dander wafting its way into the brew, but we may be overly fastidious.

The distinctive smell of a brewery bears mentioning. If you don't particularly like beer—or if you despise strong, slightly rotten smells of any sort—you may find this unavoidable olfactory dimension of the experience off-putting. For our part, Drinkology finds the deeply, richly organic odor that permeates a brewery's atmosphere comforting and reassuring.

Some breweries charge a nominal amount for their tours and tastings; others don't. Do note, when you're planning a brewery tour, that some breweries require that you go to their website to reserve a spot. *Do this,* even if it's not the tourist season and you think nobody else could possibly show up. Drinkology and company didn't make reservations for the Dogfish Head tour, which we took late on a Saturday afternoon in *mid-February*, for God's sake, and we arrived to find the joint so mobbed that we almost didn't get in. (Ever resourceful, we did make it—by pretending that we were members of the aforementioned tour-bus group!)

THE MONEY SHOT

As you will by then have been promised multiple times, you'll end the tour at the brewery's tasting bar. (At some breweries, you may also begin the tour with some samples from the bar, but you'll still end up back there at tour's end.) This segment is any brewery tour's "money shot" in two ways: (1) It's what you've been waiting for. And (2) the tasting-bar area will contain a gift shop, where you'll be encouraged to relinquish your hard-earned simoleons on brewery-branded T-shirts, baseball caps, beer glasses, and all manner of other stuff.

Don't expect a spit bucket

At the tasting bar, you'll generally be offered samples of four to six of the brewery's beers, with the tour guide (or perhaps the bartender) explaining each in turn. Sometimes the beer's on tap, sometimes it's poured from bottles, and we've found that the amount dispensed differs from place to place—anywhere from about two ounces to about four ounces per sample cup.

If you don't want to drink all of each sample that's poured—either because you don't like a particular beer or because you're driving and don't want to catch a buzz—you've got a problem. The protocol at brewery tasting bars differs from that at wineries. Wineries' bars are always set with a series of "spit buckets" at intervals along the counter, and, in fact, it's common practice among wine tasters to sniff, taste, and, without swallowing, spit the wine into the bucket, dumping whatever's left in the glass into the bucket, too. One gets the strong feeling that, in beer culture, such a practice might be considered effete if not downright candy-assed. Only one of the breweries we visited (Dogfish Head) even had a spit bucket on the bar—which the tour guide derisively referred to as the "Bucket of Shame." (Drinkology used it, proudly.) At another brewery, where we were virtually the only people at the tasting bar, the bartender insisted on pouring full four-ounce samples of each beer despite our repeated protestations that we only wanted a sip of each. In short, at most tasting bars, you'll either have to drink up or furtively find someplace to set down or dump your unfinished samples.

Of course, you may well *want* to drink up, and here we finally come to the real reason to keep on visiting breweries—or at least their tasting bars—time and time again. During the tasting, not only will you learn something about each of the brewery's products as the tour guide or bartender explains the ingredients and brewing method used in each, but you'll get to sample that brewery's beers at their very freshest and, presumably, best. (This, obviously, is also a reason to buy beers you like from the brewery's own shop.)

How to Be a Beer Geek

Looked at from one angle, beer making is cooking. An elaborate kind of cooking, but cooking nonetheless. And an *ancient* kind of cooking—one that human beings have performed since . . . well, ever since we began to cook, which was long, long before the development of anything we might recognize as modern science. Let's call this the *primitive* take on beer making and note that this "primitive" perspective has a parallel when it comes to drinking beer. For "primitive" beer drinkers—a group to which Drinkology definitely and unashamedly belongs—drinking beer is *sensory pleasure,* and we primitives tend to be fairly imprecise and colloquial in the terms we use to characterize the experience. Beers' colors are golden or red or black; the tastes are sweet or dry, malty or hoppy; the potencies are weak or moderate or strong.

But there's a whole 'nother angle from which beer making can be viewed and beer drinking approached: the *scientific* angle. This perspective, developed over the past couple of centuries of scientific brewing, views the process as a set of mathematically determined procedures and carefully calibrated techniques for achieving predictable outcomes—a very important consideration for the commercial brewer. For scientifically minded beer *drinkers*—let's call them **beer geeks**, which is what they sometimes call themselves— the experience of drinking beer, though it may be quite enjoyable, is much more intellectual and analytic. And the terms they use to describe beers—scientific terms of measurement borrowed from the jargon of the modern brewhouse—fall like Greek on the barbarous and uncomprehending ears of us primitives.

Of course, there's some overlap between these perspectives and these groups. If you're a primitive who gets it into your head to brew your own beer, you're going to have to learn about at least some of the terms the geeks so casually bandy about. And some of that geekishness is going to rub off on you. But even if you've no desire whatsoever to try your hand at brewing—you might merely want, say, to read beer literature with something resembling comprehension—it might be a good idea to have an elementary grasp of the terminology.

Yes, you can can. Beer, that is. And (some) people will drink it.

The commercial canning of food began in the early decades of the nineteenth century, but another hundred-plus years were to pass before beer and other carbonated beverages were successfully canned. The technical obstacles to creating a workable beer can were formidable. With an ordinary food can—whether it's holding pineapple chunks or lumpfish caviar—the pressures inside and outside the can are more or less equal. A beer can has a much tougher job of containment to do, because the CO_2 dissolved in the beer exerts an outward pressure of about 80 pounds per square inch (psi). Given that ordinary atmospheric pressure at sea level is a little under 15 psi, that's an awful lot of force for a can's walls to have to hold in check.

The risk of explosion wasn't the only problem the beer can's inventors faced. Beer reacts chemically with metal—especially the tinplate steel that was used for most canning before the mid-twentieth century. A successful beer can—one that wouldn't ruin the beer's taste—would therefore have to incorporate some sort of nonreactive lining to prevent the beer from coming into contact with the metal. But the technical challenges weren't the only hurdles slowing the beer can's development. There was also the not-inconsequential question of whether beer drinkers—long accustomed to draft and bottled beer—would accept the new packaging.

Can makers had been working on ways to solve the technical issues since the first decade of the twentieth century. Then, in 1920, Prohibition went into effect, squelching any and all beer-related innovation. By the early 1930s, however, it was apparent that Prohibition was a social, economic, and law-enforcement disaster, and the tinkerers at the American Can Company, anticipating its repeal, restarted their tinkering. By 1933, they had created a strong-enough can; now all they needed was a customer. The Gottfried Krueger Brewing Company proved willing to take the plunge, but only after American Can sweetened the deal by paying the cost of installing canning equipment at Krueger's Newark, New Jersey, brewery.

And so in the summer of 1934, just six months after Prohibition ended, Krueger was test-marketing its product, sending out four cans each of Krueger's Finest Beer to a thousand beer drinkers in Richmond, Virginia. The consumers' verdict was a very enthusiastic thumbs-up: 91 percent reported liking the canned beer. Maybe after thirteen years without a (legal) drop of full-strength beer, those people would've chugged—and liked—just about anything. But whatever the reason for their overwhelming approval, the beer can had been successfully birthed. In January 1935, Krueger began marketing its canned beer to Richmond's general public. (In the meantime, Union Carbide had developed a reasonably effective coating for the cans' interiors: a plastic substance called Vinylite, which American Can adopted, advertising its beer cans as "keglined.")

Canned beer caught on quick. By the end of 1935, at least thirty-seven breweries in the United States were producing it. In 1936, a brewer in Great Britain—the Felinfoel Brewery Company of Llanelli, Wales—began selling beer in cans, and by 1937 twenty-two British breweries had followed suit.

FLAT TOP VERSUS CONEHEAD

The cans in which Krueger's Finest first appeared in Richmond were **flat tops**. To open one, you had to pierce the smooth metal top with a metal punch. American Can, recognizing that this necessity could pose a problem for potential customers, came swiftly to the rescue by inventing the now-familiar **church key**: a cleverly dual-purpose steel tool with one pointy, triangular end—for puncturing those newfangled cans—and a curving, pronged end for lifting the caps off those oldfangled beer bottles.

Not all beer makers, however, were eager to leap on the beer-can bandwagon, because there was a substantial financial downside. Flat-top canning operations couldn't be run on breweries' existing bottling lines, and many makers simply couldn't afford to buy and install the new canning equipment.

The cost-saving solution? A can that could be capped like a bottle. The brilliant if ungainly design for what came to be known as the **cone-top can** (a.k.a. the **cap-sealed can**) was first developed by Continental Can Company. Because cone tops could be filled and sealed on the bottling lines that were already in place, dozens of breweries—mostly smaller companies, but including a few of the major beer makers—opted for the cap-sealing method. There were, by the way, several different types of cone-top cans, the most ostentatious of which was an especially high-necked can, called the **Crowntainer**, made by the Crown Cork & Seal Company and used by many brewers.

To the modern eye, all the cone-top cans look bizarre—more like old-fashioned containers for motor oil or shaving cream than like things that might have been used for beer. So it's surprising to learn that they stayed on the scene, in competition with the flat-tops, for two-plus decades. One major brewer, the Joseph Schlitz Brewing Company, continued to use them for "the beer that made Milwaukee famous" into the 1950s.

PULL AWAY VERSUS POP 'N' STAY

Production of beer cans all but ceased in Britain and America during World War II because of the need for metal for war matériel, though limited quantities of canned beer continued to be made for shipment to

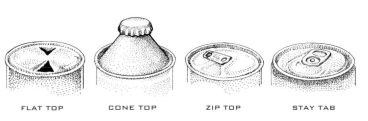

FLAT TOP   CONE TOP   ZIP TOP   STAY TAB

BEER-CAN EVOLUTION

military units. (Bottle makers' fortunes therefore briefly rebounded. War always makes *somebody* richer.) But cans returned to the consumer scene immediately following the war and continued to grow in popularity—not just in the United States and Britain but eventually around the world.

During this period, as smaller brewers went under or were gobbled up by the bigger fish—and as surviving breweries invested in new equipment—the cone-top can was gradually supplanted by the flat-top model. By 1960, the conehead was dead. But that hardly marked the end of the beer can's transformations.

The flat-top can, remember, had always been burdened by a certain inconvenience: you had to have a special tool to open it. Ever since the flat-top's introduction, people who dream about such things had dreamed of a **self-opening beer can**. That holy grail was finally attained in the early '60s, when a Dayton, Ohio, tool-and-die manufacturer named Ermal Fraze invented the **pull-tab can**. Legend has it that Fraze's determination to engineer a better beer can was fueled by an all-too-common experience. He found himself at a picnic with a cooler full of nicely chilled canned brewskis but no church key to open the god-damned things with.

The engineering riddle posed by the self-opening can was a hard one to crack. Fraze knew that the outline of the opening could be scored into the top's metal surface, but the depth of the cut had to be carefully calibrated: deep enough for the scored tab to be easily pulled away by a person of ordinary strength, but not so deep that the pressure inside the can would simply blow the thing off. There had to be some built-in finger-grip device on the tab, enabling the would-be drinker to pry it up. And the resulting aperture had to be of an elongated shape, so that the drinker's mouth wouldn't create a vacuum by covering the whole hole.

As Fraze's pull-tab can, which he perfected in 1962, demonstrates, Americans used to be a very ingenious people. The hole left when the tab is removed is keyhole shaped, wider toward the bottom and narrowing to a slit near the top, providing just enough of an airway to let the beer flow out easily. The finger-grip is a ring connected to the tab and secured to the can top by a rivet that, until broken, is an integral part of the top's surface.

By the time Fraze had his eureka moment, aluminum had replaced tinplate steel as the material from which beer cans were made, and Fraze sold the rights to his invention to the aluminum giant Alcoa. Alcoa, in turn, persuaded Pittsburgh's Iron City Brewing Company to give the self-opening cans a try. Good decision. Iron City's sales increased 233 percent within a year. Did the other beer makers notice? Yes, indeedy, and by 1965 three-fourths of American brewers were using these **zip-top cans** (as Madison Avenue christened them).

As elegant as Fraze's invention was, though, it wasn't perfect. The zip-top pull tabs had sharp edges. People sometimes cut themselves when opening the cans. People sometimes dropped the tabs into the opened cans, then swallowed them (occasionally choking to death) when the tabs floated back out as the beer was being drunk. And people, cretinous litterbugs that they are, also tended to discard the tabs wherever they were drinking—a habit that led to many injured feet at beaches. A *better* better beer can was obviously needed.

That new and improved model arrived in 1975, in the form of the **stay-tab can**, which was introduced by the Falls City Brewery in Louisville, Kentucky. It has gone on to become the standard design for carbonated-beverage cans worldwide. The name says it all: a stay-tab can's tab *stays* attached to the can when opened, because the finger-ring acts as a lever, pushing it downward, into the opening. We all know how this works, of course, and we all know that it doesn't always work perfectly. (Note to can makers: Keep trying.)

A Coda on Soda, Etc.

There is *lots* more to know about carbonated beverage cans. For instance, there's the significant role in can-design development played by the soda companies (although the beer industry has more often taken the lead role in can innovation). There are the other ways in which cans have evolved—such as the industry-wide changeover from three-piece cans (top, body, bottom) to today's two-piece cans (in which the body is a mechanically extruded cup to which the top is attached). There are all the various sizes of cans (they differ from country to country) and the various shapes (the Japanese have been especially creative in devising shapes that diverge from the Euclidean cylindrical). There are the little plastic spheres, called **widgets**, that are placed inside the cans of some Irish and British beers (especially stouts) and whose purpose is to increase the creaminess of the head when the beer is poured.

And there are the ways in which cans themselves are packaged—including the ubiquitous and notorious plastic **six-pack rings**, widely disparaged by environmentalists for strangling marine wildlife. (Untold millions of six-pack rings—along with all other manner of human-made junk—do end up at sea, of course, but the rings' ecological villainy is minor compared to the damage caused to fish, birds, and marine mammals by some of that other stuff.)

And *then* there are the graphic elements—logos, slogans, images, advertising copy—printed on the cans. One reason, not mentioned above, that cans were, from the start, such an attractive packaging option for the beer companies that adopted them was that cans can carry much more promotional information than the labels pasted on bottles. Now, seventy-five years after their debut, beer cans collectively capture quite a swath of modern graphic design and advertising history. And that— combined with their variability in size and shape, their portability, the rarity of certain cans, and, of course, their intimate connection with an emotionally fulfilling activity (drinking, that is)—is what makes beer cans *collectible.*

But none of this—beer cans' history, variety, mode of manufacture, collectibility—touches, really, on the can-related issue that's likely to be of the most consuming interest (pun intended) to the beer drinker: *Does the can affect the beer's taste?* (And, if so, how?)

On this question, the jury's out—and will likely remain so. On the one hand, it seems indisputable that, back in the old days, canning *was* at least somewhat detrimental to a beer's taste. On the other, with the arrival of new can-liner materials—today's aluminum beverage cans are coated inside with an ultra-thin layer of nonreactive glass polymer— the chance of any chemical interaction between the beer and the metal dwindles to near zero. *But,* on the third (?) hand, there are and always will be drinkers who insist that they can taste metal when drinking from cans and who will always and forever prefer bottled beer.

Part of their distaste may be physiological. It seems that certain people are just more receptive than others to the—for them, unpleasant—taste of metal. (Interestingly, there are also those who claim to be able to taste metal and who actually like it.) But the reasons for the anti-can bias are also psychological or, maybe, sociological. Some people simply consider it more decent, or urbane, or civilized to drink bottled or draft beer—associating canned-beer drinking with tailgating louts, drunkenly delinquent youth, and other unsavory types. A variation on that prejudice—if that's the right word—is voiced by some others, who identify canned beer with "crap beer."

It is true, certainly, that until very recently, almost all American canned beer was of the mass-produced kind. But since the early 2000s, there's been a countertrend among at least some craft brewers, who've decided that today's beverage-can technology is plenty good enough to protect their products' flavor—and who've realized that canning is key to expanding their markets, since so many of the public places where beer is sold and drunk (sports arenas, beaches, airplanes) ban bottles. (New Belgium Brewery, of Fort Collins, Colorado, is among the better-known craft brewers to have made the leap to cans for at least some of its products, including its signature Fat Tire Amber Ale.)

Moreover, there's even an argument to be made for contemporary cans' superiority to bottles in at least one respect. Since light is one of beer's enemies—it accelerates the rate at which beer grows stale—and since cans, unlike bottles (no matter how dark the glass they're made from), are light-tight, cans may be better than bottles at preserving the freshness of the brew. Of course, that's a logic that will probably be lost on most of cans' cultured despisers. For better or worse, matters of taste always boil down to . . . matters of taste.

Let's start with a term you're going to encounter in virtually any beer-related book, article, website, or blog you might look at: **original gravity**, or **OG**. To put it in the simplest possible terms, original gravity is a measurement of the *specific gravity*, or *density*, of wort before fermentation begins. If you're like Drinkology,

Archimedes was of a geekish bent

who remembers dramatic historical happenstances with ease but is hopeless at understanding abstract scientific formulations, you might recall the story of Archimedes, the ancient Greek scientist who discovered the principle of specific gravity while taking a bath at his home in Syracuse, Sicily, where he was in the employ of the local tyrant. Climbing into that deliciously full tub, Archimedes noticed that (1) his body sank in the water and (2) as it sank, it displaced some of the water, sending it splashing onto the bathing chamber's floor. Now, most of us, when having such a not-uncommon experience, would start worrying about having to mop up. But Archimedes was of a more geekish bent. He immediately perceived that the amount of water displaced had to do with the relative density of his body as compared to the density of the bathwater—and he immediately made the connection between this phenomenon and a physics problem that the king, his employer, had recently asked him to solve (which we won't go into here because we're already wasting too much space on good old Archimedes). Anyway, thrilled by his sudden insight, Archimedes leapt from his tub and ran, naked and presumably dripping, through the streets of Syracuse, shouting "Eureka! Eureka!" ("I've found it! I've found it!").

So, here's the thing. In the millennia following Archimedes' streaking episode, scientists came to realize that the principle he discovered could be applied to the measurement of the density of *solutions.* Dissolving various substances in water creates liquids that are denser or less dense than plain water, and scientists developed instruments for measuring these relative densities. What this has to do with beer making is actually pretty simple. Wort is basically a solution of sugar in water, which is denser than water itself. The more sugar in the wort, the higher its value on a specific-gravity scale that assigns a base value of 1 to plain water. Remember, here, that sugar is what yeast eat and, in doing so, convert to alcohol (and CO_2). By using an instrument, called a **hydrometer**, to calculate the *original* specific gravity of wort (its density *before* fermentation), you can gain a rough* idea of the alcohol content that the beer will have after fermentation. Perhaps obviously: the higher the wort's original gravity, the higher the alcohol content of the beer will be. The OG generally ranges from about 1.020 to about 1.160; to get some idea of what this range means in terms of density/sugar content, compare the OG of wort to that of honey—an extremely dense and sweet liquid—which is generally in the neighborhood of 1.400 to 1.450.

A much more precise estimate of alcohol content, by the way, can be derived by taking a gravity reading at the *end* of fermentation—this is called the **final gravity (FG)** or sometimes the **terminal gravity (TG)**—and then comparing it to the OG reading. We don't need to go into the math (which we don't understand!), but let's just say that (1) a beer's FG is always lower than its wort's OG because alcohol is less dense than water, and (2) because the rates at which yeast convert sugar to alcohol and carbon dioxide are known, a "simple" (though not to Drinkology!) equation can be used to calculate alcohol content

---

* Other factors, including, for example, the ability of a given strain of yeast to eat all the sugar in the wort, will play a role in determining final alcohol content.

once you've taken both the original and the final readings. You might, by the way, be interested to know that brewers generally take gravity readings throughout fermentation to make sure that the conversion of sugar to alcohol is occurring at the expected rate.

(And here, FYI, are a couple of other BTWs: *Original gravity* is sometimes termed **original extract**, or **OE**, because it is, in fact, a measure of the *extract*—the sugar that's been extracted from the grain—in the wort. Also, you might want to know that there are other systems besides the one just described for measuring wort's sugar content. One that you might see mention of is the **degrees Plato [°P]** scale,* which measures the amount of sugar in the wort by weight, with 1°P being equivalent to 1 percent sugar by weight. The only reason for knowing this, really, is that you might find some Eastern European beers that are identified by their rank on the degrees-Plato scale. The higher the number of degrees Plato, the stronger the beer.)

Are you feeling geekish yet? Maybe just a little? What Drinkology finds fascinating—because we don't really understand the reason for the phenomenon—is that some hard-core beer geeks tend to speak of a beer's strength by referring to its original gravity rather than the much more common (and more easily graspable) measure of **alcohol by volume**, or **ABV**. We've the feeling, though, that such people like tossing around OG numbers *simply because* the hoi polloi (i.e., the rest of us) will have no idea what they're talking about. Such tendencies make us nervous.

---

* The name of this scale has nothing to do with the Greek philosopher Plato; it was named for a nineteenth-century German scientist with the improbable name of Fritz Plato.

Yet we tremblingly soldier on. Another way in which beer is scientifically measured—and different beers are scientifically distinguished—has to do with color. For people of a geekly persuasion, the problem with ordinary color descriptions is that they're inherently inexact because different people perceive colors—and name the colors they perceive—differently. One person might see a certain ale as red, while another sees it as more amber, or more brown. *Why* this is problematic we're not quite sure, but we imagine it has to do with brewers' need to produce beer that, within a given category or brand,

Why is this a problem?

is exactly the same color from batch to batch to batch, since color is such an important component of a beer consumer's experience of his or her beloved brew.

Anyhow, there are various systems of beer color measurement (or, rather, of measuring a beer color's *value*—its relative lightness or darkness when compared to the colors of other beers). If you hear a beer geek nattering about a beer's **lovibond degree**, or its position on either the **Standard Reference Method (SRM)** or **European Brewing Convention (EBC)** scale, you know (now) that it's the beer's color that's being referred to. The numbers assigned to the various color values differ from system to system, but the systems are similar in that they all assign higher numbers to darker beers. If you're interested in polishing your GQ (geek quotient) in this area, you can find out more about these systems on the Internet.

Next up: bitterness. Beer makers have, of course, come up with a system—or, rather, several systems—for measuring bitterness, which is *mostly* (we'll come back to this qualification shortly) a function of the amount of hops added to a brew. The system you're most likely to encounter mention of is the one that gauges bitterness according to **International Bittering Units**, or **IBUs**. A measure of 1 IBU means that a chemical called isohumulone, a bitter-tasting acid found in hops, is present in a beer in a ratio of 1 part per million. In general, it's true that more hops = a higher IBU count = a more bitter beer. A relatively sweet style of beer, like a porter (see pages 166–74), may weigh in at between 20 and 40 IBUs; an extremely bitter beer, like an American "imperial" India pale ale (see pages 121–28), might have an IBU count of well over 100. But here's the qualification we spoke of a moment ago: a beer's IBU count does

A copy, but not a twin

not *necessarily* indicate how bitter it will taste on the tongue. That's because the sweetness of malt competes with, and offsets, the bitterness of hops to determine a beer's flavor. A very hoppy beer (with scads of IBUs) that is also a very malty-sweet beer (with lots of residual sugar) may, in fact, not taste very bitter at all. Meditating on this subtlety should raise your GQ considerably.

Finally, let's stray from the discussion of technical methods for measuring beer's attributes (and the terminologies employed) to focus on just one more word that you might hear spoken by a beer geek—especially a home-brewing beer geek. That word is **clone**. A beer clone is a copy, yes—but it's not like it's the identical twin of the thing it's copying. Instead, it's an attempt by a home brewer to replicate a commercially brewed beer. It's a recipe, in other words—and home-brewing books, websites, and blogs are chock-full of recipes for clones of Guinness Stout, and Pilsner Urquell, and just about every notable beer on the planet. Experienced home brewers are often highly skilled at creating beers that look and taste very much like the commercial brews they're modeled on. Still, it's unlikely that a home-brewed clone would *exactly* and in every particular match the commercial brew, since commercial brewery equipment and processes have their own effects on the way a beer looks, smells, tastes, etc. So a beer clone isn't a clone in the usual sense.

By now your mug runneth over with arcane info, and Drinkology can see your head swelling just the eensiest bit. But beware, our little beer geek in training. The short course we've just given is Beer Geekery 101, and you'll have to amass many more credits before being awarded that degree. For instance, you don't yet know what the word **kraeusen** means, do you?*

---

* Kraeusen (pron., CROY-zin), sometimes spelled *kräusen* or *krausen,* is a foamy scum that forms on top of beer during the early stage of fermentation; sometimes it's skimmed off, sometimes not. The related term *kraeusening* refers to the addition of a portion of "young" beer (beer taken from the fermenting tank during this early stage) to fully fermented beer in order to cause a secondary fermentation (see page 42). Oh, and "getting kraeusened" is beer-geek slang for getting drunk on beer.

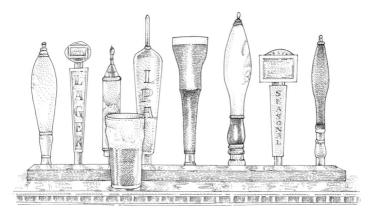

PART 2

Beer Bestiary

T HE THING THAT DRINKOLOGY, AS A BEER NEWBIE, FOUND most consternating was the sheer, mountainous number of beer styles, and also that there was no single reference (or at least none comprehensible to a neophyte) that could help us get a handle on this vast—and vastly confusing—welter of information. And so to help ourselves out, and to help you, we decided to create our own compendium. This compendium grew and grew, a little like a too-quickly-poured beer overspilling its glass, until we realized that we were going to have to make it the heart and soul of this little book. And so it is.

Beer styles are confusing not just because of their number. Worse, for the uninitiated, is that the terminology used for designating various styles is often ambiguous. The term *golden ale,* to take just one instance, is used for at least three different styles of beer; there are *many* other examples of a single term being used for several unrelated styles. Conversely, a given style of beer might be known by several different names, and there are numerous overlaps of names between and among categories. Then there are terms that *seem* to be the names of styles (e.g., *dark ale*) but that are actually much looser and vaguer rubrics under which beers of several distinct styles might fall. And then there are terms, frequently used in beer names, that mean different things in different contexts (e.g., *export*) or that don't mean much of anything at all (e.g., *spezial*). In the A-to-Z that follows, we try our best to sort some of this stuff out.

A FEW NOTES ON TERMINOLOGY

First, don't search this A-to-Z for a definition of *ale* or *lager*. Those terms—the two broadest categories into which (most) beers can be grouped—have already been defined in part 1 (see pages 8–9).

Some kind of explanation of the terms **craft brewery** and **craft beer**, which appear frequently in the pages that follow, is, however, in order. Basically, a craft brewery is a small brewery. The Brewers Association, a trade group representing American craft brewers, defines *craft brewery* as, first of all, a brewery producing fewer than six million barrels annually—a **barrel** being equivalent to two full kegs, or more than 330 twelve-ounce bottles. *Six million* barrels is therefore hardly a negligible quantity of beer, so craft breweries range greatly in size, from **brewpubs** with minuscule output (brewpubs make their own draft beers for sale on premises but often don't have the means or capacity to run a bottling operation), to **microbreweries** (which, as defined by the Brewers Association, may make up to 15,000 barrels per year, and which, though they bottle their beers and may sell them off premises, generally don't have much distribution beyond their immediate vicinities), to **regional craft breweries** (which, again using the Brewers Association categories, make between 15,000 and 6 million barrels annually and have significant regional—sometimes national—distribution of their products). Although this scheme relates specifically to American craft breweries, there are craft breweries all over the English-speaking world, as well as throughout northern Europe and elsewhere (see the sidebar on Japanese craft beers, pages 130–32). Definitions, based on production, of what constitutes a craft brewery differ from place to place, but what unites all these small breweries is that they are, collectively, a relatively *new* phenomenon—the outgrowth of the **craft-brewing movement** that began in America and Great Britain in the 1970s as a grass-roots rebellion against the hegemony of the **big brewers** (see pages 82–85) and an effort to ensure the survival of (and in some cases to resurrect) traditional, handmade, "craft" beers.

This means that the term *craft brewery* does not include, for instance, small European breweries that have in some cases operated for hundreds of years and that continue to make lovingly handcrafted beers. Such breweries have certainly provided inspiration for the craft-brewing movement—and have benefited, in terms of their own survival, from its international success—but they are not "craft breweries" per se, for the simple reason that they've been around too long. Nor does *craft brewing* include **home brewing**; although the growing enthusiasm for home brewing closely tracks the rise of the craft-brewing movement, craft breweries are commercial operations.

Abbey ales, several styles of Belgian ale that closely resemble the ales produced in Belgian Trappist monasteries. If that sentence sounds a little confusing, it's because the distinction between abbey ales and Trappist ales is more a matter of Belgian law than of significant stylistic differences. In Belgium, only the six surviving Trappist monasteries that still brew their own beer are legally permitted to call their beer *Trappist*. (See TRAPPIST BEERS for the names of those monastery breweries, as well as the lone Trappist brewery in the Netherlands.) Numerous other Belgian breweries, however, brew top-fermented ales in similar styles. Some of these breweries are operated by *non*-Trappist monasteries, but many are commercial enterprises that have licensing arrangements with monasteries that historically brewed their own beer but no longer do so. Belgian regulations regarding which beers qualify as "Certified Abbey Ales" are actually somewhat more elaborate than this, but suffice it to say that Belgian abbey ales—both the Flemish word for "abbey" (*abdij*) and the French (*abbaye*) appear on such beers' labels—are historically related to traditional monastic beers and also that many abbey-ale brewers produce ales in the three styles associated with Trappist brewers, which, in ascending order of alcoholic strength, are blonde (a.k.a. Belgian golden ale; see BLONDE ALES), DUBBEL, and TRIPEL. (They may also produce ales of other styles.)

Some Belgian abbey ales are exported; you might try ales by Affligem or Leffe if you find them at your local specialty beer shop. Also recommended by Drinkology editorial adviser Danielle Casavant is Tripel Karmeliet, an unusual three-grain beer by the

GERMAN PURITY

Seeing the words *German* and *purity* linked together in the same phrase makes Drinkology nervous. But the trepidation we felt as we approached the topic of the **German Beer Purity Law** turns out to have been misplaced. Although this centuries-old edict has its despisers (see GRUIT ALES), it's more innocuous than one might, on first hearing the name, imagine.

What the law was, originally, was a decree issued by Duke Wilhelm IV of Bavaria, on April 23, 1516, setting forth rules regarding the maximum prices at which beer could be sold and the ingredients from which it could be made—and threatening confiscation of brewers' goods if they did not obey its stipulations. The price-fixing aspects of the law are, as you might imagine, of little contemporary interest; it's the law's regulation concerning ingredients that continues, five hundred years later, to have some impact on beer making.

What the duke's decree did was to prohibit the making of beer from anything besides "barley, hops, and water." (Yeast wasn't included on the original list because no one yet knew of its existence; see pages 19–20.) The consensus among most beer historians is that the prohibition was ordered for three reasons: to ensure a steady supply of other grains (wheat, rye*) for the making of bread during a famine-prone era; to reduce beer spoilage, because hops were so much better at preserving beer than any of the other herbs then used for that purpose; and to curtail the use, by unscrupulous brewers, of poor-quality (or even dangerous) ingredients. Some even contend that the law represents the first food-safety legislation ever enacted.

---

* See WHEAT BEER and RYE BEER for more on the purity law's effects on German brewing. As the wheat-beer entry explains, an exception was soon carved out permitting certain brewers to continue making wheat-based beers—a loophole that had the effect of preserving Bavaria's tradition of wheat-beer making for posterity.

When first promulgated, the edict applied only within the duchy of Bavaria, but in succeeding years other German states issued similar decrees of their own, and a form of the law—henceforth known as the *Reinheitsgebot* (literally, "Purity Law"; pron., RHINE-heights-geh-boat)—was adopted nationally when Germany was unified in the nineteenth century. Later, as Germany reassembled itself under the Weimar Republic following World War I, Bavaria made the nationwide enforcement of the beer-purity standard a condition of its joining the new republic. This wasn't exactly altruistic on Bavaria's part, since the move drove some non-Bavarian German beer makers (whose traditional beers did not conform to the law's strictures) out of business.

Although German law—like that of other nations—still regulates brewing practices, the *Reinheitsgebot* as such no longer exists. It was, in effect, a victim of West Germany's membership in the European Union. Because the *Reinheitsgebot* forbade the sale, in the Federal Republic, of beer flavored during brewing with ingredients other than hops and because it likewise banned mass-market beers brewed from corn, rice, and other "adjunct" grains from entering the country, the European Court struck it down in 1987 as an unfair restraint of free trade. That ruling meant that Germans could now enjoy, for example, Belgian WITBIER (spiced with coriander and orange peel); it also meant that they could cozy up to a Bud (brewed, of course, from adjuncts as well as barley malt).

Despite being overturned, the *Reinheitsgebot* holds sentimental sway over many German beer drinkers as well as over German brewers, many of whom still promote their beers as conforming to the old law's standards. Whether this attachment to the past is a good thing is open to question, since sales of German-made beers have been falling in Germany in recent years—leading some observers to suggest that the *Reinheitsgebot* has the ghostly effect of stifling innovation in the German brewing industry. Such matters are, of course, of little consequence outside Germany. That said, it's clear that the 1516 Bavarian edict has had a long-lasting impact on brewing—and on beer culture—internationally. Not only did it provide the first definition of what beer could (legally) be, but it also came to influence the beliefs of beer drinkers everywhere about what beer most essentially *is*.

Bosteels brewery of Brussels that, although not an abbey ale per se, is based on a three-hundred-year-old Carmelite recipe. (That's the Carmelite religious order; the three grains are barley, oats, and wheat.) If the Belgian brews are hard to come by in your neighborhood, try some beers by North American craft brewers that are modeled on the Belgian monastic styles—often on the dubbel style, which is relatively alcoholic (generally from about 6.5 to 9 percent ABV), dark in color (but not too dark—a sultry ruby or a dark amber), and spicy/malty/fruity in flavor. Two well-known U.S. abbey ales are the Abbey Belgian-Style Ale made by the New Belgium Brewery of Fort Collins, Colorado, and the Abbey Ale made by the Ommegang Brewery of Cooperstown, New York. (The latter is one of Drinkology's favorite beers for pairing with virtually any meat-based meal.)

Alcopops, flavored alcoholic beverages (Mike's Hard Lemonade and Smirnoff Premium Malt Mixed Drinks are just two of the many brands) that are legally classified as beer in many states. Many alcopops—a neologism combining "alcohol" and "[soda] pop"—do, in fact, begin their nasty little lives as (unhopped) beer from which the malt flavor is removed and other flavorings (usually fruity) are added; these alcopops are sometimes referred to as **flavored malt beverages**, or **FMBs**. Alcopops generally range in strength from about 4 to about 7 percent ABV, but they can go higher.

Because their marketing targets young people—especially those for whom the taste of other alcoholic beverages is unpleasant or just unacquired—alcopop makers have been lambasted in some corners for encouraging underage drinking. Of course, these beverages hold little appeal for those who like the taste of (real) beer.

Altbier (pron., ULT-beer), a brown or brownish top-fermented ale associated with the German city of Düsseldorf and the surrounding west-central German state of North Rhine–Westphalia. Altbier is unusual in a couple of respects. First off, it's a throwback. For the past couple of centuries, pale, bottom-fermented lagers in the Bavarian style have dominated German brewing (see PILSNER). Düsseldorf brewers bucked that trend, continuing to make ales in the old way, or sort of. The word *Altbier* means "old beer"—but the moniker was only applied in the early nineteenth century, to distinguish this beer from the "new" lagers infiltrating the region from the south. Second, although it's an ale, Altbier is, in fact, *lagered* (i.e., stored at a cold temperature for several months before release)—so the making of this "old" beer actually incorporates the (somewhat) newer, Bavarian technique. Cold storage gives Altbier a crisp, delicate, bright-on-the-tongue character absent from many ales, but it's also sweeter, maltier, and more mildly hopped than most lagers. German Altbiers are hard to find in the U.S. (they're even difficult to find in Germany outside Düsseldorf and a few other spots), but a number of North American craft brewers have emulated the style. By all accounts, however, the best place to down an Altbier is Düsseldorf's *Altstadt* ("old city"), where more than two hundred beer joints crowd a district of less than one square mile. Note that some of Düsseldorf's Altbier brewers make a seasonal version of the beer, called a **Sticke** (pron., SHTICK-eh), or "secret" beer; Stickes are typically released in the late fall or early winter and are often maltier and higher in alcohol than other Altbiers (which usually have an ABV of a little under 5 percent).

Amber ale, a somewhat vague term for ales of an in-between color, neither pale nor dark. In fact, amber ales demarcate the middle ground just about every which way: hoppy but not too hoppy, malty but not too malty, alcoholic but usually not too alcoholic (though their ABV range is very wide—anywhere from just under 5 to well over 9 percent, at the extremity). Depending on your temperament, you can either view amber ale as a neither-here-nor-there compromise or see it as the embodiment of balance and harmony. The style is extremely popular in North America, with many breweries, large and small, producing amber ales. Note that some ales of this style are called **red ales**. American red ales, besides being somewhat redder in color than the ambers, may also be hoppier, maltier, and stronger. Especially hoppy/malty/strong American red ales may be named **double red ales** (see DOUBLE) or **imperial red ales** by their brewers (see STOUT for more on the term *imperial*).

Amber lager, another vague term (see AMBER ALE, above), used to designate a lager that's darker in color—and, usually, less dry and less hoppy—than a typical PILSNER. Amber lagers are worth investigating if you're looking for an all-occasion brew that's toothier and more interesting than a mass-market pilsner and/or if you want to begin introducing a friend who's only ever drunk, say, PBR to the wider beer world beyond. (For info on other darker-hued lagers, see BOCK, DUNKEL, MÄRZEN, SCHWARZBIER, and VIENNA LAGER.)

American pale ale. See PALE ALES.

American pale lager. See PILSNER.

American red ale. See AMBER ALE.

American wheat beer, on the one hand, a catchall term denoting WHEAT BEER brewed in America; on the other, a designation devised to highlight the differences between many American wheat beers and their European forebears. Although wheat-based beers were not unknown in nineteenth-century and earlier America, *American wheat beer* refers to wheat beers produced by craft brewers in this country from the 1970s on, some modeled more or less closely on European styles such as LAMBIC, WEISSBIER, WITBIER, etc., and others having no real Old World antecedents.

But even when an American wheat beer does take its lead from a European style, it's likely to taste significantly different. That taste difference may be partly unavoidable (for example, an American brewer may use domestic barley and wheat malts because of the difficulty or expense of obtaining European grains), but it's also partly intentional. An American HEFEWEIZEN (so called) may, for instance, be much more bitter than its Bavarian cousins for the simple reason that Americans generally prefer hoppier, bitterer beers. It may also be missing the signature **phenolic** flavors (banana, clove, vanilla) of a Bavarian Hefeweizen, because American wheat beer makers tend to avoid the special **wheat yeasts** with which German brewers ferment their wheat beers (and which contribute those flavors—odd to an American beer drinker's palate—to the finished brew).

American craft brewers are an adventurous lot, and some have pushed wheat beer's boundaries far beyond where a European wheat-beer maker would ever dream of going. There are, for example, a few dozen kinds of American **wheat wine**—high-alcohol (9 to 12 percent ABV) ales, similar to BARLEY WINE—on the market nowadays. Meant for slow sipping on chilly autumn evenings, these redoubtable beers contradict what wheat beer has traditionally been about. Such monster brews, however, constitute a tiny minority among the hundreds of American wheat beers now being produced, most of which adhere to the time-honored notion that wheat beer should be light and thirst quenching—a refreshing hot-weather beverage. In that vein, many American brewers treat wheat beers as SEASONAL BEERS, limiting their output to the warmer months and sometimes even calling them **summer beers**.

American wild ale. See SOUR BEER.

Baltic porter. See PORTER.

Barley wine, an intensely malty-flavored, thick-bodied (sometimes "chewy"), highly alcoholic dark ale. The term *barley wine* (sometimes spelled as one word: *barleywine*) has a medieval ring to it—or sounds like something Bilbo Baggins might've drunk when he was safe in his cozy hole in Hobbiton, back from battling Smaug at the Lonely Mountain. Some sources make the claim that barley wines are ancestrally just the sort of beers the Vikings drank. To which Drinkology responds, Pish-tosh. Barley wine may indeed resemble strong ales of greater antiquity, but as an identifiable, singular style, it's of fairly recent origin. Craft brewers who make barley wines—and many do, with BeerAdvocate.com listing, as of this writing, well over three hundred barley wines brewed in America alone—often give their barley wines names beginning with the word *Old* (or the worde *Olde*). As is their constitutional right. But let us note that barley wines per se were first brewed in Britain in the nineteenth century, and that America's barley-wine tradition dates *all* the way back to 1976, which is when the Anchor Brewing Company of San Francisco first released its Old Foghorn barley wine.

Note, too, in case the style's name gives you pause, that barley wine isn't *wine* at all. No grapes go into its creation. It's beer—but it's a beer that's like wine in several wises: its high alcohol content (usually between 8 and 13 percent, and therefore more akin to that of most wines than of most beers), the fact that it often receives significant aging before release and can be successfully aged in bottle for years or perhaps decades, and that it typically has the kinds of fruity flavors (dark fruit, dried fruit, stewed fruit) that people usually associate with "big" red wines (or with port, madeira, or certain sherries) rather than with beer. Though it's been done only rarely, a few brewers have even released barley wines with *no carbonation*, which doubtless has the effect of making this winey beverage even winier in character.

Barley wines are hardly the "biggest" beers, alcoholically speaking, on the planet (see BIG BEERS), but a barley wine is often the biggest beer a given brewery produces—and the barley-wine style is about as far as you can travel from a light PILSNER and still remain within the same recognizable category of stuff. While pilsners, many WHEAT BEERS (e.g., HEFEWEIZEN), and other light-colored, light-bodied, and relatively low-alcohol beers are best enjoyed in high summer, barley wines are meant to be drunk in dead, cold, dismal winter—when, if they don't exactly lift one's spirit, they do provide melancholic company. And while pilsners—particularly mass-market pilsners—are intended to be downed quickly (as you're reaching into the fridge or cooler for the next one), barley wines are meant for slow savoring, with many authorities advising that they be served in brandy snifters—and sipped as after-dinner drinks, perhaps paired with a stinky artisanal blue cheese or an ultra-chocolaty dessert.

As with some other styles, British and American barley wines differ, mainly in their bitterness—with the American versions being significantly hoppier, and therefore more bitter, than the British. (There is, apparently, no European beer style that American brewers won't "improve" with additional hops.)

Barrel-aged beers, no surprise, beers that are aged in wooden (usually oak) barrels. Time was, all beers were matured, stored, and shipped in wooden barrels. That began to change in the eighteenth century, when bottles came into fairly widespread use for beer storage and transport; a century later, the invention of noncorrosive "stainless" steel all but put the kibosh on the practice of barrel aging, except in some redoubts in Belgium and elsewhere, where it is an essential step in the production of certain traditional ales (see, for example, FLANDERS RED and LAMBIC).

Certain problems with barrel aging that had frustrated beer makers from the beginning of time were solved by nonreactive, sterilizable vessels. Because microorganisms can flourish in wood grain and on wooden surfaces, there is always the risk that a beer will go sour (though that's not a problem in the case of lambics and other beers that are *supposed* to be sour). Also, wood—especially raw oak—can impart unwanted (and strong) tastes. A growing number of latter-day craft brewers, however, are recasting these "problems" as challenges to be overcome in pursuit of days-of-yore authenticity and, of course, to achieve the subtle and complex flavors that wood aging, if successful, can bring to a brew. Some of these brewers are bravely creating their own SOUR BEERS modeled on the Belgian styles. Others are barrel aging some of their "bigger" beers (such as BARLEY WINES), which because of their high alcohol content are less prone to spoilage. Barrels used for aging beer are often treated using traditional techniques—such as charring their interiors or coating them with the resinous substance known as pitch—to reduce chemical interaction between the wood and the beer. Some brewers prefer using barrels previously employed for aging wine or whiskey; the wood of these barrels—itself "aged"—can lend unusual and desirable flavor notes. The revival of barrel aging has become a sizeable enough trend that there are now festivals devoted specifically to showcasing these beers. Among the most highly regarded of American barrel-aged beers are those made by the Jolly Pumpkin company of Michigan.

Belgian golden ale. See BLONDE ALES.

Belgian strong ale, a term applied to two different groupings of high-alcohol Belgian ales:

- **Belgian pale strong ales** (also called **Belgian golden strong ales**), whose yellow or gold color belies their formidable alcohol content (ranging from about 7.5 to 10 percent ABV). The most famous Belgian pale strong ale is Duvel—and justly so, given its beauty (its pulchritudinous assets include a gorgeous white head that just won't quit) and its complex flavor (spicy, peppery, sweet) that simultaneously manages to be perfectly comfortable and enjoyable. Duvel's one of those beers that goes down just a smidge *too* easily; its brand name, which means "devil" in a Flemish dialect, is apt.

- **Belgian dark strong ales,** which are deeper in color than the pales (but not dark brown or black) and whose ABVs occupy about the same range (usually 8 to 11 percent). The color, generally, results from the addition of sugar—caramelized sugar or dark candy sugar—to the brew. These ales, in contrast to their pale-faced kin, are more in line with ordinary expectations for a strong ale, in that they can be intensely malty (sometimes bready) in flavor. But these ales, too, are celebrated for their devilishly deceptive smoothness.

There is, by the way, some overlap between these two categories, respectively, and the TRIPEL and DUBBEL classifications of some

Belgian ABBEY ALES and TRAPPIST BEERS. As we complain in those other entries, there's a decided lack of consistency in the way these Belgian beers are named—but, hell, have more than one of any of these beers, and you'll find that you don't much care.

Berliner Weisse (pron., BARE-lih-nare VICE-eh), a sour WHEAT BEER that is authentically brewed only in the city of Berlin, Germany. Dubbed "the champagne of the north" by Napoleon Bonaparte, Berliner Weisse is extremely effervescent and is usually served in large, bowl-like glass "chalices" to accommodate its snowdrift-size (though rapidly dissipating) head. Its tartness and low alcohol content (generally less than 3 percent ABV) make Berliner Weisse a summertime, sitting-in-the-sidewalk-café-watching-

A BERLINER WEISSE
CHALICE

die-Welt-go-by sort of beverage; Berliners often sweeten it with a shot of raspberry or woodruff syrup. (Woodruff syrup—made from a highly aromatic, sweet-smelling herb—is basically unavailable in the U.S., so there's not much use in your trying to find it at the Piggly-Wiggly.) A number of American craft breweries do make beers in what they call the Berliner Weisse style (some even add fruit or fruit syrups before bottling), but these are often higher in alcohol than the German model. Besides which, they don't really have the right (well, according to German law, anyhow) to use the name *Berliner Weisse*.

Bière de garde (pron., BEE-yehr duh GARD), a northern French FARMHOUSE ALE. The Nord Pas-de-Calais region of France, from which this style hails, is hard by the Belgian border (it's sometimes called French Flanders), and bières de garde are thus similar to the Belgian ales called SAISONS. Artisanally brewed and traceable, historically, to individual farmers' individual recipes and brewing techniques, they are a diverse class of beers, varying in color (though generally of paler rather than darker shades) and in taste (though usually complexly flavored, sometimes a tad funky because of the wild yeasts that may play a role in fermentation, and only mildly hopped). French bières de garde are usually bottled in champagne bottles (complete with cork).

Like saisons, bières de garde were originally SEASONAL BEERS, brewed during the winter or very early spring (which is why they are sometimes referred to as **bières de Mars**, or "March beers"). They were then cellared (*bière de garde* means "beer for keeping") to sustain farmworkers throughout the summer and harvest seasons. Today's bières de garde, like latter-day saisons, are relatively high in alcohol (averaging between 6 and 8 percent ABV). French examples of this regional style are hard to come by in the U.S., but a growing number of American craft brewers are producing their own bières de garde/ bières de Mars, often scheduling them for springtime release.

Big beers, ultra-high-alcohol ales and lagers. Although there are many ales and a few lagers that deliver an outsize alcohol punch (refer to BARLEY WINE, BOCK, STOUT, and TRIPEL for just a few examples), the slangy designation *big beer* is more often applied to newfangled oddities that make a virtue—and, usually, a marketing splash—out of their outlandish alcohol content. In recent years, an arms race has been waged among some craft brewers to see who can brew the biggest beer of all—which, given alcohol's diuretic effect, amounts to quite a pissing contest.

The competition was set off in 1994, when the Boston Beer Company released its Sam Adams Triple Bock, which weighed in at what was then a world-record 17.5 percent ABV. That beer is no longer made (there were just three limited releases), but, in any case, the record has long since—and repeatedly—been surpassed, including by the Boston Beer Company itself. Sam Adams Millennium, released in 2000, had an ABV of 21 percent; Sam Adams Utopias—first offered in 2002, with batches (or, as they're rather pretentiously called, "vintages") being periodically released since then—has reached a 27 percent ABV.

Lately, though, those formerly astonishing figures have come to seem like small potatoes. As of this writing, there are at least ten beers in the world whose ABVs top *30 percent*, and during the summer of 2010, two beer makers released beers with an alcohol content higher than that of most distilled spirits: The End of History (yes, that's a brand name), made by the BrewDog brewery of Scotland, boasted an ABV of 55 percent. But that turned out *not* to be the end of this particular history, because not two weeks later, a Dutch brewery called 't Koelschip announced the arrival of its Start of the Future beer. A gauntlet, obviously, had been thrown down, and the future portended looks monstrous. S of the F's ABV was 60 percent, or, to put the number in hard-liquor terms, 120 proof.*

Boy, oh boy, oh boy! By which exclamation we mean, in part, that this is very much a boy's game. These big beers typically come dressed

---

* It is conceivable, of course, that this record will have been broken by the time you read this.

THE BIG GUYS

Brewing is an *immense* industry, accounting for something on the order of $200 billion in worldwide sales each year. And a very large slice of that very large market is controlled by a very *small* number of companies—a number, moreover, that's grown smaller and smaller in recent years as big beer makers have merged and merged again to form ever-larger international conglomerates and holding companies. What is currently (as of early 2011) the world's largest beer maker, Anheuser-Busch InBev, provides a good example of this process. The company was born in 2008 of the hostile takeover of the American giant Anheuser-Busch (the maker, of course, of Budweiser, Michelob, and other familiar brands) by the InBev company, which had resulted from the merger of a Belgian company called Interbrew and a Brazilian company called AmBev—each of which was itself the result of an earlier, but still fairly recent, merger.

The corporate histories of all the big brewing companies—in 2011, the top five were Anheuser-Busch InBev, SABMiller, Heineken, Carlsberg, and Molson Coors—are similarly complicated, and the interrelationships among these corporate entities and between them and their subsidiaries are mind-bogglingly complex. To give you just a couple of tastes of how weird things can be: Anheuser-Busch (now the U.S. subsidiary of Anheuser-Busch InBev) imports and distributes beers made by the Japanese maker Kirin in the United States, while Kirin imports and distributes Budweiser *and* Heineken—the latter made by Anheuser-Busch InBev's *rival* Heineken International—in Japan. Meanwhile, Miller, Coors, and Molson brand beers are marketed in the United States by MillerCoors, a joint venture (begun in 2007) between ostensible rivals SABMiller and Molson Coors. You couldn't keep all this stuff straight if you were a brewing-industry analyst. Or maybe you could—since that would be your job!—but ordinary folk like Drinkology certainly can't be expected to.

So what might an ordinary beer drinker like you want to know about the big brewers? Well, first off, you might want to know (because it's interesting and also a little scary) that any number of different brands of beer—beers that originated in entirely different places, at different times, and that are unlike one another in their taste and the method of their making—might now be owned by the same gigantic company. For example, Anheuser-Busch InBev currently owns or partly owns some *three hundred* brands, which, besides the Budweiser and Michelob brands you'd immediately associate with the Anheuser-Busch name, include beers as diverse as Boddingtons Pub Ale (a British bitter), Brahma (a Brazilian pale lager), Franziskaner Hefe-Weissbier (a German wheat beer), Hoegaarden (a Belgian witbier), Leffe Blonde (a Belgian abbey ale), and even Bacardi Silver Lemonade (an American alcopop produced under license from the Bermuda-based Bacardi rum and spirits company). Wow.

Second, you might want to be aware that the big-fish-gets-swallowed-by-bigger-fish-gets-swallowed-by-even-bigger-fish activity that's characterized the beer industry since at least the late nineteenth century—but whose speed has accelerated considerably over the past couple of decades—appears to have certain inexorable results. The first—despite what we say above about the diversity of the big beer companies' holdings—is a decline in the overall number of mass-market brands. The brewing giants tend to be impatient with any brand that doesn't maintain (or improve) its market share; if sales fall, even over a relatively short period of time, it's likely that the brand will be offloaded—sold to a competitor—or "retired." The history of big brewing over the past hundred-plus years is littered with the corpses of defunct brands, and there's no reason to believe that trend won't continue. Of course, the big brewers are also always introducing *new* product lines, but those, too, are quickly terminated if they don't meet market-performance expectations.

Third—and, again, we say this despite the inarguable diversity of the big brewers' holdings—you might want to consider a claim made by many beer lovers: that ongoing consolidation within the industry leads, gradually, to a homogenization of what that industry produces. Consolidation begets standardization, and different beers, especially beers within a given category, tend, over time, to taste more and more alike.

And, fourth, you might want to think about the economic repercussions of brewing-industry consolidations. As in any industry, mergers tend to be followed very quickly by efforts to create "synergies" and to "streamline" operations, which are pretty ways of talking about plant closures and employee layoffs. For instance, as reported by *Forbes,* the merger of InBev and Anheuser-Busch resulted, within just a few months, in 1,400 U.S. Anheuser-Busch workers losing their jobs.

Given this litany, you'd be forgiven for concluding that Drinkology has nothing good to say about the big brewers. But that's not true. Beyond our admiration for many of the individual beers owned by the big brewers, there's this: the big beer companies are masters of *quality*

in the trappings of connoisseurship of the über-male variety: limited (sometimes extremely limited) releases. Unusual, "collectible" packaging (The End of History came wrapped in a case constructed of animal skins). High price tags (in some cases hundreds of dollars per bottle). Buying one of these beers, in other words, carries some seriously macho bragging rights.

control. They go out of their way to guarantee their products' freshness and consistency. Freshness is of primary importance for most beers, and only large brewers can mount the kind of effort required to ensure that their beers—no matter where you buy them—haven't been sitting on retailers' shelves for untold months, getting staler all the while.

Consistency, of course, is both a vice and a virtue. There's something charming and "real" about inconsistency in a beverage or food. Wine lovers, for example, take endless pleasure in the endless variability of vintages—and find a deep connection to the earth and its ever-changeable climate in these infinite variations of character and quality. That's connoisseurship. On the other hand, even connoisseurs are plain old consumers at least some of the time, and there's something in each consumer that yearns for stability and predictability. If we like—or are accustomed to—Brand X applesauce, we want every jar of Brand X applesauce to taste *the same.* If Bud's the beer we drink, we want every bottle of Bud to taste *exactly the same* as every other bottle of Bud we've ever had. And—because of the standardization of recipes and processes, but also because of the scrupulous taste-testing to which the big beer makers continually subject their products—it surely *will.*

Bitter, an English term for a fairly diverse grouping of PALE ALES. Interestingly, the name *bitter* derives not from brewers' lingo but from drinkers' argot. From sometime in the early nineteenth century on, English pub-goers got into the habit of asking for "a pint of bitter," even as breweries continued to call these beers pale ales; it wasn't till about the time of World War II that the term began to be used commercially. (Also interesting, we think, is that most bitters aren't particularly bitter—the sobriquet might first have been used merely to distinguish these moderately hoppy ales from an extremely lightly hopped ale, commonly available in Victorian-era pubs but rare today, called **mild ale**.)

Bitter is intertwined with the English soul—which resides in a pub, most beer sold in England being dispensed in public houses—

Bad manners in a London pub

in ways that Drinkology cannot unravel. (We're also very bad at pub etiquette. We once made the grave error of leaving a few pounds for the barman at a London pub as a tip after a long night's bitter-drinking binge—which few pounds he huffily returned, informing us in no uncertain terms that he had a job and didn't require our charity, thank you.) Those confessions out of the way, we understand from the authorities we've consulted that, although bitter may be emulated elsewhere, it really must be made from British malts, British hops, and British yeast in order to merit the name *bitter*.

Beyond specifying the Union Jack credentials, however, those same authorities admit that the term *bitter* can cover quite a range of beers—some drier, some sweeter; some hoppier, others less so; some golden hued, others of a deep copper or even a chestnut color. They are all "pale," however, in the sense that they are *clear* (not opaque, as PORTERS and STOUTS appear), and they are also alike in that they're meant to be drunk *young*—within just a couple of months of being released by the brewery.

Although the character of a bitter made by one brewery may differ considerably from that made by another, British bitter makers generally adhere to a system that distinguishes among bitters of varying strengths. Usually, the lightest bitter (in terms of alcohol content) that a brewery makes is called its **ordinary bitter**. Topping out at about 4.1 percent ABV, these beers are sometimes called **session bitters**—because their relative weakness enables one to enjoy several over the course of a drinking session without toppling over. The next rung up on this ladder belongs to **best bitter** (ranging from 4.2 to 4.7 percent ABV), but this might, however, be denominated **regular bitter** if the brewery doesn't happen to make a weaker one. On the top rung stands **premium bitter** (a.k.a. **strong bitter** or **extra special bitter**), with an ABV of 4.8 percent or higher. Ordinary bitter is far and away the most popular of these substyles; it's also the driest, hoppiest in flavor, most acidic, and lightest bodied—flavor tends to grow rounder and sweeter and body to intensify as one mounts the scale. (Historical note: Way back when, a very low alcohol bitter, called **boy's bitter**, was also commonly brewed, but this substyle has virtually disappeared.)

Black lager. See SCHWARZBIER.

Blonde ales (or **blond ales**), ales whose color is, well, blond(e). The colors of blonde ales, like those of blond hair, cover a mini spectrum of shades ranging from pale straw to deep gold. Beyond this obvious, almost meaningless definition, a blonde ale might belong to one of the following categories: (1) an **American blonde ale**, a light-bodied, crisp, lagerlike style akin to (or the same as) an American GOLDEN ALE; (2) a Belgian TRAPPIST BEER or ABBEY ALE that is light in color and, usually, relatively lower in alcohol than the other beers made by a Trappist or abbey brewery (see DUBBEL and TRIPEL for more on this); or (3) a Belgian pale strong ale, whose delicate complexion belies its brute strength (see BELGIAN STRONG ALE). There are also French and Australian blonde ales.

BOCK

Bock is one of those beer-related terms that can befuddle the wannabe beer expert. First off, there's the matter of its history. There's some serious disagreement about where bock beer first came from:

1. Many sources, print and electronic, state unequivocally that its birthplace was the north-central German city of Einbeck, which was, in fact, a great brewing center in the late Middle Ages (in the 1300s, the town had something like six hundred breweries; today it has one). According to these sources, the word *bock* is a shortened, corrupted form of *Einbeck.*

2a. Other sources say, just as unequivocally, that, no, this can't be true. They point out that bock beers are mostly lagers and claim that since the lagering method hails, originally, from Bavaria, in southern Germany, bock must have originated there.

2b. Some sources split the difference, saying that, yes, bock did originate in Bavaria, in or around the city of Munich—but that the Bavarians, in brewing the strong, dark *lager* they called bock, were attempting to emulate the strong, dark *ale* that they'd been in the habit of importing from Einbeck before the Thirty Years' War destroyed much of northern Europe (and, as collateral damage, Einbeck's brewing industry) in the early seventeenth century. (Advocates of this version of events may also agree that *bock* is etymologically traceable to *Einbeck*: "bock," they say, is "-beck" as mispronounced in the Bavarian dialect.) And then . . .

3. There are others who say that—no, no, no—bock has nothing whatsoever to do with Einbeck. This camp points out that the word *Bock,* in German, also means "billygoat," adding, too, that bock beers were, historically, SEASONAL BEERS. Huh? So what's the connection? Well, they say, bock beers were originally brewed (in Bavaria) in the early winter, during the astrological house of Capricorn—signified, of course, by the *goat*—and then lagered through the cold months for springtime release.

We don't know about you, but this kind of stuff drives Drinkology straight to drink. And the difficulty of precisely defining bock doesn't end with its historical roots. There's also the question as to what "bock" means, *descriptively.* Although it's true that many beers whose makers call them "bocks" are dark brown in color, not all are. There are pale bocks and copper-colored bocks, as well. And although most bocks are barley malt–based lagers, not all are. There is also WEIZENBOCK, which is a top-fermented wheat ale. And although most bocks are only lightly hopped, at least one variety (Maibock; see next page) has a pronounced hops flavor. And, again, although many bocks remain seasonal beers, many others are nowadays produced year-round, since modern refrigeration has made the necessity of wintertime lagering moot.

This stuff drives us straight to drink

So does the word *bock* mean anything at all? Well, yes, it does. It means at least this: a beer that is relatively strong, alcoholically (in Germany, bock of any type may also be referred to as **Starkbier** [pron., SHTARK-beer]—that is, "strong beer"), and one whose recipe and method of making are somehow related to the beer-making tradition of Bavaria (no matter whether the tradition *originally* originated in Bavaria or not). So, for example, if you're in a tavern and overhear some beer snob angrily denouncing Michelob Amber Bock (made by Anheuser-Busch), saying, "How dare they call this bilge a *bock*? It's not very dark, and anyway it's colored with caramel, and besides it's got rice in it, and moreover it's not all that strong, and blah blah blah," you might point out to that unhappy person that, in fact, Michelob Amber Bock, being relatively stronger than plain old Michelob (5.2 percent ABV as opposed to 5.0, but still) and being a lager (which means that it is somehow related to Bavarian beer-making tradition, however remotely), has every right to claim the bock moniker. Do not, however, sue Drinkology when this conversation degenerates into a barroom brawl.

Now, there are a number of distinct substyles of bock, and, mercifully, these are a little—no, a lot—easier to define. In ascending order of alcoholic strength, these are

- **Maibock** (pron., MY-bock), a pale, relatively hoppy bock beer traditionally released by Bavarian breweries during the month of May (hence the name, which means "May bock"). Also known as **Hellerbock** or **Helles Bock** (both variants mean "pale bock"), Maibock is substantial yet refreshing—meant for drinking when the weather's neither chilly nor hot. Maibocks generally range between 6 and 7 percent ABV. Numerous American craft brewers have copied the style, sometimes calling these brews **golden bocks** or **blonde bocks**.

- **Doppelbock** ("double bock"), a dark, malty, caloric, high-alcohol beer (usually ranging from 6.5 to 9 percent ABV) that was first brewed in the early 1600s by monks in a Munich cloister to be drunk as "liquid bread" during the Lenten fast. (Drinkology understands that the calories in Doppelbock would've supplied the monks with the energy to keep belting out those Gregorian chants, but wouldn't that ABV have urred-slay their Atin-lay?) Interestingly, Doppelbock appears to have been invented independently from the bock style. The monks made their toothsome beer; they began selling it to the Bavarian public; somebody noticed that it was a lot like bock beer, but stronger; and so it was accorded the name *Doppelbock* after the fact. The monks in question, by the by, were *Minim* friars, a name that implies that they were to be "minimal"—humble, poor, and beneath the world's notice. To which end they created a far-from-demure beer that eventually became world famous: Paulaner Salvator Doppelbock, still brewed in Munich (though no longer by monks). The Minims belonged to the order of Francis of Paolo, hence the name "Paulaner." In Latin, *Salvator* means "Savior," which Drinkology thinks is a pretty good name for a beer. And while we're on the subject of names. . . . Emul*ators* of the Bavarian Doppelbock style are in the *habit* of giving their beers names that, like Salvator, end in "-ator." Some of these have a portentous ring—e.g., Liberator, Consecrator. Sometimes they're tongue-in-cheek—e.g., Seeyoulator and a coffee-flavored Doppelbock called, yes, Perkulator.

- **Eisbock**, which is pronounced ICE-bock and which means . . . "ice bock." Eisbocks—which, like all the Bavarian bock styles, are widely imitated by craft brewers here—get their name from the method of their making. After fermentation, a batch of Doppelbock is partly frozen; the ice that forms—the ice is entirely water, since water freezes at a higher temperature than ethyl alcohol—is removed; and the resulting **freeze-distilled** beer is therefore both beefier in flavor and higher in hooch. Eisbocks begin at about 9 percent ABV but can range upwards of 40 percent ABV or even higher—crossing over into distilled-spirit territory (see BIG BEERS).

Bock beers are so different from one another, and each bock's character is so dependent on the brewery making it that we decided that the American bock we'd recommend should be one that, though it's available nationwide, is deeply identified with a particular brewery and a particular place: Shiner Bock, made by the K. Spoetzl Brewery of Shiner, Texas. It's a favorite in the nearby (well, *sort of* nearby; we *are* talking about Texas) beer-crazy city of Austin, and a favorite of Drinkology drinking buddy Jack Lamplough, who says, "Some beers have an unmistakable sense of place. For me, Shiner Bock is as much a part of being in Austin as the great music, spicy food, and Texas heat. Easy drinking and slightly sweet, it goes down great with barbecue and Tex-Mex. The first sip never fails to put me in a Lone Star state of mind."

Bohemian lager. See PILSNER.

Brown ales, ales that are the color ale is supposed to be. We're kidding, of course—ales may be golden, ales may be red, ales may be black—but when Drinkology thinks of ale, the image that first appears is a brownish drink—as opposed to when we think of lager, which conjures the image of a much brighter, yellowish beverage (even though we know that there are several darker lagers). We're speaking here of archetypes—and we submit that, for us, the archetypical ale is brown.

As it turns out, the archetype squares with the prototype. Detailed records of beer-making procedures in most places date back only a couple of centuries, so determining the attributes of earlier ales—their colors, their flavors—is often largely a matter of guesswork. We do know that ale, historically, was brewed in numerous—undoubtedly a multiplicity of—styles. But we can reasonably guess that most if not all these styles were, basically, brown. The development of truly pale-colored ales (and of pale lagers) awaited the introduction of pale malts in the seventeenth century (see PALE ALES). Before then, barley malt was dried—*roasted* is probably the more apt word—over open fires (see RAUCHBIER), which means that the malt, once dried, was always at least somewhat *brown.* And brown malts make **The motherhood is metaphorical** brown ale. Yes, there were ways of lightening an ale's color; by making it partly of wheat, for example (see WHEAT BEERS), or by limiting the amount of time the wort spends in the kettle (less cooking = less caramelization of sugars = lighter color). But these techniques amount to exceptions to the rule. As some commentators have put it, "Brown ale is the mother of all beers."

That motherhood, however, is metaphorical. Here's the complicated part: the brown-colored ales of long ago are, in truth, somewhat tangentially related to what we call *brown ale* nowadays. For one thing, today's brown ales—the two main English varieties, as well as **American brown ales**—are made mostly of pale malts. (Pale malts can be used as the base for dark brews so long as some dark malt is included in the grain bill, for color.) For another, although today's brown ales hearken back to an earlier era of beer's history, they're a relatively recent creation. The antique style of English brown ale (which *had* been made of brown malt) pretty much ceased to exist during the nineteenth century, when the popularity of pale ales obliterated most other traditional British ale styles. Modern brown ales, first brewed in England at the turn of the twentieth century, represent a reaction against pale ales' takeover—an attempt to recapture the past, albeit using the newer pale malt as a base.

Present-day English brown ales differ according to whether they come from northeastern England (specifically the Yorkshire and Northumberland regions, including the city of Newcastle) or southern England (in or around London). Brown ales of the **southern style**—malty, sweet, minimally hoppy, and low in alcohol (2.8 to 4.1 percent ABV)—are rarely seen in America. Those of the **northern style**—also malty, but somewhat drier, hoppier, and stronger (4.2 to 5.4 percent ABV), and often having a decided caramel or nutty flavor—are better represented on U.S. beer retailers' shelves. One very popular northern-style brown ale, the Nut Brown Ale made by the Samuel Smith company of Tadcaster, in North Yorkshire, is a Drinkology favorite. (A third English-style brown, called **mild ale**, doesn't travel well and is virtually unknown on this side of the Atlantic.)

The scores of brown ales now produced by North American brewers, though generally modeled on the northern English style, occupy too great a spectrum of dryness/sweetness, hoppiness, flavor (some have coffee or nut additions to the brew), and alcohol content (4 to 8 percent) to characterize neatly. Color is diverse, too, ranging from dark amber (there's some overlap between this style and AMBER ALE) to a rich, chocolaty brown. Many (not all) brown ales are unfiltered and may appear hazy when poured. Though brown ale is now made all over, Texas is a particular center of brown-ale brewing in the U.S., and Pete's Wicked Ale, made by Pete's Brewing Company of San Antonio, is a particularly well-known example.

Finally, note that what we here call "brown ale" is not to be confused with the Belgian ale style known as OUD BRUIN, or Flanders brown. There are also some other Belgian ales called "brown"; these generally resemble ales of the DUBBEL style.

Budweis. See PILSNER.

California common beer, a.k.a. **steam beer,** a moderately to very hoppy, dry, especially effervescent American-born lager. California common beers are darker lagers (amber or coppery in color), are typically moderately alcoholic (in the 4 to 6 percent ABV range), and have feisty, never-say-die heads.

Invention is the offspring of necessity, and the inventors of "steam beer" (whose names are lost to history) had substantial necessity to contend with. These brewers arrived in San Francisco Bay along with the mid-nineteenth-century Gold Rush crowd, which was thirsty for the lager beers whose popularity was just then sweeping the country. The brewers had the proper yeast for brewing lager; what they didn't have was any reliable method of controlling temperatures during fermentation—so crucial to the usual lager-making method. Year-round ambient temperatures in this part of California were simply too high, and ice for cooling fermentation rooms was simply unavailable. So they did what they had to, fermenting their wort with lager yeasts at the higher temperatures associated with ale fermentation—and ended up with a distinctive style coupling lager's refreshment with some of ale's rougher edges.

No one knows for certain where the name *steam beer* came from. Perhaps from the beer's high level of carbonation. The casks in which it was briefly conditioned had to "blow off steam" when tapped, and the beer was notoriously difficult to pour because of all the gas it contained. Or perhaps from the method used by some steam-beer brewers to chill the wort when transferring it from brewkettle to fermentation tank. They pumped it up to the brewery's roof, where it ran through open troughs—cooled by winds blowing in from the Pacific and creating a cloud of vapor around the rooftop—before descending back into the brewhouse.

Whatever the name's origin, steam beer caught on among the locals (out of necessity, maybe?), and by century's end, there were more than two dozen breweries in the Bay Area making it. Prohibition all but killed this indigenous style, however. Just one maker, the Anchor Brewing Company, survived that thirteen-year-long legal drought—only to see its fortunes dwindle over the following decades. In 1965, unable to withstand the competitive pressure from the big beer-makers, Anchor was about to close up shop. And then . . .

In what's generally regarded as a milestone moment of brewing history, Anchor was bought up by a whippersnapper by the name of

Fritz Maytag. This young Stanford grad (and, conveniently, heir to the Maytag washing-machine fortune) didn't know anything about the brewing business; he just knew he liked Anchor Steam Beer, which he'd gotten into the habit of drinking at a favorite San Francisco restaurant. Long story short: within ten years, Maytag had turned the company around and established a national presence for its signature brand (and started brewing other unconventional beers, besides). In the opinion of many, Maytag's takeover of this ailing small brewery marks the launch date of the contemporary craft-brewing movement.

Maytag just knew he liked Anchor Steam

So why is this entry called "California common beer" rather than "Steam beer," which is the better known and more historically appropriate appellation? Well, Anchor, which had long been the only company making steam beer, trademarked the name in 1981. Other U.S. craft brewers who make beer in this style—there appear to be about ninety, currently—can't use the term. (Though some skirt trademark regulations through wordplay. For example, the Triumph brewpub of Princeton, New Jersey, occasionally offers a brew it calls Esteemed Beer.) *California common beer* is the official designation used by the **Beer Judge Certification Program (BJCP)**, a brewing-industry standards-setting organization, though the brand names of beers of this style rarely use the term.

Cask-conditioned ale, an unpasteurized, unfiltered ale that is racked (transferred) directly from the fermenting tank into a container called a **cask**, where the ale matures and becomes carbonated—is "conditioned"—through the ongoing activity of yeast remaining in the ale. The length of time that the ale is allowed to mature differs according to style. Lighter, lower-alcohol cask-conditioned ales may be ready for serving within just a few weeks; stronger brews may be allowed to mature for up to a year.

The preservation of the tradition of cask-conditioning ales has been a cause célèbre in the U.K. for the past four decades. By the early 1970s, virtually all British brewers had adopted the practices of pasteurizing, filtering, and kegging the ales destined to be served at British public houses, or pubs. This move toward industrial brewing methods (which included the growing use by British beer makers of nonmalt adjuncts in their brews and of artificial-carbonation techniques) did not sit well with some members of the British drinking public, who found the sterilized, filtered ales much less flavorful than traditional "real" ales—and much too fizzy, besides.

In 1971, four young British beer drinkers decided to do something about the trend before natural, "real" ales became extinct. The organization they founded, **CAMRA** (originally the **Campaign for the Revitalisation of Ale**, later changed to the **Campaign for Real Ale**), has since then enjoyed great success, becoming the U.K.'s own grassroots equivalent of the craft-beer movement in the United States. Besides promoting traditional brewing, CAMRA, which now has more

A CASK

than 100,000 members, supports pubs that serve "real" ales and has mounted successful efforts to change Britain's beer laws to make it easier for small brewers to survive; the group also publishes the annual *Good Beer Guide* that's an invaluable resource for the beer tourist in Britain. (For much more info, visit www.camra.org.uk.)

Cask-conditioned ales are "real" in the sense that they're made from natural ingredients but also in the senses that they are *alive* (the yeast remains active) and that they are dispensed naturally—a cask's contents are not artificially pressurized, and the beer flows into the tap via gravity (the cask is positioned behind the bar and above the level of the tap) or, if the cask is located in the pub's cellar, by being hand-pumped into the tap with a device called a **beer engine**. Although casks were historically made of oak, today's casks are made of metal (or, in some cases, plastic); they differ from kegs (see pages 266–67) in that they are barrel-shaped rather than straight-sided and have two openings rather than one—not just the hole at one end of the cask into which the tap is fitted but also another hole, called a **shive**, in the side, which is opened before the cask is tapped. (A peg called a **soft spile** is inserted into the shive immediately after opening, allowing some of the CO_2 to vent away and allowing the pub's **cellarman**—who keeps watch on the bubbles forming around the spile—to judge when the cask is ready to tap, at which point the shive is plugged by an airtight **hard spile**.) Real ales are also fragile; they become stale within just a few days of the cask's being tapped.

Cask-conditioned ales remain mostly a British phenomenon, though some American craft brewers have adopted the method, and an increasing number of American bars are outfitting themselves to serve them.

Cassis. See LAMBIC.

Chicha, a South American (specifically Andean) corn beer. You don't want to know how chicha is made, but we'll tell you anyhow. In the traditional method (still followed in some Andean communities) maize kernels are chewed—by human beings, in their grotty human mouths—and the masticated paste is formed into little cakes. The chewing serves the same purpose as malting would—to break down complex starches in the grain into simpler, fermentable sugars. (Saliva contains enzymes that perform this function.) The chewed-corn cakes are then boiled, and this stew is fermented; the resulting cloudy yellow beverage is fairly low in alcohol—hard to get drunk on, unless you drink piles of it, which Andean men did (and do) at days-long village festivals.

Drinkology is torn between repulsion and fascination. Knowing that the boil kills the bacteria in the chewed corn doesn't really quiet our urge to squirm. Still, we'd like to try chicha. The ever-adventurous Dogfish Head brewery of Milton, Delaware, has made occasional batches—the staff, apparently, gets together for a chew fest—using organic heirloom maizes from South America and flavoring the brew with strawberries (which is likewise traditional). Anyhow, its labor-intensiveness means that DFH's chicha is released in extremely small quantities, which sell out very quickly (which is sort of surprising when you consider the ick factor).

Chocolate stout. See STOUT.

Christmas ale. See SEASONAL BEERS.

Cider. See pages 101–2.

Cream ale, an American ale style that is brewed in such a way as to resemble an American pale lager (see PILSNER)—light, crisp, and (at best) inoffensive. As with pale lagers, cream ales' grain bills often incorporate adjuncts like rice or corn, although some craft brewers make malt-only versions. But what really links this style to lagers is that, although it's top-fermented and thus truly an ale, cream ale is lagered—that is, stored at a cold temperature for some period before release. This **hybrid** style, created to appeal to lager drinkers, also usually matches pale, pilsner-style lagers in strength, with most cream ales weighing in somewhere in the range of 4.5 to 5.5 percent ABV. (For info on a German ale style that resembles American cream ale, see KÖLSCH.)

APPLESEED VERSUS BARLEYCORN

Johnny Appleseed was a real-life guy; he really did plant thousands upon thousands of apple trees throughout the early American "West" (western Pennsylvania, Ohio, and Indiana); and he really was thought of as a hero by his fellow frontierspeople. But what the real Johnny Appleseed—a nickname bestowed on one John Chapman by his grateful beneficiaries—was doing wasn't the stuff of children's literature or kiddie movies. The apples from the apple trees that Chapman raised in his nurseries and sold to settlers were intended for one purpose and one purpose only: making **hard cider**. Mr. Appleseed was a folk hero because his activities kept the frontier awash in booze, which, when you think about the hardships of pioneering life, seems pretty goldarned heroic indeed.

Cider—the alcoholic kind, as opposed to the unfiltered fresh apple juice you buy at your local farm stand when the weather turns nippy—has been made for millennia in Europe and was a mainstay of American life from the colonial period up until Prohibition. As food writer Michael Pollan put it in his 2001 book *The Botany of Desire,* apples, in pre-Prohibition days, "were something people drank." Cider, like beer, was a safer drink than water in those unsanitary days—but it was easier to make than beer. Basically, making cider involves crushing and pressing apples and fermenting the squeezed-out juice; the fermented cider can then be filtered to clarify it, but it doesn't have to be. Prohibition quashed hard-cider making in this country—apples were rebranded as a health food. Its revival here is fairly recent, and hard cider hasn't even begun to recapture its former popularity. Woodchuck Hard Cider, made by the Woodchuck Cidery of Middlebury, Vermont, is the best-known American cider; founded in the 1990s, the company produces several varieties, including a **pear cider** and some interesting seasonally limited releases. (Pear cider, BTW, is sometimes called **perry**.)

We mention cider in a book about beer for two reasons: (1) Cider presents a light, refreshing, and somewhat beerlike alternative for people who don't like the taste or aroma of hops, and (2) cider, because it's made only from apples, is gluten-free, which means it can be safely imbibed by gluten-intolerant folks (as, of course, can gluten-free beer; see pages 112–13). Oh, and there's another reason. We rather like cider, especially the Organic Cider (dry, effervescent, and equipped with a pleasant sting of alcohol) made by the Samuel Smith brewery of North Yorkshire, England. Cider-making flourishes in the U.K. as nowhere else. British cideries produce a variety of styles; cider is more or less universally available in British pubs; and we'd tell you even more about it if this weren't, after all, a book on beer.

Dark ale, a vague descriptive term rather than a particular style of ale. The vagueness of the designation applies even to color, since an ale called "dark" might be dark amber, or brown, or blackish. Dark ales include Belgian dark strong ales (see BELGIAN STRONG ALE), DUBBELS, and other dark-colored Belgian ales, as well as some North American BROWN ALES.

Dealcoholized beer. See pages 160–62.

Doppel. See DOUBLE.

Doppelbock. See BOCK.

Dortmunder (pron., DORT-moon-der), a deep golden German lager, also known as **Dortmunder Export** or "**Dort**." Beer experts seem to disagree about whether Dortmunder—which takes its name from the German town of Dortmund, in the Ruhr River valley, where it originated—qualifies as a distinct beer style. German PILSNER-style lagers, which include the Pils beers of northern Germany and the Helles ("pale") beers of the south, occupy a continuum, with those of the north being more bitter and hoppy and those of the south more sweet and malty. Dortmunder resides in the middle of this continuum. What really distinguishes it from the other German pilsner subtypes is its relatively high alcoholic strength (about 5.5 percent ABV) and a mineral flavor, perhaps even slightly sulfurous, conferred by Dortmund's hard water.

Dortmund was a notable brewing center from the Middle Ages on, but the origin of the style (or substyle) now known as Dortmunder is much more recent: the late nineteenth century, when German beer drinkers (like beer drinkers internationally) turned away from traditional, dark, top-fermented ale ("old beer"; see ALTBIER) and embraced the new lighter-colored and -bodied lagers emanating from Bohemia and Bavaria. Dortmunder is an artifact of that revolution in taste. It was first brewed in 1873, and its comparative robustness, commentators claim, is a function of the roughneck market at which this new lager was aimed: the workingmen who worked the coal mines and manned the steel mills of the Ruhr valley, long Germany's most heavily industrialized region. Interestingly, now that those mines have largely been closed and the mills shuttered, the region's taste in lager has changed. Nowadays, the Ruhr consumes much more Pils than it does Dortmunder. Not only that, but the various local breweries (Hansa, Kronen, Ritter, Stifts, Their, *und so weiter*) that produced their own variations on Dortmunder have, over recent decades, been bought up by two large brewing conglomerates, DAB (Dortmunder Aktien Brauerei) and DUB (Dortmunder Union Brauerei). Some of those old brands are still marketed—as "product lines"—by the DAB and the DUB, but you'll find critics who claim that their individual characters have been snuffed out and, further, that it's now the craft-brewing movement in Germany and North America that's keeping "authentic" Dortmunder alive. Great Lakes Dortmunder Gold, made by the Great Lakes Brewery of Cleveland, Ohio, wins consistently high marks among craft-brewed Dortmunder-style beers.

Double, a descriptive term used in the names of some beers to indicate that a greater-than-usual amount of malt for a given style was used in the mash (to pump up the beer's alcohol level), or that the beer is hoppier than standard beers of that style, or both. (Note that "double" also appears in the names of some craft-brewed ales that ape the DUBBEL style of Belgian ABBEY ALES and TRAPPIST BEERS.)

As a descriptor, *double* is pretty loose—sometimes its inclusion in a beer's name means that the malt count (and/or hopping) was actually doubled, sometimes that it was increased by some significant amount but less than twice the usual. Makers of INDIA PALE ALES (some of whose fans believe that there can never be too much of a good thing) are especially partial to creating double—and also TRIPLE—variations on the brew, but you'll also find PALE ALES and other beers touting themselves as doubles or triples. Since no rules govern the use of the terms *double* and *triple*, there's actually a great deal of overlap, in terms of both alcoholic strength and bitterness, between these categories. Some double and triple IPAs are strong enough to qualify as BARLEY WINES.

Dry stout. See STOUT.

Dubbel (pron., doo-BELL), a designation applied to some Belgian TRAPPIST BEERS and ABBEY ALES. The term *dubbel* (meaning "double" in Flemish) belongs to a one-two-three naming convention in which a given brewery makes ales of three alcoholic strengths. If naming systems were rational, the least strong brew would be called an *Enkel* (Flemish for "single"), but that term is not used nowadays. Instead, the lowest-alcohol beer in the range might be called a **blonde** (see BLONDE ALES), or, depending on the maker, it might be called something else. (BeerAdvocate.com refers to this category of beers, which are straw to light amber in color, as **Belgian golden ales**.) In any case, this least-strong ale is the brewery's "standard" ale. Don't make the mistake, however, of thinking that these blonde ales are *weak*; they actually range from 4 all the way up to 7 percent ABV.

A dubbel is, obviously, stronger. Dubbels range from 6.5 to 9 percent ABV. It's also an entirely different sort of beer—a malty, sometimes fruity, often full-bodied and rather dark ale that may also have a caramel flavor if candy sugar is added to the mash (which some breweries do). Even stronger than a dubbel is a TRIPEL ("triple"). Tripels typically range from 8 to 12 percent ABV.

For the beer neophyte, the problem with this naming system is that it's sort of theoretical; almost nobody employs it as described. Trappist breweries and brewers of abbey-style ales may make more than three ales, or they may make fewer; they may use different systems of nomenclature; they may, in addition to a blonde, dubbel, and tripel, also make an ultra-strong ale called a **quadrupel** ("quadruple," obviously). (Or they may make a quadrupel but not a tripel—the variances are legion.)

Despite all these caveats about the "system," however, dubbels do represent a distinct style (though one that overlaps with the style called **Belgian dark strong ale**; see BELGIAN STRONG ALE) and a style that is widely emulated, in the U.S., Canada, and elsewhere by craft brewers who take their cues from Belgian brewing traditions.

Dunkel (pron., DOON-kull), a German word, meaning "dark," that is most often applied to Bavarian dark lagers, also sometimes called **Munich dunkel lagers** (but there are also *dunkel* wheat beers; see DUNKELWEIZEN). Historically, dark lagers predate pale, PILSNER-style lagers, so you can think of Dunkel as the original lager style. Although they are now not nearly so popular as pale lagers, Dunkels have survived in their homeland, and many well-known German brewers—including the likes of Beck's, Paulaner, St. Pauli Girl, and Spaten—make Dunkel beers. The darkness of a Dunkel is relative. It is generally dark copper or reddish-brown in hue (compare SCHWARZBIER), the coppery or ruby shade resulting from the use of slightly caramelized Munich malts, which are in between pale and dark malts on the malt color spectrum and are noted for producing reddish-toned beers. Because Dunkels are lagered, they're markedly smoother than many ales of a similar hue. They also have a reputation for a complexity of flavor conferred by putting the mash through repeated decoctions (see page 37 for more on decoction mashing). On the whole, they're just a wee bit stronger, alcoholically, than pale lagers, averaging from 5 to 5.5 percent ABV.

Dunkelweizen (pron., DOON-kull-VITES-zin), a dark Bavarian WHEAT BEER that also goes by the illogical names Dunkel Weissbier (= dark white beer), Dunkles Hefeweiss (= dark yeast white), and other, similar variants. A coppery color, Dunkelweizen is certainly darker than much other WEISSBIER, but not nearly so dark as a PORTER or STOUT. Like other German wheat beers, it's made mostly from wheat malts, but it gets its signature hue from the darker-roasted barley malts included in the grain bill. Those dark malts also confer a malty—even bready—taste absent from lighter Weissbiers. The darkest Dunkelweizen is the type called **Schwarze Weisse** (= black white; pron., SCHVAR-tzeh VICE-eh), a moniker that's not only oxymoronic but also inaccurate, in that the beer, though deeply colored, isn't even vaguely black. Munich's Hofbräu brewery makes a Schwarze Weisse that's relatively easy to find in the U.S.

Eisbock. See BOCK.

Export, a designation whose meaning differs according to context. Sometimes the word is attached to a beer style—as in Dortmunder Export. Sometimes it's part of the name of a given brand or line produced by a particular brewery—as in Guinness Special Export Stout. It can mean

1. a beer that's somehow different from the beers a brewery ordinarily produces and that's aimed at a different or new *domestic* market (which appears to be the case with Dortmunder Export, which was developed in the late nineteenth century to satisfy the changing tastes of the Dortmund breweries' regional clientele; see DORTMUNDER), or

2. a beer that's specifically aimed at a *foreign* market (Guinness Special Export Stout was created by the Irish brewer for the Belgian market), or

3a. a beer that's high in alcohol (e.g., Steel Reserve 211 Triple Export Malt Liquor, whose name goes one better by adding the extra-strength designator TRIPLE into the mix), or

3b. a beer that's higher in alcohol than other beers of the same basic type (e.g., Scottish export ale; see SCOTTISH ALE), and/or

4. it may, in some (many?) cases, amount to no more than a marketing term intended to class up a particular brand.

Extreme beers, experimental (sometimes outright gimmicky) craft beers that push the envelope in terms of their alcohol level, taste, ingredients, and/or the methods used to brew them. The moniker *extreme beer* can't be defined with any precision. It doesn't just mean that a beer is "big," alcoholically, though extreme beers include BIG BEERS. It might also mean that a beer is bittered/spiced with an outrageous quantity of hops, or brewed with twice or three times the amount of malt generally required for a particular style, or flavored with unusual additives (lavender? ginger? raisins? seaweed? oysters?). Extreme beers are cutting- (or bleeding-) edge concoctions that demonstrate their brewers' creativity . . . or, occasionally, an extremely dim notion of what beer drinkers might actually care to drink.

Farmhouse ales, traditional ales with rural/agricultural roots. The term does not identify a particular style. Rather, a farmhouse ale is one whose origins can be traced back to the home-brewing practices of farmers, for whom making beer was, in years past, a common wintertime pursuit. A number of Belgian beer styles (e.g., LAMBIC, SAISON) and one (less well-known) French style (BIÈRE DE GARDE) originated in agricultural communities, and present-day craft makers of what they call farmhouse ales (e.g., Michigan's Jolly Pumpkin Brewery) are often particularly indebted to these Belgian/French peasant brewing traditions.

Faro. See LAMBIC.

Flanders brown. See OUD BRUIN.

Flanders red, a.k.a. **Flemish red ale** or **Flemish red-brown ale,** a sour, spontaneously fermented Belgian ale. Lactic-acid-producing bacteria play an important role in its fermentation, and their interaction with the wild yeasts also present in the oak fermentation vessels produces a beer that's at least as unusual as Belgian LAMBIC. Flanders reds, which are barrel aged (see BARREL-AGED BEERS) and are often **blended beers** (younger ale is mixed with older ale to cut the sharpness), are sometimes called "the most winelike" of beers (compare GUEUZE). But we don't taste wine. We taste a drink that, neither exactly beerlike nor exactly winelike, belongs in a category unto itself—a palate-surprising admixture of citrusy, even vinegary, sourness and sweet fruit flavors (berries, cherries). We like it a lot, without, however, being certain that we could drink several in a row. Flanders reds' appealing red-brown color results from the use of "red" malts; ABVs are 5.5 to 6 percent; and the degree of sourness ranges from the mildly tart to the tongue-stabbing. Though Flanders reds can be difficult to obtain stateside, you might find those made by Rodenbach or Duchesse de Bourgogne. A few American craft brewers have tried their hands at making ales in this style. Try the La Folie ale made by the New Belgium brewery of Fort Collins, Colorado, or, better, La Roja, by Michigan's Jolly Pumpkin brewery (the latter, a truly eye-opening beer, was called "the weirdest beer—maybe the weirdest beverage—I've ever had" by the friend with whom we shared a bottle). Note, finally, that there's a similarity between the Flanders red style, made in western Flanders, and the eastern-Flanders style called OUD BRUIN ("old brown").

Framboise. See LAMBIC.

Fresh-hopped ales, a.k.a. **fresh-hop ales.** See HARVEST ALES.

Fruit and vegetable beers, barley- or wheat-based beers flavored during the brewing process with fruits or fruit syrups or with vegetables. The range of fruits that have been used is very wide: berries (blackberries, blueberries, cranberries, grapes, raspberries, strawberries, etc.), orchard fruits (apples, apricots, cherries, peaches, etc.), citrus fruits (grapefruits, lemons, limes, oranges), even watermelons, mangoes, and bananas. (We found ourselves wondering whether anybody'd yet made a kiwifruit-flavored beer; although we couldn't find any commercial examples, we did find discussions of the topic on home-brewing blogs.) The range of vegetables is somewhat narrower, including root vegetables like carrots and sweet potatoes, as well as (somewhat unsurprisingly, given some beer makers' he-man proclivities) jalapeño peppers. Among North American craft brewers, pumpkin ale is a very popular SEASONAL BEER (guess which season); such ales often incorporate pumpkin-pie spices in the flavor mix. (Drinkology, BTW, is unsure whether pumpkin is a fruit or a vegetable.)

If you're the sort of person (a guy, most probably) who thinks that beer should be flavored only with hops and that any other sort of flavoring is "inauthentic," you're not just narrow-minded; you're wrong. Hops weren't used in brewing until the Middle Ages—by which time beer had been around for umpty-ump thousands of years and had often been flavored with fruit as well as many other things (see GRUIT ALES; SPICED AND HERBED BEERS). And even after hops became the standard beer-flavoring agent, a number of traditional European styles (e.g., fruit-flavored Belgian LAMBICS as well as Belgian WITBIER) continued to incorporate fruit in the brew. And if you think that adding fruit to beer is sort of "fruity," we (1) have nothing to say to you and (2) hasten to remind you that various malts and yeasts, in and of themselves, are capable of imparting quite a range of fruitlike flavors to beer. (All this aside, we do admit that there's something gimmicky/trendy about the number and variety

BAD NEWS BEERS

Barley contains the protein known as gluten. So does wheat (even more of it, actually). So do rye and oats. Notice that we're quickly exhausting the list of grains from which most beers are mostly or partly made. If (1) you like beer and (2) you have a gluten-intolerant autoimmune disorder (celiac disease is the most common of these dangerous allergies), this is very bad news, since it means you cannot drink beer without risking a flare-up of symptoms, including fatigue, abdominal pain, and diarrhea.

Or, to be more accurate, it means that you can't drink beer made from any of the usual suspects. The good news is that the brewing industry (the big beer makers and a goodly number of smaller outfits) has responded to the increasing prevalence of gluten intolerance by creating a growing number of **gluten-free beers**, which are made from various gluten-free ingredients (or combinations thereof), including buckwheat, corn, rice, quinoa, molasses, lentils and other legumes, and—especially—sorghum. (Interestingly, sorghum, which is a prime constituent of many of the new gluten-free beers, has long been used in brewing in Africa, where it is a major cereal crop.)

of fruit and vegetable beers being made by craft brewers today; as of this writing, almost eight hundred such beers receive ratings on BeerAdvocate.com.)

It's hard, of course, to generalize about fruit and vegetable beers, since they represent so many different styles. Many, however, are brewed in such a way as to diminish maltiness—and many are only very lightly hopped (or have no discernible hops character)—so as not to compete with the fruit flavor. Also important to note is

Or, to be more accurate, this is *sort of* good news. One limitation of the gluten-free beers now on the market is that they fall into a very narrow range of beer styles—so far as we can tell, they're all either PILSNER-style pale lagers or GOLDEN ALES. The other, perhaps more serious, limitation is that, on the whole, they appear to be not very good. A scan of opinions posted on sites like ratebeer.com and BeerAdvocate.com reveals scads of thumbs-downs and precious few thumbs-ups. A typical comment: "I wouldn't recommend [brand name here] to anyone who isn't gluten intolerant."

One serious caution: if you are gluten intolerant and want to try some gluten-free beers, be careful. The designation "gluten free" can mean different things, depending on where such a beer is made, with certain countries allowing brewers to use the term for beers that do, in fact, contain gluten, albeit at very low levels. These beers, which are better termed **low-gluten beers**, may or may not be harmful to you, depending on the degree of your sensitivity.

But, hey, if "better safe than sorry" is the name of this game, we have even better advice for you. Learn to like wine.

that fruit beers need not be particularly sweet and can, in fact, be quite tart and dry if the fruit is added during fermentation and its sugars allowed to fully ferment, as is the case with some lambics (see KRIEK). Finally, a point of information: the term *fruit beer* does not apply to styles of beer—for example, BERLINER WEISSE and kvass (see pages 163–64)—to which fruit syrups or juices are traditionally added when the beer is being served.

Golden ale, a term that may designate one of three different types of ale: (1) Belgian BLONDE ALE, also sometimes called a **Belgian golden ale**, (2) Belgian pale strong ale (see BELGIAN STRONG ALE), or (3) **American golden ale**, also called **American blonde ale**. Here, we focus on the third, American type:

American golden ales might be described as crossover beers. Unlike most American PALE ALES, they're generally lightly hopped; they're also generally of a moderate alcoholic strength (4 to 5 percent ABV). These qualities, coupled with golden ales' lagerlike color and crispness, make them ideal entry-level ales for the beer drinker who's used to PILSNERS or light beers but who wants to try something else without getting too radical about it. Big, mass-market brewers make golden ales (Molson Golden Ale is an example), but the style has also become increasingly important to craft brewers interested in broadening their client base beyond the beer cognoscenti. Not that a cognoscente wouldn't appreciate a well-made golden ale—especially in the summer, because these ales are such great thirst-quenchers. Some craft brewers make golden ales specifically for summertime release. (When it comes to golden ales, Drinkology drinks locally: the

Summer Blonde golden ale released seasonally by the River Horse Brewery in Lambertville, New Jersey—just down the road a piece from our house—is a favorite.)

Note that the lagerlike KÖLSCH ales of Cologne (Köln), Germany, have a great deal in common with American golden ales.

Gose (pron., GO-zuh), a.k.a **Goslar** or **Leipzig Gose,** a top-fermented wheat ale (see WHEAT BEER) brewed mostly in Leipzig, Germany. Gose isn't a well-known style (we're guessing the German Goses are nigh unto impossible to find in the U.S.), but it's worth including on our list of beer styles for three reasons: (1) It's a highly unusual beer in that it's flavored with coriander and salt—yes, *salt*, (2) the style has in recent years been emulated by at least a couple of dozen American craft breweries, and (3) it's a beer style that actually went totally extinct but was then brought back into existence. The story of its resurrection is interesting. First brewed in the central German city of Goslar (from which it takes its name) in the eighteenth century, Gose really caught on in Leipzig, in eastern Germany, eventually becoming Leipzig's "hometown" beer, dispensed in numerous local taverns devoted specifically to the brew. But between the turn of the twentieth century and World War II, Gose's popularity collapsed, and by the mid-1960s it simply wasn't made anymore. Some twenty years after its disappearance, a fellow named Lothar Goldhahn, in what must've been a rare instance of entrepreneurship in communist East Germany, decided to re-create it—and came up with a recipe by conducting interviews with Leipzig old-timers. In 1986, Gose was reborn, and it's now made by a few breweries in Leipzig and even one in its original birthplace, Goslar. Nice comeback.

By the way, don't confuse Gose with Belgian GUEUZE—which, although it has a similar-sounding name and is also a sour wheat ale, is not directly related to the Gose style.

Gruit ales, a.k.a. **gruited ales** or **grut ales**, ales flavored with herbs other than hops. Many a modern-day beer drinker might find the idea of a beer brewed without hops a travesty—a beverage unworthy of the name "beer." In point of fact, though, hops were a relatively late arrival in beer-making history. First mentioned in an eleventh-century document, the use of hops in brewing spread slowly, gaining significant ground in central Europe with the introduction of the German Beer Purity Law (see pages 68–70) in the sixteenth century but not becoming (more or less) universal in Europe until the mid-seventeenth century. Before hops' ascension to become the *single* bittering and spicing agent used in almost all beers, lots of other flavorings were used. In medieval Europe, various herbs and combinations of herbs, called *gruits* or *gruts,* played the role later accorded to hops alone.

Beer historians commonly credit hops' takeover to their superiority to other herbs as a brewing additive, citing, especially, their strongly preservative character. Not only do hops do a good job of bittering and spicing beer, they say, but because hops are better at helping beer *keep* than any other botanical, their gradual adoption by brewers everywhere was a natural and easily comprehensible progression. Some present-day partisans of gruit ales—which have undergone quite a revival in the craft- and home-brewing worlds— look at that same history, however, and discern darker forces at play. According to these people's more complicated and rather grim version of events, the promulgation of hops represents an effort on the part of governments, in concert with religious authorities, to keep their subject populations tame and docile. Hops were, they claim, an instrument of oppression.

The evidence marshaled by these conspiracy theorists (Drinkology uses the term descriptively, not pejoratively) is severalfold: First, they say, hops proved useful in modifying behavior because of their demonstrated soporific and even *emasculating* effects; the herbs commonly used in gruit ales, by contrast, stimulated their drinkers and had the power to intensify sexual desire and male potency. (For more on hops' purported testosterone-suppressing effect, see page 223.) Second, they point to the near-simultaneity of the German Beer Purity Law (1516; see pages 68–70) and the beginnings of the Protestant (specifically Lutheran) Reformation (1517), speculating (1) that Protestants, being of a puritanical bent, wanted to deprive people of sexual pleasure, and (2) that Protestants, being of an anti-Catholic bent, wanted to deprive the Roman church of a significant source of income by promoting the use of hops, since Catholic monasteries often controlled regional markets in gruit-ale herbs. Some of these theorists go so far as to link the switchover from gruit herbs to hops to the transformation of beer making from a largely domestic activity (performed largely by women) to an increasingly commercial activity (performed solely by men); in this view, the witch-hunting and -burning craze of early modern Europe was nothing short of a campaign to rid Europe of age-old botanical knowledge (so-called witches often being skilled herbalists) toward the end of instituting a New World Order.

Drinkology, not being a historian, can't really assess these arguments, but we're just an eensy-teensy bit skeptical, remembering, for example, that Martin Luther was a pretty lusty guy (he talked dirty, and when he left the monastic life behind, he quickly found himself a gal) and that the beer purity law was first introduced in Bavaria—a region of Germany noted for being a *Catholic,* not Protestant, stronghold. We're sure, of course, that the gruit-ale conspiracy theorists could muster lots of data to counter our quibbles, but, the thing is, we really don't want to get into a fight. We're all in favor of the gruit-ale revival for the simple reasons that we like it that home and craft brewers are exploring the folkways of the past and that they're making beer in lots of different ways.

We don't want to get into a fight

The gruits used to flavor historical gruit ales could be compounded of countless different herbs, but three herbs in particular—sweet gale, yarrow, and wild rosemary—were widely used. Also, the brewing of unhopped beers did manage to survive hops' onslaught in some corners of Europe, for instance in Finland (see SAHTI). In Scotland, the making of traditional **heather ale**—bittered by the very plant that so poetically blankets the highland moors—was outlawed when the English took over the country in 1707 but has recently been revived, with the Fraoch Heather Ale made by the Williams Bros Brewing Company of Alloa, Scotland, being the best-known brand. Williams Bros also makes several other so-called **Scottish gruits**, and a number of North American craft brewers have emulated the Scottish styles.

Gueuze (pron., GUR-zeh or GOO-zeh or gooz), a blended Belgian LAMBIC. Truly "the champagne of bottled beers," gueuze *looks* like champagne (both in its champagne-style bottle and in its color and bubbliness when it's poured), and, to some palates, it even *tastes* like champagne—dry and citrusy-tangy. Gueuze, whose name is of obscure origin but may be derived from the same root as our word *geyser,* is a blend of "young" lambic (aged six months to a year) and old lambic (aged three years). It undergoes a second fermentation in bottle (just like champers), and it shares champagne's fizzy thirst-quenchingness. *But* (and this is a big "but") it does *not* smell like champagne. The fruitiness of its aroma is compounded with something on the order of . . . skunk. (Some people, trying gueuze for the first time, have trouble making it past the nose.) Oh, and because it's not disgorged or filtered, gueuze (unlike champagne) is cloudy. If stored in a cool, dark place, gueuze can keep for years— maybe even decades. You're likely to have some trouble finding gueuze stateside, though the Lindemans Brewery's René Cuvée gueuze appears to be somewhat widely distributed; this particular beer has a weaker odor than some other gueuzes, but its sourness is bracing. Gueuze, BTW, is the beer traditionally used in the Belgian stews known as carbonnades.

Harvest ales, SEASONAL BEERS (usually PALE ALES or INDIA PALE ALES) spiced with freshly harvested hops rather than the dried (often pelletized) hops ordinarily used in brewing; also referred to as **fresh-hopped ales** or, sometimes, **wet-hopped ales**. Unless they're dried, hops lose their potency soon after they're picked, which means that the fresh, "wet" hops for a harvest ale must be delivered to the brewery very soon after being picked and that harvest ales are, of necessity, brewed in small batches for limited releases.

Beer drinkers of the "hophead" orientation especially love these beers, which capitalize on fresh hops' powerfully grassy and citrusy aromas and flavors. Well-known examples include Sierra Nevada's Northern Hemisphere Harvest Ale, brewed in the fall, which uses fresh hops grown in Washington State's Yakima Valley—not too, too, too far away from the Chico, California, brewery—as well as Sierra Nevada's Southern Hemisphere Harvest Ale, brewed in the spring, which uses fresh hops flown in from the down-under end of the planet (specifically, New Zealand). Which, to our mind, makes for a pretty big carbon footprint for a style that's s'posed to revel in the bounty of the (local) harvest season. (Ahem.) A number of craft brewers in the Northeast—among them, Harpoon (of Boston) and Southern Tier (of Lakewood, New York)—make well-regarded harvest ales from hops grown in New York State.

Hefeweiss (pron., HOOF-uh-vice). See HEFEWEIZEN, below.

Hefeweizen (pron., HOOF-uh-VITES-zin), the most popular type of Bavarian WEISSBIER. Hefeweizen means "yeast wheat," and the name succinctly captures what's distinctive about the style. It's an *unfiltered* wheat beer whose sediment of yeast cells creates a haze when the beer is poured. For many beers, cloudiness is a fault; for Hefeweizen, it's not just a virtue—it's a raison d'être. Besides the yeasty haze (which is intensified by the wheat proteins in the beer), Hefeweizen's trademark traits include a strong and long-lived head (the wheat protein is also responsible for beefing up the head's tensile structure), a silky mouthfeel, mild hops character, and a smattering of flavor notes often including banana and clove. Bavarians sometimes raise the refreshment potential of this already-refreshing beer by mixing it, fifty-fifty, with lemonade, but they rarely add a slice of lemon to a glass of Hefeweizen (as some non-German enthusiasts recommend).

The Hefeweizen style—sometimes called **Hefeweiss** (= yeast white) or other, similar variations on the name—has gained fans around the world, and you're likely to find Hefeweizens made by several German breweries at your local beer retailer. Among the best known (and one that Drinkology quite likes) is Franziskaner Hefe-Weisse, from a Munich brewery that can trace its origin back to the fourteenth century. Beers made in the Hefeweizen style by North American craft brewers are often released, as SEASONAL BEERS, during the summer.

Helles. See page 153.

Herbed beers. See GRUIT ALES, SPICED AND HERBED BEERS.

High-gravity lager. See page 169.

Imperial stout. See STOUT.

INDIA PALE ALE
Among its many fans, India pale ale is usually referred to as "IPA"—it's the only beer style, so far as we're aware, that has an acronym. (No, PBR is not a *style* of beer.) These days, the IPA style marks one of the great divides in the beer-drinking world. You either love it (in which case you really, really love it), or you hate it (in which case you may either really, really detest it or only somewhat detest it). Those who love IPAs tend—or such is our impression—to openly or secretly disparage those who dislike IPAs. IPAs, you see,

are *butch* beers, and saying that you like them seems automatically to give you a kind of street cred among the style's partisans—like having a gang tattoo or something.

The India pale ale style creates such discord for one reason only: its hoppiness. IPAs are *very* hoppy beers. Or, rather, *some* IPAs are very hoppy beers; other IPAs are *extremely* hoppy beers, and still others are *unbelievably* hoppy beers. (Some ultra-hoppy—and, often, ultra-alcoholic—IPAs are dubbed DOUBLE IPAs, TRIPLE IPAs, or **imperial IPAs**; for more on the use of the word *imperial* to describe a beer, see STOUT.)

Modern-day "hopheads"—as they're wont to call themselves—admire IPAs for their indisputably hoppy flavor. What's interesting, though, is that the original motive behind the style's development had nothing to do with the bitterness produced when extra hops are added to the brew. It had to do, instead, with hops' preservative character.

Running a well-oiled empire requires some lubrication, and the British, back when they had a well-oiled empire, used alcohol as a lubricant. For the sailors who ruled Britannia's waves, there was rum. For the civil servants who did the colonies' paperwork, there was gin (mixed with quinine-laden tonic water to tamp down those inconvenient malarial symptoms in the empire's hotter climes). And for the ordinary soldiers who did the empire's grunt work of putting down rebellions and whatnot, there was beer.

Beer, however, has a distinct disadvantage when compared to rum or gin. It doesn't travel nearly so well as distilled spirits, and that was a real problem in the eighteenth century, when beer brewed in Britain but destined for British troops stationed in India

PASSAGE TO INDIA

Nearly everything about the early history of India pale ale is debated by beer historians. For instance, some call IPA the world's first "export" beer—not in the sense that no beers were ever previously exported by their makers but rather in the sense that it was the first beer *expressly created* for export. Others quibble that this isn't really so, since it was an accident of time and place that led George Hodgson to off-load some of his October beer (which he'd already been making and trying to sell to London customers) on the East India Company.

Some experts claim that IPA shipments were not destined specifically or primarily for the British army serving in India, because soldiers represented a minority of colonial personnel in India—there simply weren't enough soldiers there to account for all those casks of ale recorded as having been shipped to India in the late 1700s and the 1800s. *All* the Brits in India drank beer, they say. And that may well be true. Still, there was a huge upsurge in the amount of British beer exported to India in the late 1850s, during the years of the Indian Rebellion (formerly better known as the Sepoy Mutiny). Why? Well, presumably because of the huge influx of British troops during that period. Soldiers, it does appear, drink beer.

Historians also counter the notion that IPA was uniquely suited to surviving the voyage to India, noting that quantities of British-brewed PORTER were also drunk on the subcontinent in the late eighteenth and early nineteenth centuries and that porter seems, based on shipping documents, advertisements, etc., to have weathered the trip quite well. Point taken. Even so, the IPA style did become phenomenally popular in India, and ever more so throughout most of the nineteenth century. When, beginning in the 1820s, British expats began building breweries in India itself, they brewed . . . India pale ale. And they continued to do so until PILSNER-style lagers established worldwide dominance. (Drinkology has read that no IPAs at all are now produced in India—all Indian breweries having switched to lager production over the past century-plus—but we can't absolutely vouch for that.)

Why was the IPA style so indisputably popular among Brits stationed in India? Well, it seems to Drinkology that it's because IPA is—when compared to porter, say—such a *thirst-quenching* beer. Think about it: India is mostly a hot place. Imagine yourself in a hot place, with a merciless semitropical sun beating down on your pith helmet. If someone offered you a beer, letting you choose between a light-amber-colored, sparkling IPA and a blackish, heavy, syrupy porter, which would you reach for? 'Nuff said. (In this last connection, it's interesting to note that India pale ale may have been the first type of beer to be artificially chilled. There are several mid-nineteenth-century reports of British colonials immersing containers of the beer in tubs containing a solution of water and saltpeter—a common cooling technique in the days before refrigeration.)

had to weather a half-year-long sea voyage—south to the Cape of Good Hope and then north again through the Indian Ocean—often suffering large temperature changes en route. It often went bad. The solution to this problem was devised—inadvertently, it appears—by a brewer called George Hodgson, whose brewery was fortuitously located in Bow, in London's East End, very near the docks from which the ships of the British East India Company set sail. One of the beers Hodgson made was based on a home-brew recipe he probably got from his employees: country boys—former servants or children of servants at country estates—who'd recently migrated to the big city. Called October beer (because it was brewed in the fall, serving as a **stock beer** that the landed gentry would cellar and drink all year long), this ale was pale, strong, and very well hopped. Hodgson sold some of his October beer to the East India Company, and a miracle occurred. Not only did the beer *survive* the passage to India, but its taste actually ripened and improved along the way. (Note: It wasn't just the extra hops that aided the beer's survival; the higher-than-usual alcohol content—alcohol itself being a preservative—also helped.)

Don't mess with the big guys

Hodgson had a hit on his hands. Orders poured in. But the popularity of the beer was eventually to prove the Hodgson company's undoing. After several immensely profitable decades of doing business with the East India Company, the Hodgson brewery decided to eliminate the middleman, and in the 1820s it began shipping its beer to India itself. Well, as Drinkology always says, Don't mess with the big guys. Hodgson's move did not sit well with the old boys at the East India Company, and to fight the brewery's attempt to cut them out, they began negotiating with a number of brewers in the English town of Burton-on-Trent, in Staffordshire, a spot long famed for the high quality of its ales. Burton's brewers—which included the Bass company, among others—had longstanding experience in the export trade, having made much of their income over the previous century selling beer to the Baltic and Russian markets. But those markets, on account of the Napoleonic wars and subsequent skirmishes and trade embargoes, had dried up, and Burton's brewers were thirsty for a new customer base.

At the East India Company's urging, Burton's brewing companies copied the pale, alcoholic, hoppy style of ale that Hodgson had himself copied from a home-brew recipe. And another miracle (at least from the Burton brewers' and East India Company's perspectives) occurred. The Burton brewers' India pale ales were *even better* than Hodgson's. It was the sort of miracle, however, that succumbs to scientific explanation. The IPAs of Burton-on-Trent turned out to be superior to those of Hodgson's London-based brewery because Burton's hard, mineral-laden water was better than London's for making this particular beer style—better for converting starch to sugar during mashing (resulting in a higher-alcohol ale) and better at extracting only limited color from the malt (resulting in an even paler ale).

As the Hodgson brewery went under, the Burton brewers' operations expanded, first by leaps and then by bounds as India pale ales (and, later, other PALE ALES made in Burton) grew in popularity on the domestic British market. (A possibly interesting aside: IPA's rising popularity coincided with a switch, by publicans and their public, from serving and drinking beer in metal vessels to using glassware. The chicken-or-egg question: Did IPA—so much lighter in color and more effervescent in appearance than older-style ales—gain in appeal because it looked so good in transparent glasses, or did beer glasses come into wider use because IPA looked so good in them? Or was it just a coincidence?)

It's said that IPA made the Bass company's fortunes. By the 1880s Bass had become the largest beer maker in Britain. But, like Hodgson's before them, Bass and the other Burton brewers couldn't keep exclusive hold on the franchise. When a scientist by the name of C. W. Vincent invented a method for "Burtonizing" water—making the mineral content of any water equivalent to that of Burton-on-Trent's—it became possible to brew Burtonesque IPA anywhere. By the turn of the twentieth century, nearly every British brewer was making an IPA.

U.S. brewers jumped on the bandwagon, too, although in America the IPA style never really recovered from Prohibition, with one notable exception: Ballantine India Pale Ale, which survived into the 1980s. A highly regarded ale, its disappearance continues to be mourned by some graybeards among the beer-loving set. India pale ale's stateside rebirth, and the development of distinctively American IPAs, happened with the craft-beer movement. As it turned out, those first makers of reborn IPA were suckling a giant. Over the last few decades, IPA (in several variations) has become one of the most popular beer styles among craft-beer brewers and drinkers. As of this writing, the website BeerAdvocate.com rates more than *two thousand* different IPAs.

It's fitting, Drinkology thinks, that India pale ale, which was born as a home brew, is also probably the style most favored by beginning American home brewers today. The story told by our friend Tony Moore, who writes about his initial home-brewing experience on pages 302–27, may be typical. The first craft beers Tony ever drank were IPAs—they introduced him to the pleasure of "real" beer. So when he decided to brew his own, IPA was, inevitably, what he most wanted to try.

And now for the full disclosure (not that you asked for it). Drinkology doesn't really care for the IPA style. Our perhaps sissified palate just can't get past all those **IBUs** (see page 62), and the hoppier the IPA, the more we dislike it. In our not-so-humble opinion, a beer like Dogfish Head's 120 Minute IPA, which is continuously hopped over *two hours* of brewkettle boiling, then dry hopped, and *then* aged with *yet more* hops—and which has an *18 percent* ABV, besides—is a ridiculous beer. Sort of in the way a thirteen-inch penis is a ridiculous penis. Still, we're just humble enough to admit to being out of sync with the times—and to recognize that one man's poison is, so to speak, another man's meat. And so we humbly requested suggestions, from our IPA-loving consultant Danielle Casavant, as to some craft India pale ales you might want to try. Her short list:

Celebration Ale (Sierra Nevada Brewing Co., Chico, California)

Crooked Tree (Dark Horse Brewing Co., Marshall, Michigan)

Double Daisy Cutter (Half Acre Beer Co., Chicago, Illinois)

Furious (Surly Brewing Co., Brooklyn Center, Minnesota)

Huma-Lupa Licious (Short's Brewing Co., Bellaire, Michigan)

Nelson (Alpine Beer Co., Alpine, California)

Pliny the Elder (Russian River Brewing Co., Santa Rosa, California)

Unearthly (Southern Tier Brewing Co., Lakewood, New York)

Union Jack (Firestone Walker Brewing Co., Pasa Robles, California)

Irish red ale, a.k.a. **Irish ale,** the signature SESSION BEER of Ireland. Irish red ales, which range from amber to a deep, garnet-toned hue, are *gentle* beers—mildly alcoholic (averaging about 5 percent ABV), mildly hopped, and mildly malty. Many Irish reds, the experts like to say, possess "toffee-like notes," which, to put it in American English, means they can have a detectable buttery/caramel flavor (which is contributed by the roasted malts that give Irish reds their color). Brewed in Ireland by both big and small beer makers (some of which make a similar red lager), this crowd-pleasing, easygoing PALE ALE style is widely copied elsewhere; in America, Irish reds are made by scores of brewpubs, microbreweries, and larger craft brewers, including, among others, the Boston Brewing Company (Sam Adams brand) and the Matt Brewing Company (Saranac brand) of Utica, New York.

Irish stout. See STOUT.

Kellerbier (pron., KELL-uh-beer), a well-hopped, darkish German lager. The style, which hails from the German region of Franconia (basically, northern Bavaria), is unusual in a couple of ways. It is stored in cellars (the name means "cellar beer") inside wooden barrels with *open* **bung holes**, allowing CO_2 to flow out as fermentation slowly continues during this cool-temperature lagering. In Franconian *Biergartens* (where most German Kellerbier is drunk), the beer is served by tapping these casks; it emerges uncarbonated, because the gas has escaped, and quite cloudy, because the residual yeast has not been filtered out. Franconian drinkers don't have to stare at the haze, however, since they typically tipple their Kellerbier from earthenware steins rather than from glasses.

EASTERN PHILOSOPHY

On the face of it, Japan is not a place you'd expect to find a craft-beer movement. That's not because the Japanese don't like beer. They certainly do. Beer is *the* most popular alcoholic beverage in Japan, accounting for about two-thirds of the booze guzzled there. But almost all of that beer—the vast, vast majority—is produced by the four biggest Japanese brewing companies: Asahi, Kirin, Sapporo, and Suntory. And, according to expat bloggers in Japan who report on such things, Japan's leading beers are the most homogeneous, tastewise, in the world. The flagship brands are all light, dry, relatively low-alcohol PILSNERS, and they are virtually indistinguishable from one another.

Moreover, the Japanese are also fond of some truly drecky-sounding beverages known as **pseudo-beers**. There are two categories of these relatively low-cost alcoholic beverages: *happoushu* (literally, "foaming alcoholic drink"), which has a malt content that's too low to allow it to be called beer under Japanese law, and *happousei* (also called **third beer**, or, weirdly, **liqueur**), which is a brewed, beerlike beverage containing no malt whatsoever. (It's made from soybeans and other stuff.)

So, given Japanese consumers' thirst for insipid beers and beerlike drinks, along with their apparent desire that big-brand beers taste as much alike as possible, it's surprising to learn that the craft-beer movement is alive and, on a minuscule scale, doing reasonably well in Japan. In 2010, there were about a hundred microbreweries in the country making what the Japanese call *ji birū* ("local beer") in a wide range of styles, including their own variations on the pale, dry pilsners so beloved by Japanese drinkers.

Editor's note: This sidebar was composed before the March 2011 earthquake and tsunami that devastated so much of northern Honshu. As of this writing, it is unknown how that catastrophe has affected the Japanese brewing industry.

Japan's present-day craft brewers got a late start. Before a 1994 relaxation of Japanese licensing laws, which had previously prohibited breweries producing less than two million liters annually, it wasn't even possible to start up a small brewing operation in Japan. The first company to do so, in 1995, was Echigo Brewery, in Niigata City (more or less due north of Tokyo, on the opposite side of the island of Honshu).

Fortuitously, Drinkology happened, while researching this book, to receive an invitation to a Japanese microbrew beer tasting at the Japanese Culinary Center in New York City, which event featured several of Echigo's beers as well as beers made by another Japanese microbrewery, the Coedo Brewery of Kawagoe, just outside Tokyo. Since Japanese microbreweries' products have such limited, scattershot distribution in the United States, we jumped at the chance to sample some beers that we might otherwise never encounter. The gathering was lots of fun, and the food—each beer served was paired with a different dish, including *two* desserts—was exceptional. Our opinions of the beers themselves, however, were somewhat mixed.

The first beer poured—Echigo's Koshihikari lager—was a disappointment. Praised by the event's emcee as having "raised the bar for Japanese rice lager," this simple pilsner-style lager tasted . . . well, it tasted much like any other pale lager that uses rice as an adjunct. Drinkology found it bland to the point of anonymity, and our tablemates concurred. Granted, it was okay with the tuna tartare it was paired with, but pilsners *do* go well with mild-flavored fish dishes, so this wasn't much of an achievement.

Luckily, that first beer represented the low point of the tasting. Drinkology briefly wondered whether any craft brewer ought even to try to make pilsners—what's the point?—*until* we sampled a pilsner called Ruri produced by the Coedo Brewery. Paired with a decidedly un-Japanese (but scrumptious) sausage-and-sauerkraut dish, this refreshing, slightly bitter, remarkably well-balanced beer reminded us again of why the pilsner style became so popular. Without asserting itself, the beer held its own against the (very) hot mustard sauce that accompanied the sausages, demonstrating that good beer doesn't have to bully your tongue.

Without going through each of the evening's offerings, we'll mention two other standouts: One was Coedo's Beniaka, a beer whose recipe incorporates sweet potatoes. That's right, sweet potatoes. (Sweet potatoes are the major crop in the prefecture where the brewery is located.) This orangey-red (i.e., sweet potato–colored) lager is Coedo's signature brew, and it was great to sample a "gimmicky" beer that didn't taste *argumentative*. The other standout was the Echigo Stout—a subtle, beautifully made, creamy STOUT that seemed to have been created to be drunk with the delicious, gooey-centered chocolate fondant cake it was paired with.

When Drinkology had first received the invitation to the tasting, we'd been struck by its wording. "You will be amazed," it said, "at how mild Japanese beers are." *Mild?* we thought. *They think that American beer enthusiasts will be enticed by the word* mild? As it turned out, though, that wasn't such a bad way to characterize all the evening's beers—the good and, yes, the not so good. Certainly, the best of the offerings—Coedo's Ruri and Beniaka lagers and even the Echigo Stout—showed that subtlety and delicacy can be true virtues in a beer. Too many American craft brewers want their beers to shout; it's nice to know that a beer can succeed by whispering.

Bottled German Kellerbiers—it's possible you might find the St. Georgen Bräu brand at your specialty beer retailer—are, however, lightly carbonated and partly filtered before bottling. Like most German styles, Kellerbier has been copied by some North American craft brewers; their Kellerbiers, however, are sometimes higher in alcohol than the German versions (which are in the 5- to 5.5-percent ABV range) and also sometimes much more highly carbonated.

Two regional variations on Kellerbier—**Zwickelbier** (pron., TSVICK-ul-beer), which is a lightly hopped but more effervescent variety (the carbonation resulting from the barrels' bung holes being plugged during lagering), and **Zoiglbier** (pron., TSOY-gul-beer), which is darker and more heavily hopped than other Kellerbiers—are rarely found outside Franconia because they don't travel well.

Kölsch (pron., kerlsh [more or less]), a pale, moderately alcoholic (usually about 4.8 percent ABV) German ale originating in the city of Köln (Cologne) and, according to German beer law, allowed to be brewed only there. Although Kölsch's appearance and flavor aren't so unusual—it looks like PILSNER and resembles it in taste, though it's usually less hoppy and less dry—it qualifies as an unusual beer style because it is a *lagered beer that is* not *a lager*. That is, it's a top-fermented ale that is stored (lagered) at a cold temperature for several months before release.

American craft brewers, not subject to German *Diktat,* have produced hundreds of Kölsch-style beers here. German Kölsch *is* exported, and you may find several brands at your local specialty beer shop. But by all accounts, the place to drink Kölsch is Köln, because of the city's distinctive beer culture—a culture in which you, the patron, are abused and are expected to take pleasure in it. Apparently, when one enters a beer hall or beer garden in Köln, one sits at a table and then patiently and silently waits to be attended; to ask to be served is considered bad form. When the waiter—a blue-shirted gentleman called a *Kobe* (the word roughly translates as "pilgrim")—deigns to approach your table, you *must* order a Kölsch, or risk being denounced as a "foreigner." (There may be other sorts of beer on the menu, but you must not drink them.) The beer will be served in a narrow, straight-sided glass called a *Stange* ("stick"). When you finish your beer, the *Kobe* will automatically replace it with another—unless you situate your beer mat (coaster) atop the empty *Stange* to indicate that you've had enough. While serving, the *Kobe* will probably crack jokes at your and your party's expense; it's a time-honored part of his job to insult you. And, when you leave, you must tip him (you must actually place the money in his hand—no leaving it behind on the table); a tip of 5 to 10 percent is standard. (Drinkology isn't sure what happens to you if you don't tip, but, Germany being Germany, we don't care to imagine.)

What fun! Book us on the next flight to Cologne.

Kriek (pron., kreek), a cherry-flavored Belgian LAMBIC beer. (A few Belgian krieks use OUD BRUIN, rather than lambic, as the base beer.) In the traditional method of making kriek, whole (i.e., unpitted) sour Morello cherries are added to young lambic after it has begun to age in barrel; the fruit sugars cause the beer to re-ferment, eventually producing a beer that is intensely cherry-colored and -flavored but not sweet. (The pits and other fruit residues are removed before bottling.) A scarcity of Morello cherries, which are native to Belgium and sometimes called "Flemish" cherries, has led some present-day kriek makers to substitute other varieties—and has led yet others (including Lindemans, which is the brand you're likeliest to find in the United States) to flavor their kriek with cherry-flavored syrup, which results in a sweet-'n'-sour beer whose taste resembles that of Luden's cherry cough drops. Drinkology shamefacedly confesses to liking even these sweet krieks, but, for a slightly more "authentic" taste—a tad drier and funkier—try to lay your hands on the kriek made by the Boon (pron., bone) brewery, also fairly widely available here.

Kristallweiss. See KRISTALLWEIZEN, below.

Kristallweizen (pron., krees-TAHL-vites-zin), a Bavarian WEISS-BIER. The name, which means "crystal wheat," says it all. This wheat beer differs from its better-known sibling, HEFEWEIZEN, in that it is filtered, meaning that it pours clear rather than cloudy. (Kristallweizen is also called **Kristallweiss**, "crystal white.") Because the yeast cells are removed before bottling, Kristallweizen is artificially carbonated, unlike Hefeweizen, which is naturally carbonated in bottle. That, coupled with its clarity and relatively undemonstrative flavor, make Kristallweizen the Weissbier that comes closest, in look and taste, to a PILSNER. If you search, you might find a retailer in your vicinity that carries the Weihenstephaner brewery's Kristallweissbier.

Kvass. See pages 163–64.

LAMBIC

Lambic beers are among the oddest beers in the world—in the opinion of many, they are *the* oddest. Now, "odd" does *not* mean "not good"; Drinkology quite likes the lambics we've sampled, but the taste is definitely not for everyone. For one thing, they're decidedly sour, and even when that sourness is offset or partly disguised by fruit flavoring, as it is in some lambics, a tart edge remains. For another, lambics are decidedly *un*hoppy; they usually have no discernible hops character, because only **aged dried hops**—which add no flavor or bitterness to the brew but do confer the preservative effect—are used in their making. So, if sour tastes appeal to you and you can tolerate the idea of beers with no hops flavor, you'll probably like lambics; if not, then probably not.

There are a number of subcategories of lambics—faro, GUEUZE, KRIEK, etc.—but all lambics share a place of origin and a method of fermentation. The place is the Payottenland (also spelled Pajottenland) region of Belgium—a string of villages and intervening farmland along the river Senne (also spelled Zenne), just southwest of the capital, Brussels. (There's also one lambic brewery—Cantillon—in Brussels itself.) The fermenting method is **spontaneous fermentation**. And these two attributes—place of origin and fermenting method—are two sides of the same coin.

Some beer writers (and some brewers, including home brewers) like to insist that *any* type of beer can be made *anywhere*—that the key to making a successful beer of whatever style is to follow a proper recipe, which includes, of course, acquiring the right ingredients. Drinkology won't weigh in on whether this opinion is correct or not—*except* in the case of lambics. Regarding lambics, it is definitely *in*correct, and for a very simple reason: unless you establish a brewery in the Payottenland, you *cannot get* all of the essential ingredients. Specifically, you cannot get the right combo of **"bugs"**—wild yeasts and other **microflora**, including various strains of bacteria—that reside in the Payottenland and are essential to a lambic's fermentation.

In fact, making a proper lambic might be a sizeable challenge even were you to build a (new) brewery along the river Senne, and that's because the yeasts and other critters that turn lambic wort into lambic beer hang out in the very nooks and crannies of lambic breweries' fermenting rooms. They're there in the cobwebby timbers, they're there in the walls of the wooden fermentation tanks—and they've been flourishing there, in some cases, for hundreds of years. (As you might guess, lambic-beer brewers tend to resist modernization—or even overly meticulous cleaning—of their facilities, lest the balance of this age-old mix of microorganisms be upset.) Lambic beers, in short, have what wine lovers call **terroir**. They taste indelibly of where they come from.*

> ### They're there in the cobwebby timbers

---

* You can, of course, try to replicate lambics elsewhere, by inoculating wort with commercially available versions of the yeast and bacteria species that play the major roles in lambics' fermentation—or by doing as the Belgians do, and exposing your wort to the open air. Several North American craft brewers now make lambic-like beers (see SOUR BEER), as do a number of especially fearless home brewers. (Some home brewers even cultivate their own bacteria—you know, *in petri dishes*—which strikes Drinkology as taking the DIY thing just a nanometer too far.) No matter how good they are, however, non-Belgian "lambics" are *not* lambics; they're better termed **lambic-style** or, even better, **pseudo-lambic** beers, since the mix of bugs a non-Belgian brewer achieves is unlikely ever to be the same as any of the mixes infecting the fermenting rooms of the Senne valley.

Appropriately, the word *lambic* (sometimes spelled *lambiek*) is most probably a toponym—meaning a word derived from a place name. The place in question is the town of Lembeek, one of the little cities in the Senne valley where lambics are brewed. (Other etymologies have been proposed, but they aren't as poetically satisfying.) If you want to get all authentic about it, you'll pronounce *lambic* like this: lom-BEEK. But Drinkology consorts mostly with American beer drinkers, who mostly say LAM-bick.

Lambics, which are WHEAT BEERS of a sort (their grain bills generally mix about two parts barley malt to one part raw, unmalted wheat), are distinctive in other ways, as well. For one, fermentation of lambics occurs only from October through April, because exposing the wort to the air during the hotter months would amount to an invitation to *other* bugs—yeasts and bacteria that aren't members of the fermenting room's neighborly menagerie but invaders that flourish in the ambient atmosphere when the weather's warm—to crash the party, and to spoil the beer. Lambics are also aged for a considerable time—one to three years—in wooden casks, often casks previously used to age port or sherry. And lambics are usually **blended beers**. (Unblended lambics do exist. A couple of pubs in Brussels have unblended lambic beer on tap, and at least one maker—the aforementioned Brussels brewery, Cantillon—bottles and exports an unblended lambic, with the seriously pretentious name of Grand Cru Bruocsella.)

What a lambic is blended *with* depends on the substyle it belongs to. Fruit lambics are mixed either with whole fruit (whose sugars set off another fermentation, leading to a fruity-but-dry result) or fruit syrups (making for a sweeter, but usually far from cloying, result). Well-known fruit lambics include kriek, which is cherry flavored; raspberry-flavored **framboise**; and black-currant-flavored **cassis**; as well as apple- and peach-flavored varieties. (Note that another Belgian sour ale, OUD BRUIN, is sometimes used as the base beer for kricks and framboises.)

Fruit lambics are the ones most commonly available from U.S. beer retailers—especially the fruit-syrup-flavored lambics from the Lindemans Brewery, which in 1979 became the first lambic brewer to market its products here. But don't make the (common) mistake of equating lambics with fruit beers. Just as not all lambics are fruit-flavored, not all fruit beers are lambics. (See FRUIT AND VEGETABLE BEERS for more info.)

Faro is a type of lambic sweetened with candy sugar. Faro beers used to be so popular among the citizens of Brussels that the style was regarded as the city's own hometown brew—and was sometimes disparaged by foreign visitors, including nineteenth-century French poet Charles Baudelaire, who compared drinking faro to downing a gulp of river-water from the Senne (then one of Europe's most foully polluted waterways). Faro's popularity waned in the twentieth century, but the style has recently undergone a revival. Some U.S. specialty beer retailers carry a faro made by the Lindemans Brewery.

Perhaps the most unusual substyle of this unusual style of beer, however, is GUEUZE, in which old lambic (aged for two to three years) is blended with "young" lambic (aged for at least six months but maybe even a whole year—but that's not much time for a lambic) and then bottled. Because the younger beer hasn't fully fermented, gueuze undergoes a second fermentation in bottle—like

Lambics may seem exotic and classy (an impression likely to be underscored by their prices, which begin at about nine bucks—granted, that might be for a 750-milliliter bottle—and range upward to the high teens), but they are essentially *peasant* beers. They're seasonal, top-fermented FARMHOUSE ALES whose brewing traditionally kept farm families occupied during the time between harvest and planting. Lambic's origin disappears into the mists of time, but it's safe to say that it's been brewed in Flanders (the Flemish-speaking part of Belgium, along whose southern boundary Payottenland is situated) for many, many centuries. If you've ever seen the painting *Peasant Wedding,* by the Flemish/ Netherlandish old master Pieter Bruegel the Elder, you may recall that it shows, along its left-hand edge, a man pouring beer from a jug into a tankard (and several wedding guests who, sitting at table, are hoisting tankards of their own). Well, the beer depicted in that 1568 painting was in all probability a lambic-style beer.

AFTER
BRUEGEL

champagne. In gueuze, lambic's trademark tartness is often comple-
mented (if that's the right word) by a sometimes profound **funki-
ness**, apparent especially on the nose. Commentators have likened
gueuze's odor (which *is* the right word) to farts, stinky feet, and,
slightly more politely, moldy old leather.

Lambics are often bottled in champagne bottles—thick-walled,
with **punts** (the indentations in the bottom), and stoppered with
corks. Sometimes the cork is held in place champagne-style—with
the little metal cage called a **muzzle**—in which case you should
open the bottle carefully, as you would a sparkling wine. Sometimes,
though, the cork is topped with a metal cap, and you'll need both a
church key and a corkscrew to get it out. It makes aesthetic sense to
drink lambic beers from champagne flutes or, better, tulip-shaped
champagne glasses.

Lambics, which are moderately alcoholic (generally between
4 and 6 percent ABV), fizzy, and sometimes cloudy (because unfiltered), are widely regarded as particularly
complex in flavor—the complexity resulting **"Sprite for adults"?**
not just from blending but from the mul-
titude of microorganisms contributing their different by-products
during fermentation. That complexity, along with the winelike
flavor of some lambics and, of course, the absence of hops character,
makes them appealing brews to some wine lovers who otherwise
disdain beer. Lambics' tartness—they can be so lemony-limey as
to taste like Sprite for adults—makes them great summer thirst
quenchers. And the indisputable oddness makes drinking a lambic
(or, better, several different kinds of lambics) a merit-badge-worthy
experience for any dedicated beer-world scout.

For info on other types of Belgian sour ale, see FLANDERS RED and OUD BRUIN.

"Lawn-mower beer." See PILSNER.

Leipzig Gose. See GOSE.

Light beer. See pages 154–56.

Low-carbohydrate beer. See pages 154–56.

Low-point beer. See pages 162–63.

Maibock. See BOCK.

Malt liquor. See pages 168–71.

Märzen (pron., MEHRZ-en), a.k.a. **Märzenbier** or **Oktoberfest** (and sometimes **Märzen-Oktoberfest**), a Bavarian lager that is relatively dark in color, malty, hoppy, and (as measured against other lagers) alcoholically strong, with about 5 to over 6 percent ABV. *Märzen* means "March," as in the month, so how come it's also called *Oktober*—as in October—*fest*? Although it's seemingly contradictory, the pairing of two months that fall half a year apart makes historical sense. Back in the days before refrigeration, the brewing of beer in Bavaria was limited (by custom but also by law) to the cooler months. The final batches were brewed in March (hence *Märzen*) and stored (lagered) in caves cooled with blocks of ice carved from local ponds during the wintertime. These "March" beers were more strongly hopped and brewed to be higher in alcohol than beers made earlier in the brewing season because they had to last throughout the summer and into the following fall, when brewing would recommence. (Recall the preservative capability of both hops and alcohol.) Then, round about October (hence *Oktober*) brewers had to empty their casks of any remaining beer to prepare them for the next season. The need to drink up all that leftover beer provided the perfect excuse for a party (hence *fest*).

Of course, the advent of mechanical refrigeration eliminated the climatological rationale for SEASONAL BEERS like Märzen-Oktoberfest. It did not, however, impair people's need to party. The Oktoberfest held annually in the Bavarian capital of Munich from late September through early October—which celebrated its two-hundredth birthday in 2010—is not just the grandpapa of all beer festivals; it's also the world's largest such gathering, now drawing six million revelers who collectively put away something like two million gallons of beer over the festival's two weeks. (For an account of a rather more modest—but, in a way, no less frenzied—beer fest, see the sidebar on pages 243–55.)

Today, Märzen-style lagers are made by many brewers in Germany and Austria (where the style has become particularly popular); most German and Austrian brands are available year-round, though a few makers (notably Munich's famous Paulaner and Spaten breweries) stick to the old tradition of autumn release. As do most North American craft breweries that include this style of lager among their offerings. (It's mostly just called Oktoberfest here, though you'll find a few American brewers who use the less-familiar-to-us Märzen moniker.) American Oktoberfests are—unsurprisingly, given American beerhounds' insatiable hops craving—generally a bit hoppier than the Bavarian brews. Note, finally, that some American breweries make *fake* Oktoberfests—

which, although they may resemble beers of the Märzen style in color and flavor, are top-fermented ales rather than lagers.

Milk stout. See STOUT.

Monastic beers. See ABBEY ALES, SCHWARZBIER, TRAPPIST BEERS, and the information on Doppelbock on pages 90–91.

Near beer. See page 162.

Nonalcoholic beer. See pages 160–62.

Oatmeal stout. See STOUT.

Oktoberfest. See MÄRZEN.

Old ale, a strong, dark, lusciously malty, and sometimes slightly sour or acidic English style of barrel-aged ale (see BARREL-AGED BEERS) that emulates the "keeping" ales of the eighteenth century and earlier. Ales of this style are also called **strong ales** or, sometimes, **stock ales** (because the ales on which they're modeled were, historically, kept "in stock" by breweries as the ale matured in barrel; see PORTER for more on this practice). Most British old ales weigh in somewhere between 8 and 10 percent ABV, putting them midway, alcoholically, between strong BITTER and BARLEY WINE; North American craft versions of the style are sometimes even stronger, creeping into barley wine territory. Like barley wines, old ales are meant for slow sipping—preferably on a cold night while one sits before a roaring fire (which is why some old ales are called **winter warmers**).

Before the nineteenth century (when PALE ALES came to the fore and the making of older styles was largely abandoned), British brewers often made ale of two different strengths: an "old" or "strong" stock ale and a **mild ale** that was alcoholically weaker and lighter in color and that was meant to be drunk young. Because the old ale had lingered in barrel, undergoing a slow secondary fermentation often involving the activity of *Brettanomyces* yeasts (see SOUR BEER) and lactic acid–producing bacteria, it often had a sharp, acidic bite that some drinkers found unpleasant. Because of this, pubs often mixed the older and the younger, milder ale together in different ratios to suit individual customers' tastes. Today's old ales are generally smoother than those old old ales must've been, though some do have a definite tang (and, in fact, a few brewers inoculate their old ales with *Lactobacillus* bacteria to produce that authentically tart snap).

Drinkology's resident beer expert, Danielle Casavant, who literally resides in Michigan, recommends you try one of her home-state favorites: the crimson-colored, 10.2-percent-ABV Third Coast Old Ale made by the Bell's Brewing Company of Kalamazoo. Among English old ales, she's fond of Fuller's Vintage Ale (brewed in limited batches and meant to be cellared for three or four years after bottling).

Oud bruin (pron., OAT-brun), a.k.a. **Flanders brown ale**, an aged Belgian sour ale. Oud bruin (the name means "old brown") is darker in color and usually maltier in flavor than FLANDERS RED ales, and, unlike Flanders reds, which are BARREL-AGED BEERS, oud bruins are nowadays generally aged in stainless-steel tanks rather than oak. Although oud bruins constitute a small class of beers, they are diverse. Some are only vaguely tart, others are astringently sour; some are copper colored, others a deeper, richer brown. Their

GREEN BEER

And, no, by that heading we don't mean beer that's been dyed green
with food coloring for beer-guzzlers' favorite holiday, Saint Patrick's
Day. We mean, of course, **organic beer**.

For the most part, farmers of barley and other beer grains, as well
as of hops, continue to rely heavily on pesticides and chemical fertilizers, so organic beer remains a relative rarity. Nonetheless, a slowly
increasing number of organic and partly organic beers are appearing
on the market. In North America, organic beer makers seem most
heavily concentrated in the Pacific Northwest—unsurprising, given
that region's progressive reputation and its people's greater-than-
average support for local, sustainable agriculture. Portland, Oregon,
plays host each June to the North American Organic Brewers
Festival, at which about thirty beer makers (most from the Northwest
but a few from outside the region) were represented in 2010. A trend
toward using organic ingredients is also showing up in Europe. To
spotlight just two examples: The two-hundred-year-old German
brewer Pinkus-Müller, based in Münster, turned to organic brewing
as early as 1980. And Samuel Smith, a brewery in North Yorkshire,
England, makes several all-organic products.

Of course, using organic ingredients to the greatest extent possible
is just one measure of a brewer's commitment to sustainability. The
sources, kinds, and quantity of energy a brewery uses; the brewery's
sponsorship of or participation in sustainability initiatives; and its
methods of disposing of waste products (e.g., giving away spent grain
to local farmers to use as forage for livestock) are equally important.
Brewers who engage in sustainable activities of one kind or another

tend to advertise their environmentally responsible efforts on their websites, so it's fairly easy to find out whether your favorite beer's maker is running an earth-friendly operation.

Beyond buying organic beer, beer drinkers can reduce their own carbon footprints in ways small and large, for instance, by saving empty bottles and giving them to a home-brewing friend (many home brewers recycle bottles rather than buying new ones) or by making a pledge to drink only beer that's brewed locally—which, when you consider the amount of energy consumed in transporting it around the country and the globe, might be the greenest consumer strategy of all.

No discussion of "green" beer could be complete without a mention of **hemp beer**—which is beer that's *flavored* with hemp seeds and not, as one might be tempted to think, brewed from hemp. (Hemp beers, brewed in a number of styles, are, like other beers, made from grain mashes.) Hemp, of course, is the absolutely favorite plant of the ecologically oriented, since this miraculous "weed" can be easily grown without chemical fertilizers or pesticides and can be used as raw material for a vast range of products including building materials, paper, plastics, clothing, and so on. Partisans of hemp beer like to point out that using hemp to flavor beer makes perfect sense, since the hemp and hops plants are closely related. The nutty, sometimes creamy notes hemp seeds contribute to a beer are, however, different from hops' flavors (and do note that hemp beers are generally hopped as well as hemped). Be aware that although some hemp beers are organic, not all are; unfortunately, the mere addition of hemp seeds to a beer does not miraculously make the beer sustainable.

strength ranges from about 4 to 8 percent ABV. (None of the Belgian oud bruins, however, has a pronounced hops character.) Most oud bruins are **blended beers**: a brewery will combine older and younger beers to achieve its brand's signature mix of sour and sweet. Celebrated for aging particularly well in bottle, oud bruins can keep for years if cellared properly, and they are therefore sometimes referred to as **provision beers**. Also, some brewers use oud bruin as the base for fruit beers such as cherry-flavored KRIEK and raspberry-flavored framboise (see LAMBIC, as well as FRUIT AND VEGETABLE BEERS).

The best known of the traditional oud bruins is probably Liefmans Goudenband, made by the Liefmans brewery (established 1679) of Oudenaarde, Belgium. A few big brands (Heineken, Grolsch) produce versions of the style, and oud bruin is fairly widely imitated by North American craft brewers.

Pale ales, ales that are brewed solely or primarily from pale malts. "Pale ale" is simultaneously one of the world's most popular types of beer and a difficult term to define precisely, because it embraces such a large and diverse family of styles. The thing that all these ales have in common, however, is that all are descended, in one way or another, from the pale ales first brewed in England in the middle to late seventeenth century, which had a transformative impact on beer making worldwide.

What made pale ale possible was a revolutionary change in the way barley malt was dried, or kilned. Before the mid-seventeenth century, malt was dried over wood fires, resulting in grain that was brown in color (see BROWN ALE) and roasted and smoky (see

RAUCHBIER) or even somewhat scorched in flavor. But in the mid-1600s it was discovered that malt could be hot-air dried in a kiln fueled by **coke** (and, no, that doesn't mean the soft drink but rather an altered, clean-burning form of coal), resulting in a brewable grain that was much lighter in color than previous malts, lacked their roasted/smoky flavor, and could be mashed much more efficiently, producing greater quantities of fermentable sugars in the mash tun. (That's why pale malts—including the ultra-pale variety known as **pilsner malt**—serve as the **base malts** for most barley-based beers brewed today, including very dark beers, which derive their color and distinctive flavors from the presence of much smaller proportions of darker **specialty malts** in the grain bill.)

By the early years of the eighteenth century, the use of pale malts in brewing had become commonplace in Britain, although the older, darker kinds of ale continued to be made and another hundred years, give or take, would pass before pale ales secured first place in the British market. The entry on INDIA PALE ALE recounts some of that history, but note that the IPA style (bitterly hoppy, alcoholically powerful, and brewed largely for export) actually predates the style called British pale ale—better known as BITTER. This latter style represented an accommodation, by British brewers, of the desires of their domestic clientele—who liked the clarity and crispness of India pale ale but preferred a less strong and less bitter brew. (The irony is that the beer called bitter is less bitter than its predecessor.)

The technique for producing pale malts spread far and wide, working great changes on Continental and nascent American brewing practices. In America, pale ale proved very popular, becoming

U.S. beer drinkers' beverage of choice (and made by hundreds of brewers nationwide) until it, in turn, was swept aside by the even lighter, crisper PILSNER-style lagers. Few U.S. pale ales survived into the twentieth century, and fewer still made it through Prohibition (the XXX and India pale ales made by the Ballantine Brewery were notable exceptions; the former is still made, though now—after several changes of brand ownership since the 1980s—by the Pabst Brewing Company).

Despite pale lager's inroads in Britain from the late 1800s on, pale ale was never in danger of disappearing there. But it took another revolution—that sparked by the craft-brewing movement—to restore its place in the hearts, minds, and throats of American drinkers. In this connection, 1980 stands as a landmark year, for that was when the newly founded Sierra Nevada Brewing Company of Chico, California, first released its Pale Ale, immediately establishing a gold standard for the hundreds of craft brewers who followed suit. Although these American beers are inspired by the British pale ales, they're different enough as a class to qualify as a new substyle: **American pale ale**. Golden to orangey-amber in color, the American versions are, in general, more assertively hopped and, on average, a little stronger than their British cousins (a number cross over, in strength and hops character, if not in name, into India pale ale territory).

Besides the styles already mentioned, others that fall under the broad pale-ale umbrella include AMBER ALE, GOLDEN ALE, HARVEST ALES, IRISH RED ALE, and SCOTTISH ALE; for info on Continental pale ales, see BELGIAN STRONG ALE, BIÈRE DE GARDE, BLONDE ALES, SAISON, and TRIPEL.

Pils. See page 153.

PILSNER

Pilsner may or may not be "the king of beers," but it's certainly a tyrant. If you've ever drunk a beer—even just one beer in your life—the chance is pretty damned good that you've drunk a pilsner. That's because the pilsner style of lager, which didn't even exist 175 years ago, is now the overwhelmingly dominant style of beer worldwide. Pilsner's hegemony reminds Drinkology of an old Monty Python comedy routine—the one in which a cheese-shop customer throatily declares cheddar to be "the single most popular cheese in the world!"—and not just because of pilsner's similarly impregnable dominion. Just as cheddar can be a tasty and sophisticated cheese (try a sharp, crumbly, nicely aged Irish farmhouse cheddar if you don't believe us), so can pilsner be a delicious and worthy beer. Trouble is, most commercial pilsners—like most commercial cheddars—are anything but.

Budweiser's a pilsner-style beer. So are Miller and PBR. So are Molson, and Foster's, and Harp. So are Heineken and Grolsch and Amstel—the three Dutch brands so popular here and elsewhere. So, for that matter, is Singha (from Thailand). And Efes (from Turkey). And Tsingtao (from China). And Kingfisher (from India), and Kirin (from Japan), and . . . [insert the name of almost any other big-name, mass-produced beer, from almost anywhere]. The best-selling beer in the world is a Chinese pilsner whose name you may never have heard: Snow Beer. Light beers are pilsner-style beers, though of a degraded sort (see pages 154–56). It's no exaggeration to say that ninety-some percent of all beer brewed and consumed today, all around the globe, is pilsner-style beer.

So what *is* pilsner, anyway? And how did a beer style introduced in 1842—and considered highly unusual at the time—become so universally popular as to nearly obliterate every other style of beer? How, in other words, did *pilsner* become almost synonymous with *beer*? The history of pilsner's rise, spread, and conquest closely tracks the history of beer itself since the mid-nineteenth century. In fact, pilsner's rise, spread, and conquest *is* beer's history from the mid-nineteenth century on—at least up until the beginnings, several decades ago, of the craft-beer movement, which can rightly (albeit only partly) be viewed as a revolt against pilsner's totalitarian rule.

Which is kind of ironic, since pilsner itself originated in a revolt.

In 1838, the good citizens of Pilsen, a city in Bohemia (now Plzeň, in the Czech Republic), were growing more and more unhappy about the quality of the local beer. Apparently, it wasn't only bad, it was uneven. Sometimes it was tolerably bad, sometimes intolerably so. So they did what good citizens too long deprived of good beer might reasonably do: they rioted—dumping barrels of the swill into Pilsen's presumably quaintly cobblestoned streets.

Did the city fathers quash the uprising with tear gas, dogs, and fire hoses? No they did not. Instead, they wisely commissioned the building of a new Citizens' Brewery (*Bürger Brauerei*) dedicated to the proposition that Pilsen's burghers should have better beer. And they wisely hired a Bavarian brewer, Josef Groll (or Grolle—sources differ on the spelling), to run the operation, which opened in 1839. The Bavarians, just over the border to Bohemia's west, had been brewing lager beers for some time, and Herr Groll, though young (only twenty-two when he took the job in Pilsen), obviously knew his stuff. What's more, he was not afraid to play around with ingredients, combining newly avail-

In applying the term *pilsner* to a huge, multinational army of beers, Drinkology is taking certain liberties. Properly, the name Pilsner (capitalized) belongs only to beer brewed in the town of Pilsen. Specifically, that means Pilsner Urquell ("original Pilsner")—a name trademarked in 1898 by Pilsen's brewers, who realized that worldwide copying of the pilsner style was watering down their brand. Respecting Pilsen's claim to the name, some beer experts refer to similar beers produced elsewhere (whether in Bohemia itself or much farther afield) as **Bohemian lagers** and to pilsner-style beers made by the big commercial U.S. breweries as **American pale lagers**.

German pilsner-style beers, by the way, have their own nomenclature. Such a beer, when it's from the north of Germany, is generally called a **Pils**—German brewers stopped using "Pilsner" when they were sued by the Czech Pilsner brewers. When it's from southern Germany, a pilsner-style beer is usually called a **Helles**, which means "pale." (There are subtle differences between a typical Pils and a typical Helles, with the former tending, for example, to be more hoppy/bitter than the latter.)

Oh, and *pilsner* is sometimes spelled *pilsener*—with two *e*'s. Just thought you'd like to know.

able very pale malts with locally grown Saaz hops (farmed in the vicinity of the nearby Bohemian town of Saaz, now Žatec). These ingredients, coupled with Pilsen's very soft (i.e., mineral-free) water and the lagering method that Groll had learned as an apprentice, resulted in a brand-new style of beer. Groll rolled out his first batch of what would ever after be known as pilsner on October 4, 1842.

Five of the ten top-selling beers in the United States are light beers. Together, those five light beers account for nearly *half* of all the beer sold here, and one brand—Anheuser-Busch's Bud Light—trounces everybody else, accounting for almost 20 percent of the entire domestic beer market. (Bud Light is quite the slugger internationally, too—one out of every six beers drunk on this poor, benighted planet is a Bud Light.)

These are phenomenal figures when you consider that untold thousands of beers representing hundreds of different styles are brewed in the U.S. alone. And the numbers grow even more astounding when you stop to think that light beers—as a class—are sneered at, derided, even outright despised by most people who claim to be real beer lovers. So *why* are they so popular? Are light beers' massive sales merely another example, if an especially egregious one, of the triumph of marketing over taste?

Drinkology's definitive answer: yes and no.

Light beer—pilsner-style beer that's lower in calories and carbohydrates than the standard brew—has only been around since 1967, when a brand called Gablinger's Diet Beer was brought to market by the now-defunct New York–based Rheingold Brewing Company. The man who invented the method for making for lower-cal/lower-carb beer, a Dr. Joseph L. Owades, was something of a marketing prodigy. Owades made it his aim to sell beer to people who *didn't like beer.* He's reported to have said, "When I got into the beer business, I used to ask people why they did not drink beer. The answer I got was twofold: One, 'I don't like the way beer tastes.' Two, 'I'm afraid it will make me fat.' . . . I couldn't do anything about the taste of beer, but I could do something about the calories."

Dr. Owades was, however, being much too modest. He certainly *did* do something about the taste when he set about removing a goodly portion of beer's calories and carbs. In the process, he created a type of beer that doesn't taste like very much at all. And, apparently, that's just what a very large slice of the drinking public (perhaps including many folk who wouldn't touch a "real" beer) *wants*. So the complaint that light beer doesn't taste like beer may well be entirely beside the point.

That's not to say that light beer caught on instantly. Owades's marketing genius was a little ahead of its time, and the Gablinger's brand flopped. So Owades lent the formula to an acquaintance at the (also now-defunct) Meister Brau Brewery, in Chicago, but Meister Brau Lite tanked, too. Then one of the giant brewers—Miller—bought Meister Brau. Miller's brew team tinkered with the recipe and in 1975 brought out Miller Lite. With Miller's marketing muscle behind it, the brand succeeded, and the other big makers soon followed suit—and have continued, over the decades, to introduce new brands of light beer.

Specific brewing methods are—no surprise—closely guarded secrets, but it appears that all light beers are made in more or less the same way. Enzymes are added to the mash that break down carbohydrate compounds called **dextrins** into fermentable sugars. Ordinarily, these carbs remain in the wort—yeast can't eat them—and they provide much of the color, flavor, and body (and some of the calories) of the finished beer. But when the dextrins are chemically altered, yeast *can* eat the resulting, simpler sugars. Perhaps counterintuitively, the wort for light beer is actually higher in sugar than the wort for regular pilsner, but that just means that there's more food for the yeast to convert to alcohol. At the end of fermentation, light beer is significantly higher in alcohol (it is, in brewer's lingo, more **attenuated**) than a non-light beer made from the same ingredients would be—*and* it's significantly lower in the stuff that makes beer taste like beer. It's also lower in calories, but not all that much lower—generally less than 30 percent—

because much of any beer's caloric content comes from the alcohol, not the carbs.

Most people, even those who typically drink light beer, would probably agree that light beer tastes "watery," and, in fact, it *is* watered down. Light beer makers long ago decided that they didn't want these ostensibly healthier products to pack a greater per-serving wallop than regular beer, so they reduce the ABV by adding water to the fermented brew. It's no wonder, then, that light beers are so insipid. If you take a mash that would, in any case, result in a comparatively mild-flavored beer, then dose it with enzymes that strip away some of that flavor, and *then* add water to the fermented brew . . . well, what can you expect?

Less, however, is definitely sometimes more, as the phenomenal worldwide sales demonstrate.

Herr Groll's beer was unlike any ever brewed before: a light-bodied, moderately alcoholic, pale gold, crisp, sparkling, and wonderfully *clear* beverage whose hops character was more noticeable on the nose than on the tongue.

It was drunk in Pilsen with gusto. It was soon imitated throughout Bohemia and in neighboring Germany. It made early cameos in London pubs (though the Brits, at first, didn't like the wan new import very much). And, by the 1870s—after pilsner-style Bohemian lagers began winning international beer competitions—it was taken up by American brewers, among them Adolphus Busch of St. Louis, who named his new pilsner-style lager Budweiser after another Bohemian town, Budweis (now České Budějovice, which we have no idea how to pronounce).

The American would-be emulators encountered a serious problem, however. Bohemian pilsners were brewed with malted two-row barley, which was then unavailable on this side of the Atlantic. They found they couldn't duplicate Bohemian pilsners' remarkable clarity using the six-row barley they typically relied on—it was much richer in protein than two-row and inevitably resulted in a hazy beer. So the Americans, intent on capturing the Bohemian lagers' see-through appearance, tinkered with their recipes, adding varying amounts of what are called **adjuncts**—other grains, notably rice and corn—to the mix of grains used. They succeeded insofar as they were able to produce a look-alike beer; they failed insofar as their "pilsners" or "Bohemian lagers" tasted different from the original: weaker, less assertive. They wanted a beer the color of straw, and they got it; trouble was, they got one that tasted strawlike, too.

That taste difference appears not to have mattered much (or at all), given American-style pilsners' ultimate marketing triumph. In fact, given Americans' oft-remarked fondness for bland-flavored foods and beverages, it may well have helped. And during the late nineteenth century, several other factors also helped propel pilsner-style beer to national dominance:

1. the development of mechanical refrigeration (because pilsners, like all lagers, require cool temperatures for fermentation and conditioning);

2. efficient rail transport (enabling brewers making pilsner-style beers to distribute their products far and wide);

3. large-scale German immigration to the United States (German immigrants disliked the stronger English-style ales that Americans drank before the new lagers' arrival);

4. the **"tied" system**, in which the big beer-makers ran franchise taverns that were allowed to sell only the beers made by the brewers licensing the franchises; and, curiously . . .

5. the temperance movement.

You read that right: *the temperance movement.* Light in color, light in taste, and (comparatively) light in alcohol content, pilsner-style beers were perceived as a far cry from ale—and were indeed a very, very far cry from the hard liquor that was the temperance movement's nemesis. Touted as "temperance beverages" by their brewers and even promoted as such by some temperance-movement activists, the new light lagers were presented as wholesome, "non-intoxicating" drinks suitable for imbibing in the family-friendly, German-style beer gardens that proliferated in cities across America in the late 1800s. Ale's proper precinct—like rum's and whiskey's—was the dark, dank, and disreputable saloon, where shiftless men gathered to shirk their familial and civic duties. The new beers, by contrast, could sinlessly be drunk by respectable people—the gentlemen and the ladies, too—in the sunshine and open air. (And this wasn't just an American phenomenon. By the late nineteenth century, some British brewers were likewise exploiting pilsners' ostensible power to defeat the social scourge of alcoholism. As one ad for a British pilsner-style lager unambiguously if disingenuously put it, the new beer could "diminish intoxication and do more for the temperance cause than all the efforts of total abstainers.")

There isn't enough space in this little book to document the whole story of pilsner's world conquest—but we should note that its dominion in the U.S. was certainly helped along by Prohibition. Not, of course, that brewing pilsners was permitted during Prohibition—its manufacture, like that of virtually all alcoholic beverages, was *verboten*. But Prohibition's injuries to the U.S. beer, wine, and liquor industry were felt hardest by the little guys. The bigger pilsner brewers—which were the largest brewers in the country by the time Prohibition was enacted—sometimes had the money, facilities, distribution networks, and business savvy to diversify (while, of course, downsizing) and thereby survive. When Prohibition ended, they faced much less in the way of competition. (The tale of the big brewers' triumph is, by the way, wonderfully well told in Maureen Ogle's 2006 book *Ambitious Brew: The Story of American Beer*.)

We've said a lot of negative stuff about pilsner-style lagers, but let us not leave you with the impression that Drinkology hates pilsners. Without quivering, Drinkology will admit that, in default mode, we sometimes order a Bud (and, as much as it pains us, we keep Bud Light in the fridge for the in-laws, who don't much like anything else). There are pilsners we actually like: Singha, for one (we wouldn't drink any other beer with a Thai restaurant meal), and Tsingtao (with Chinese food), and especially the Jamaican pilsner Red Stripe (for just having a beer). We even have a soft spot in our heart for Tecate—the absolutely insipid Mexican pilsner that once, long ago, made a disastrous vacation we took in the Rio Grande Valley tolerable. (The wedge of lime we squeezed into each can helped.) And we don't have anything personal against **"lawn-mower beers"** as

To Chronicle Small Beer

The term *beer* has a legal definition, but general parlance never precisely squares with the language of the law, so there are lots of beverages that are called "beer" but that aren't really beer, or not quite. Some of these aren't (or aren't quite) beer because their alcohol level is too low. Some—and here we're thinking of root beer, ginger beer (and ale), birch beer, etc.—aren't beer, at least not in that legal sense, because they're made from something other than fermented grain. In this sidebar, though, we focus on the "near" (and nearly near) beers—malt beverages that fall short of being beer because they don't contain enough booze.

"Nonalcoholic" "Beers"

Low-alcohol grain-based "beers" include, at their very lowest alcohol level, the drinks commonly referred to as **nonalcoholic beers**. Actually, "nonalcoholic" is sort of a misnomer, since these beverages aren't entirely alcohol-free. Rather, they're *very, very low* in alcohol: on average, about 0.5 percent ABV. Granted, that's not nothing, but it's actually only a little higher than the ABV of fresh-squeezed orange juice. (Surprised to learn that orange juice contains some ethyl alcohol? Well, think about it. Natural yeasts are floating around *everywhere* in the atmosphere, so as soon as the skin of a fruit of any kind is pierced, yeasts "invade" and immediately begin converting the fruit's sugar to CO_2 and C_2O_5OH.)

Most of today's so-called nonalcoholic beers are produced following a method that, up through fermentation, closely resembles the brewing of PILSNER-style beers, although there are also a number of non-pilsner-type nonalcoholic beers on the market. The difference is that the process of making a nonalcoholic beer includes a final step, before bottling, in which the alcohol is removed. This is often accomplished through **reverse osmosis**, a technique about which you are required to know absolutely nada—but which you may be interested to know involves passing the beer through a semipermeable membrane that permits the water and alcohol to flow through while holding back the beer's other constituents; the water and alcohol are then separated from one another through distillation, and the water is returned to the "retained" components. The website of one of the leading brands of nonalcoholic beer, O'Doul's (brewed by Anheuser-Busch), states that the alcohol is removed "naturally." Drinkology offers no comment except to note that synthetic reverse-osmosis membranes do not, so far as we know, occur in nature.

Makers of dealcoholized beers are wont to claim that the alcohol-removal process does not affect taste. Beer lovers—who know that *any* intervention can affect a beer's character—tend to dispute this, assigning nonalcoholic beers failing grades in flavor, body, color, etc. But, as with every other category of thing, there are better and worse nonalcoholic beers, and here Drinkology will make a recommendation. If you're going to drink a nonalcoholic beer, try a Clausthaler (brewed by the Binding-Brauerei company of Germany). It's the one preferred by those among Drinkology's reformed-alcoholic friends who permit themselves to drink nonalcoholic beer (and, yes, we do have reformed-alcoholic friends as well as nonreformed-alcoholic friends). We've sampled Clausthaler and some of the other brands, and we agree. It's better.

Historically, today's nonalcoholic beers are the latter-day progeny of Prohibition. The Volstead Act—the law passed by Congress in 1919 that spelled out the specifics of the constitutional amendment prohibiting the manufacture or sale of intoxicating (take special note of the word *intoxicating* here) beverages—did not regulate beverages containing 0.5 percent alcohol or less. And so, in an attempt to stay afloat after Prohibition went into effect, many breweries resorted to making extremely low-alcohol "malt beverages," or "cereal beverages"—in effect, beer-flavored soft drinks. These drinks—universally referred to as **near beers** and marketed under wonderfully silly-sounding brand-names like Graino, Barlo, Cero, and Mulo—never proved especially popular, and breweries that depended solely on this survival strategy tended to go under.

A CONVENIENT LEGAL FICTION

And Prohibition—or, rather, the *end* of Prohibition—spawned yet another category of low-alcohol beer: **3.2 beer**, so named because it has an ABV of 3.2 percent. By the early 1930s, more than a decade after the ban went into effect, the United States was sick to death of Prohibition—not only had it proved impossible to enforce, but it was robbing federal and state treasuries of liquor-tax revenues that were sorely needed during the Great Depression. Repeal was beginning to seem inevitable. The trouble with the repeal of a constitutional amendment, however, is that *it takes a long time,* requiring the approval of three-quarters of the country's state legislatures. What was obviously needed, in the uncertain interim before repeal could be effected, was a convenient legal fiction.

Congress supplied that helpful ruse in late 1932, by amending the Volstead Act to redefine what counted as an intoxicating beverage. (We told you above to pay attention to that word *intoxicating*.) According to the newly revised law, beverages containing up to 3.2 percent ABV were *not* intoxicating. They had been, but now they were not. The Orwellian logic of this decision aside, Congress's endgame weakening of Prohibition made a lot of people (especially the country's suffering brewers) very happy. Beer—*real* beer, albeit with a lower than normal alcohol content—could once again be legally brewed, sold, and guzzled.

Interestingly, 3.2 beer (also known as **three-two beer** and **low-point beer**) has persisted long past Prohibition's repeal, which finally occurred on December 5, 1933. With national Prohibition lifted, much of the job of regulating the sale of alcohol was handed over to the individual states, which is why, even today, there are vast differences between states regarding where, when, and even whether one can purchase this or that kind of alcoholic beverage. So, in 2011, there remain a handful of states that allow higher-alcohol beers to be sold in liquor stores but prohibit the sale of beer with an ABV greater than 3.2 percent in grocery and convenience stores. The major U.S. brewers are delighted to accommodate, producing low-point versions of their signature brands specifically for distribution to those retailers in those states.

THE RUSSIAN SOFT DRINK

Although Prohibition fostered the creation of near beer and then, as repeal approached, 3.2 beer, the making of other kinds of low-alcohol beer and beerlike beverages predates Prohibition by centuries. You may, for instance, have heard of **kvass** (sometimes spelled *kvas*)—a traditional drink in Russia and in parts of Eastern Europe, especially the Baltic states. It's probable that kvass resembles the ancestral beers of Mesopotamia in that it's made from bread rather than malted grain (see page 5). The bread (usually rye) is dried, then steeped in hot water and strained from the liquid, which, when cool, is fermented with yeast; fruit (especially raisins) and herbs (especially mint) are often added to the finished brew.

Because of kvass's low alcohol content, generally less than 2 percent and often considerably less, Russians consider it a soft drink, suitable even for children. (But do note that we're talking about those vodka-sodden *Russians* here.) Over the past couple of decades, kvass's popularity in Russia first waned as Coca-Cola and Pepsi conquered the soft-drink market in the former Soviet Union, then rebounded as resurgent nationalism led some Russians to reject the "cola-nization" of their country. (Coca-Cola of course responded by developing and marketing its own brand of kvass in Russia, beginning in 2008.) If your travel plans don't include the former Soviet bloc, you can buy kvass at some Russian grocery stores. A very few American craft brewers have released their own versions, but distribution has been limited. (See RYE BEER and SAHTI for info on other beers made using rye.)

Don't Drink the Water

Even if you've never heard of kvass, you've probably encountered the term **small beer**. And it's likely that you first heard it (as Drinkology first did) in a non beer related context, since the phrase *small beer* has been used, at least since Shakespeare's day, to derisively denote something trivial. That's how Iago (the villain of Shakespeare's play *Othello*) uses it in the speech from which this sidebar takes its title. In a misogynist rant delivered to the play's tragic heroine, Desdemona, Iago declares it women's destiny "to suckle fools and *chronicle small beer*"—that is, to pay too-scrupulous attention to the unimportant (from a man's point of view) aspects of running a household.

There's a valid observation lodged in Iago's vituperation. Small beer (a.k.a. **small ale** or **weak ale**) was, in Shakespeare's time and for centuries beyond, such an essential beverage that every British household kept some on hand—the equivalent, in today's terms, of making sure there's a half gallon of milk in the fridge. (That was true in

Britain's American colonies and the early American republic, as well. Ben Franklin drank small beer for breakfast; George Washington brewed his own at Mount Vernon.) Small beer was an everyday, any-time-of-day beverage—not just because it was low-alcohol, somewhat nutritious, and cheaper than stronger ale but also because it was *safe* to drink, which wasn't the case with most water in the era before modern municipal water-supply systems.

Small beer, traditionally, was brewed from a second, third, or some-times even a fourth mashing of a single batch of grain. When the same grain is used for multiple mashes, it produces worts that, consecutively, contain less and less fermentable sugar—resulting in beers with pro-gressively less alcohol. So "small" beer isn't beer meant to be served in Munchkin-size mugs; it's beer that's intentionally brewed to be *weak*.

Not everyone disparages small beer. Although much drunk by ordinary folk, it has had its royal defenders. Queen Elizabeth I much preferred it to ale. And some of today's craft brewers, interested in exploring a multiplicity of beer styles of the past, are experimenting with small-beer recipes, partly in reaction against the general trend toward ever "bigger" (= more alcoholic) beers and partly out of the recogni-tion that there's a lot to be said for a well-made beer that won't get you drunk (or not so powerfully or quickly). Notably, San Francisco's Anchor Brewing Company makes a small beer—called, forthrightly, Anchor Small Beer—that's brewed from a second mashing of the grain used in its Old Foghorn BARLEY WINE; although Anchor Small Beer, at 3.3 per-cent ABV, is somewhat higher in alcohol than historical small beers, the difference between it and Old Foghorn, at 8 to 10 percent ABV, gives you an idea how far the wort's fermentable-sugar content can fall from a first to a second mash.

weak, watery, but parched-throat-mending pilsners are sometimes called. We just think it's a damnable shame that so many of the world's people think that *this* (and this alone) is beer.

PORTER

It's a little-noted fact that civilization depends on there being a group of people—men, usually—who earn their living by toting things from one place to another: loading, unloading, delivering, taking away. In a world where transportation is largely mechanized, that class has shrunk in size. But in busy cities in the days before the Industrial Revolution, it was, of necessity, enormous. In eighteenth-century London there were thousands upon thousands of such men. And, as a group, they tended really to like a thick, robustly malty, highly nutritious, highly alcoholic, blackish-brown style of beer that first appeared in London sometime around 1720. They drank so much of it that the brewers who made it became very wealthy, and the beer style itself acquired the name of the working men who favored it. They were, of course, called *porters*.

The history of porter-style beer is complicated. Some credit its invention to a single brewer—a certain Ralph Harwood, of Shoreditch High Street, in the part of London known as the City. According to that—probably legendary—account, Harwood was trying to emulate a drink, then popular in London pubs, called "three threads," which was a mixture, performed by the publican, of three different kinds of beer drawn from different casks. Harwood purportedly called his new brew by a name that strikes the modern ear as ludicrous, salacious, or both: *entire butt*. At the time, however, the name would have conveyed that the taste of the three-threads combo was reproduced, in Harwood's brew, by one beer drawn from a single ("entire") cask ("butt").

But, as we say, that story—which first appeared in the early 1800s—was probably made up, and porter-style beers were probably independently created by a number of London beer makers a century earlier. While its precise origins are obscure, however, porter's rapid rise in popularity among eighteenth-century drinkers couldn't be clearer. The style spread around the British Isles, then immigrated to America at about the same time that colonial discontent was fermenting into revolution. (A porter brewed by an émigré brewer who'd landed in Philadelphia was reportedly one of George Washington's favorite beers.) Porter's arrival in Ireland is particularly significant, historically. Extra-strong porter, you see, was commonly called "stout porter"—a term that eventually got shortened to just STOUT. So Guinness Stout is actually, ancestrally, a porter—though one of greater-than-usual strength. (When engaging in barroom banter, you might try impressing, or irritating, your homies with the syllogistic-sounding axiom, "All stouts are porters, but not all porters are stouts.")

Ludicrous, salacious, or both

Porter remained an extremely popular style through much of the nineteenth century, but its popularity waned, precipitously, with the ascendance of brighter, crisper, PALE ALES and, later, PILSNER-style lagers. By the turn of the twentieth century, few porters were being made in either England or America. (Ireland, however, remained a porter redoubt.) It wasn't until the craft-beer movement of the past several decades that international interest in the style was rekindled.

Malt liquor can be accurately described as a pale, dry, light-bodied, very mildly hopped, mass-market PILSNER-style lager with higher-than-usual alcohol content (ranging from about 5.5 to above 8.2 percent ABV). It doesn't taste like much, but then many mass-market pale lagers don't either. And its alcohol content, while significant, is lower than that of many traditional European beers and latter-day craft-brewed beers. Sounds pretty innocuous, yes?

Think again. Because malt liquor can *also* be accurately described as *the* bad boy of beer. In fact, it's the bad boy of booze, period. No other legal intoxicant—at least not since the temperance movement's campaign against "demon rum" in the 1800s—has inspired such rage, scorn, derision, denunciation, and out-and-out hatred. Alcohol in any form is, as we all sadly know, capable of ruining individual lives; what sets malt liquor apart is that its detractors have accused its makers of attempting to destroy *entire communities*.

It didn't start out that way. Along with just a few other beer styles (CALIFORNIA COMMON BEER [steam beer], CREAM ALE, light beer), malt liquor is an American original. It was created by a couple of Midwestern breweries around the time of World War II. The Grand Valley Brewing Company of Ionia, Michigan, introduced Clix Malt Liquor in the late 1930s, and the Gluek Brewing Company of Minneapolis followed suit in the early '40s with one called Sparkling Stite. Like many other mid-century American "advances," malt liquor was a feat of engineering. Brewers had to tinker with the chemistry of the brewing process, concocting a mash containing a relatively small proportion of barley malt and a relatively great proportion of nonmalt adjuncts (e.g., corn, rice, and dextrose, or **brewer's sugar**) and adding enzymes to break down complex starches into fermentable simple sugars. The purpose of this is simple: to give the yeast plenty to eat so that they'll make *lots* of C_2H_5OH. This technique actually resembles that for brewing light beer (see pages 154–56), except, of course, that malt liquor isn't watered down after fermentation. As with light beer, malt liquor's adjunct-laden, **high-gravity** mash—with a higher-than-usual amount of fermentable sugar—results in a beer without much body or flavor. (Note, too, that some malt liquors are billed as **high-gravity lagers**—a name that sounds imposing but just means that the wort was especially yummy from the yeast's perspective.)

What's ironic, historically, about malt liquor's current rap sheet—as the cheap, get-real-drunk-real-quick choice of the destitute, demented, and downtrodden—is that it was, during its first two decades, targeted at an affluent, aspirational market and pitched as a civilized alternative to proletarian beer. Early ads compared it to champagne and suggested it be served at cocktail parties. The name of one of the earliest malt-liquor brands, and the first to be commercially successful, says it all: *Country Club*. (It's still made, now by the Pabst conglomerate.)

So how did malt liquor accomplish its downscale migration from the suburban, no-minorities-need-apply golf clubs of mid-century America to the inner-city ghettoes and barrios with which it's associated today? Part of the blame (if it's blame you want to assign) can be laid on *market research*. Back in the 1960s, brewers and the ad agencies that worked for them decided to take a look at who was buying their products. They discovered that malt liquor sold better in poorer African-American neighborhoods than in richer white ones, and so they refashioned their advertising accordingly. That advertising, wholesome enough to begin with, grew edgier over time—with, for example, the St. Ides malt-liquor brand commissioning gangsta rappers to create spots in the early 1990s.

BAD BOY

But to return to the '60s for a moment. During that decade, one brewer, the National Brewing Company of Baltimore, Maryland, decided to test the federal government's enforcement of a regulation on the books since the end of Prohibition—to wit, that beer could not be named or advertised in such a way as to promote its alcohol content. Brewers could—in fact, had to—disclose the alcoholic strength on beer containers' labels, but they could not *name* a beer Loaded, or Tipsy, or Three Sheets to the Wind, and they couldn't run ads that said, in effect, "Drink this and you'll get absolutely polluted!" Well, in 1963, the National brewery introduced a new malt liquor, which it called Colt 45—a name that sounds an awful lot like the name of a gun. (Purportedly, it was named for a Baltimore Colts football player whose jersey bore the number 45, but anyway. . . .) And the logo that National's execs chose? A bucking bronco, encircled by a horseshoe. Following the letter but perhaps not the spirit of the law, the Bureau of Alcohol, Tobacco and Firearms *approved* this branding.

The further course of malt liquor's history was largely shaped by these events: the discovery of the power of targeted marketing to specific demographic groups, and the branding of malt liquors in ways that, at least metaphorically, emphasize their added "kick." Oh, and two other factors have certainly played a role: the low price (people without much money tend to buy stuff that, you know, doesn't cost much) and the *big* bottles. (Malt liquors are sold in cans and bottles of many sizes, ranging from twelve to sixty-four ounces, but the forty-ounce bottle—the "forty" or "four-O"—is emblematic, as is the twenty-two-ounce "double deuce," which friends who know about such undignified things tell us fits neatly into a brown paper bag for illicit sidewalk guzzling.)

Let's review: Take a certain category of beer, and advertise it in ways designed to appeal to certain ethnic and other groups (not just urban blacks, but later Latinos, as well as reckless young men of whatever persuasion); give these beers brand names like Colt 45 and King Cobra and Steel Reserve and Hurricane; sell them cheap (which you're able to do because, despite *malt* liquor's name, it contains comparatively little malt—a more expensive ingredient than corn or other adjuncts); *and* put it in huge bottles (some of which are outfitted with extra-wide mouths for easy down-the-hatch pouring). And so what happens?

Well, one thing that happens is that certain people—certain upstanding and morally minded people—object. They say that you're trying to get people *addicted* to the stuff. They say malt liquor's a "gateway" to illegal drugs. They call it bad names, like "liquid crack" and "death in a bottle." They raise, in other words, holy hell. And that no doubt increases malt liquor's cachet among those who want to be perceived as devilish, lawless, and badassed.

Two notes: (1) Not every beer labeled "malt liquor" is the malt liquor we've been talking about here. The category gets muddled by the alcohol laws of a number of states, which specify that the words *malt liquor* appear on the label of any lager whose ABV is higher than 5 percent. So, depending on where you live, you might find that the label of an imported German BOCK beer (for example) identifies the brew inside as "malt liquor." It is, however, quite a different animal. (2) If you're going to drink malt liquor (which, assuming you're of age, is entirely your business), do yourself a favor and make sure you drink it *cold*—as near freezing as possible. There are better and worse malt liquors, but many are notorious for their "off" tastes—especially on the finish and the aftertaste—and these unpleasant flavors become more noticeable as the beer warms up.

A few other points about porters: Among the places porter traveled to were the Baltic states—the three little countries (Estonia, Latvia, and Lithuania) perched at Russia's northwestern corner along the Baltic Sea. Baltic brewers went crazy for porter, and many continue to make them. (A few—especially Lithuanian porters—now wend their way onto American store shelves.) What's especially interesting about **Baltic porters** is that, although porter is generally an ale (that is, top-fermented, using ale yeast), most Baltic brewers switched, at some point, to bottom-fermenting lager yeast, resulting in, to Drinkology's taste buds, a noticeably different sort of brew—somewhat lighter in color and body, more sour, and even slightly metallic.

Drinkology also found it interesting to learn that porter was among the first English beers to be "matured"—that is, aged in cask—on breweries' premises before being distributed to pubs. (Prior to porter, beers *were* sometimes aged, but the job of storing beer until it became "stale"—a term of approval in the eighteenth century—generally belonged to the pub owners.) The mellow quality that porters acquired through brewery aging may have added to early porter drinkers' enthusiasm.

Like French-kissing a chain-smoker

Today's porters are *very* dark beers, though more translucent than stouts, often showing red or amber highlights in the glass. In general, they're a little less potent than their ancestors, hovering in the 5 to 6 percent ABV range. Their flavors occupy the darker end of the flavor spectrum, with raisinlike, apple-cidery, chocolaty, and coffee-like (even espressolike) notes. One well-known English porter—Fuller's London Porter—is so tobaccolike in the nose and on the tongue that drinking it is like French-kissing a chain-smoker.

(And since Drinkology is a nostalgic former cigarette fiend, we rather like the quality.)

Pseudo-lambic. See LAMBIC.

Quadrupel (pron., kwah-droo-PELL), an extremely strong Belgian ale. (The name, obviously, means "quadruple.") For information on the beer-naming convention that includes the designation *quadrupel,* see the entries DUBBEL and TRAPPIST BEERS.

Rauchbier (pron., ROWK-beer), a Bavarian beer style notable for its smoky flavor. The first time Drinkology had a "smoke beer" (which is what *Rauchbier* means in German), at a local brewpub, we ignorantly assumed it was the brewmaster's gimmicky innovation. Little did we know that smoky-tasting beer has a venerable history. The smokiness of smoke beer results from its malt (or a portion of the malt used) being dried directly over an open fire, and—here's the thing—this is the way that malt was usually dried in the centuries before the development of modern kilning techniques, which instead subject the malt to indirect heat. Ergo, most beers made before the last few hundred years probably tasted, to some degree, of wood-fire smoke. Abandoned elsewhere, the age-old method survived in the northern Bavarian city of Bamberg, where a small number of breweries continue to produce smoke beer of several kinds. Most Rauchbiers are lagers, but Bamberg brewers also produce smoke WEISSBIERS. Most have an alcohol content of around 5 percent ABV, but there are also stronger (BOCK) varieties. Rauchbiers are meaty beers—by which we mean they literally taste of smoked meat. Drinkology prefers its bacon in crunchy, chewable form, but we can appreciate the love that some drinkers feel for these unusual beers. Of German smoke beers, the Aecht Schlenkerla Rauchbier ("Original Schlenkerla Smoked Beer"), named after an old pub in Bamberg, is probably most widely available in the U.S. You might also look for Rauchbiers (of several different types) produced by Bamberg's Spezial brewery. Scores of American craft breweries also now make smoke beers, including many smoke PORTERS, which wed British and German beer-making traditions.

Real ale. See CASK-CONDITIONED ALE.

Red ale. See AMBER ALE, FLANDERS RED, IRISH RED ALE.

Roggenbier. See RYE BEER.

Rye beer, an ale or lager that incorporates a lesser or greater proportion of rye malt in its grain bill. Rye has been used in brewing (especially in northerly latitudes, where it is a more dependable cereal crop than barley or wheat) since God knows when. It is nearly impossible, however, to make a beer *entirely* from rye, which, like wheat (see WHEAT BEER), is a "naked," or hull-less, grain, meaning that the use of rye all by itself can readily lead to a stuck mash (see page 13).

A few traditional northern European beers are rye based (e.g., kvass; see pages 163–64) or have some rye in them (e.g., SAHTI). The best-known European rye-beer style, however, is the German **Roggenbier** (pron., RAH-gen-beer; literally, "rye beer"), which, though it dates back to medieval times, was not made for nearly five centuries following 1516, when the German Beer Purity Law (see pages 68–70) banned the use of any grain but barley for the making of beer. Roggenbier was revived by a number of German breweries in the late twentieth century; originally an ale, it is now made in both ale and lager versions. Typically unfiltered, Roggenbiers are noted for their **turbidity**, the haze caused by all the residual yeast swirling around. Like HEFEWEIZENS, which are also usually unfiltered, Roggenbiers are summertime quaffing beers. (They may also, like Hefeweizens, have a slightly banana-like taste.) The alcohol content is typically moderate, in the area of 5 percent ABV; they're coppery to reddish brown in color; and they're often spicy-tangy on the palate—which makes sense, given the liberal use of rye malts in their grain bills (usually 50 percent or more). Unfortunately, German-made Roggenbiers are hard to find in the United States, and one of the best known, the Roggen brewed by Munich's Paulaner brewery, has recently been discontinued (or "retired," as the beer experts say).

Which is not to say that it's hard to find a rye beer on this side of the Atlantic. Although American craft brewers' enthusiasm for rye beers has, after waxing, recently waned, hundreds of rye beers are still brewed here. Many American rye beers, like their German cousins, are only mildly hopped (to let the rye flavors shine through), but some craft brewers are upping the ante, producing highly hopped versions that resemble INDIA PALE ALES.

Sahti (pron., SAH-tee), a traditional Finnish ale made primarily from barley malt—but often with some rye in the mix—and flavored with juniper. The juniper gets into the beer in an unusual way. After steeping in a wooden barrel, the mash is ladled into a trough called a *kuurna* (sort of a primitive lauter tun), where a bed of juniper twigs strains out the solids, simultaneously infusing the wort flowing through it with a piney, resinous flavor. The wort is not boiled, which means that much of the grain's protein makes it into the finished, fermented brew, rendering the beer extremely hazy. Brewed in Finland since the 1500s, sahti is now brewed commercially there (as well as by "sahti masters" in rural Finnish communities). Despite its high alcohol content (between 7 and 10 percent ABV), sahti has a very short shelf life, so very little Finnish sahti makes it out of the country. One Connecticut importer brings extremely small quantities of sahti made by the Lammin Sahti Oy company of Lammi, Finland, to the U.S., so there's a slender chance you might find a bottle at a specialty retailer in the Northeast. A very few American craft brewers (e.g., Delaware's Dogfish Head, Colorado's New Belgium) have experimented with the style.

Saison (pron., SAY-zaw[n]), a class of Belgian FARMHOUSE ALES defined more by geographical origin—saisons hail from Wallonia, the French-speaking southern part of Belgium—than by a shared character. Their diversity testifies to the fact that, historically, saisons were brewed by individual farmers using their own recipes, equipment, and methods. The brewers all had the same purpose, however: to make a beer that could nourish and quench the thirsts of the farmhands who worked their fields during the summer and the harvest season (without, however, getting the workers drunk, which is why saisons of the past were low-alcohol beers, averaging about 3 percent ABV). The epitome of SEASONAL BEERS, saison was brewed in fall and winter to be drunk in summer. (The name in French means, literally, "season.") Because these relatively weak beers had to keep for many months, they were more heavily hopped (to preserve them) than most other Belgian beers.

Belgian saisons are still made by small-scale artisanal brewers, but their production, during the last century, declined almost to the point of nonexistence before the style (if that's the right word) was discovered by latter-day beer enthusiasts and craft brewers. In recent years, Belgian saisons, as well as North American craft-brewed ales taking their cues from the rural Wallonian tradition, have become very popular, with BeerAdvocate.com rating more than five hundred examples. Today's saisons—both Belgian and American—are a lot stronger than their down-on-the-farm ancestors (most fall between 5 and 8 percent ABV but some range upwards of 9.5 percent), but the diversity remains. Some saisons are very pale, some golden, and some amber; some have a tart edge, others don't. As a class, they're noted for their spiciness; in the case of the Belgian saisons, that spice usually comes from the use of traditional yeast strains, but North American craft brewers often add actual spices to achieve a similar complexity. Among American saison-style ales, Drinkology is *very* fond of the Bam Bière made by Michigan's Jolly Pumpkin Brewery—an incredibly mouth-smacking brew.

For a related style, see BIÈRE DE GARDE.

Schwarzbier (pron., SCHVARTS-beer), a very dark German lager. The name means "black beer," but Schwarzbiers aren't necessarily black—just a lot darker than other lagers, including lagers of the related DUNKEL style. Although Schwarzbiers visually resemble PORTERS and STOUTS, they don't have the hefty body or the toasted or "burnt" flavors associated with those British ales; instead, as befits a lager, typical Schwarzbiers are refreshing and clean tasting, fairly light bodied (well, for such a deeply colored beer), and dry (never cloying) on the finish. They are also only moderately strong, generally falling in the 4.5 to 5.5 ABV range.

Schwarzbier's birthplace is central/central-south Germany, specifically the regions of Franconia (northern Bavaria) and Thuringia. The style has ancient roots, reaching back to the dark beers made in the monastic brewhouses of medieval times—or even further back, since archaeological finds show that beer has been made in this part of Germany for at least three millennia. Two well-known examples of the style, the Kloster Mönchshof ("Cloister Abbey") Schwarzbier made by the Kulmbacher brewery of Kulmbach, Germany, and Köstritzer Schwarzbier, made by the Köstritzer brewery of Bad Köstritz, can trace their ancestries directly to monastic breweries.

The Schwarzbier style has, however, evolved. Monks in the Middle Ages would've brewed ales, since bottom-fermenting lager yeast hadn't yet been discovered. And they would've made their dark ales from dark-roasted malts rather than the not-yet-invented pilsner malts on which Schwarzbier is primarily based today. (That's why the style, in Germany, is sometimes called **Schwarzpils**. Dark malts do, however, still play a role in Schwarzbiers, contributing color as well as chocolaty or coffeelike notes to these brews.)

The style has been widely copied by North American craft brewers, who often call such beers **black lagers**. Magic Hat, Sam Adams, Saranac, and Spoetzl are just a few of the better-known brands whose lines include them.

Scottish ale and **Scotch ale,** two different styles—well, kinda sorta different styles—of ale, both originating in Scotland. Of all the many puzzles presented by beer nomenclature, Drinkology has found this one perhaps the most difficult to figure out. The references we've consulted are both individually confusing and collectively contradictory, which makes us feel like flinging ourself into Loch Ness—or even to spend some time rewatching the grosser bits of *Trainspotting*—rather than trying to write this entry. But here goes:

Scottish ales are PALE ALES that emphasize maltiness rather than hops bitterness. Some authorities claim that this is because, historically, hops were hard to come by in Scotland (where they are not grown); others say that, no, this isn't true, and that Scottish ales of the nineteenth century were as well hopped as pale ales produced elsewhere in Great Britain. (Aargh.)

Today, Scottish breweries produce ales in a range of different strengths that are distinguished by name *and* by a numbering system based on the old (and, to foreigners, incomprehensible) shilling currency system, so sensibly abandoned by the U.K. in 1971. In the past, these shilling-based denominations, shown on the table that follows, were used to differentiate one beer from another according to the selling price of a **hogshead** (that's a big barrel) of each beer, which price wasn't necessarily indicative of the beer's strength; nowadays, the shilling designations *are* indicative of relative alcoholic strength—though that's not as clear-cut as it might sound, since different breweries use the shilling system in different ways. (Aargh.) In any case, here's the list of name-and-shilling designations and the alcoholic strengths that they generally (but not always) indicate. (What you've got to know before looking at this list is that the slash-and-dash mark [/-] is a symbol for "shilling." What you might also want to know is that a Scottish person ordering an ale would most likely use the old slang word "bob" ["a pint of sixty bob"] instead of saying "shilling." Aargh.)

Name	Shilling Designation	Strength
Light	60/-	Under 3.5% ABV
Heavy	70/-	3.5–4.0% ABV
Export	80/-	4.0–5.5% ABV

We're not done. Even stronger than the Scottish export ale is the category known as *Scotch* ale, identified by shilling designations ranging from 90/- to 160/- and ranging in strength from 6 percent up to about 10 percent ABV. The thing is, Scotch ale isn't just the *strongest* kind of Scottish ale; it's also kinda sorta a different kind of beer: darker, fuller bodied, and sweeter—its signature sweetness resulting from a very long boil, during which some of the sugar in the wort caramelizes.

In Scotland, ale belonging to the Scotch ale category is often referred to as **wee heavy**, which of course infuriates Drinkology, since "wee" means "little," whereas a wee heavy is heavier than a heavy. But we must learn to just accept rather than to try to understand.

Many of the ales made in the Scotch ale style by brewers in the United States and elsewhere outside Scotland are notable for having a smoky taste that results from the presence of smoked malts in the grain bill (the Sam Adams Scotch Ale made by the Boston Brewing company is an example). The smokiness resembles that of

Scotch whisky, and ales brewed in this manner are also sometimes called **whisky ales**. What's peculiar is that this smoky character is only very rarely found in Scotch ales hailing from Scotland itself.

We just want to give up, which we shall do momentarily—but not before recommending a Scottish Scotch ale to you: the Traquair House Ale made by the Traquair House brewery of Innerleithen, Scotland. (The brewery was originally a domestic beer-making operation at this noble estate, which bills itself as the "oldest inhabited house in Scotland.") Fermented in oak tanks, Traquair House Ale is an amazingly rich brew (and also a potent one, at 7.2 percent ABV).

The killer, of course, is that the brewers of this exemplar of the *Scotch* ale style themselves identify it as a *Scottish* ale. Loch Ness, here we come. (Splash!)

Seasonal beers, ales and lagers brewed during, released during, created especially for, or best enjoyed during specific seasons of the year (whether calendar seasons or holidays). So sorry for the can't-catch-your-breath wordiness of that definition—it's just that the term *seasonal beers* covers such a vast multitude of styles. According to the Brewers Association, a U.S. craft-brewing trade group, seasonal beers nowadays represent the largest and fastest-growing category of American craft beers—a fact that manages to be both interesting (because it demonstrates U.S. beer enthusiasts' growing openness to trying a wide variety of beers) and sort of meaningless (because the category is so very broad).

Before the development of modern technologies of refrigeration and air-conditioning, brewing was of necessity a mostly seasonal activity, often ceasing during the summer months because of the

The "Essence" of Beer

At some level, it doesn't make sense to like whiskey but not beer. Or vice versa. That's because whiskey *is* beer. Or, rather, whiskey is beer (minus the hops) that's been distilled. You might think of it as the "essence" of beer.

Although processes for making different whiskeys differ in a hundred particulars—the kind or kinds of grain used, the type of still employed, the number of distillations the spirit undergoes, the way in which the raw whiskey is aged—the basic procedure is everywhere the same. And, up until distillation, it's basically the same as that used in beer making.

Like beer, whiskey (spelled *whisky* if it's made in Scotland, Wales, Canada, or Japan) is a fermented-grain beverage. And, like most beer recipes, most recipes for whiskey include at least some malted barley in the mix. Scotch and Irish whisk(e)y use only malted barley; in American whiskeys like bourbon and rye, other grains predominate (for example, the grain mix for bourbon must, by law, contain at least 51 percent corn), but even they incorporate some barley malt.

So to make whiskey, as to make beer, you begin by grinding the grain; then you steep, or *mash*, the ground grain in hot water to extract fermentable sugars; then you separate the liquid—which, as in beer making, is now called the *wort*—from the spent grain; and then you boil the wort for a period of time, cool it down, and transfer it to a tank where yeast is added and fermentation commences. (Whiskey makers are, by the way, every bit as proprietary about the yeast they use as are brewers.) When fermented, the liquid is called—you guessed it—*beer,* because that's what it is. Not hopped, of course, but beer nonetheless. (Some whiskey makers refer to the fermented liquid as **wash**. But that doesn't mean it's not beer.)

It's at this point that whiskey and beer making diverge. For the brewer, the fermented liquid is the *almost* finished product (although different beers undergo different conditioning or maturation processes before release). For the whiskey maker, however, beer is the raw material for **distillation**, a process of *controlled evaporation*. In the smallest nutshell: the beer is heated in a **still**; as it boils, the vapor that steams away has a higher concentration of alcohol than the liquid remaining behind because of alcohol's lower boiling point; then, this high-alcohol vapor is allowed to condense and is collected. (Stills are actually somewhat complex contraptions, and distilling processes are considerably more complicated than this brief description, but this is the gist.)

Raw whiskey—fresh from the still—is colorless. Whiskeys acquire their color, which can range from a pale, strawlike shade to a deep amber-brown, from being aged in oak barrels or casks for a period of time ranging from a few months for some corn whiskeys to upwards of thirty years for some super-premium scotches. In many cases, these casks are "recycled"—for example, casks formerly used for aging sherry or port are favored for the aging of certain whiskeys. Cask aging doesn't just color the liquor; it also changes its flavor, smoothing away its sharpness and adding the toasted, nutty, caramel, vanilla and other tastes associated with this or that whiskey.

But whiskey doesn't have to be aged to be drunk. In America, colorless "new make" whiskey is often referred to as **white dog**—or as **moonshine**, if it's been produced illegally by unlicensed distillers. Time was that almost nobody except moonshiners and their yokel clientele drank raw whiskey, but fashions do change, and lately there's been a vogue for white dog, some of it produced by small craft distillers and some released unaged by bigger whiskey makers looking to cash in on the trend. Aficionados claim, with justice, that drinking good white-dog whiskey lets you appreciate the grain from which the spirit is made, since grain flavors—corn, wheat, rye, or barley—get subdued (if they don't actually disappear) when whiskey is aged in barrel.

danger that beer would spoil in the heat. Beyond that general prohibition on summertime brewing, however, many traditional beers were crafted in specific ways to accommodate seasonal requirements (e.g., **Lenten beers** such as Doppelbock, pages 90–91, were brewed to be especially hearty because they were meant to sustain monks during the Lenten fast). *Or* they were made in a certain way at a certain time during the brewing season to ensure that they would keep through the summer (see, for example, BIÈRE DE GARDE, MÄRZENBIER, and SAISON).

Such calendrical imperatives, whether religious or climatological, hardly exist any longer, though it remains true that the brewing of spontaneously fermented beers (see LAMBIC and SOUR BEER) remains restricted to the cooler months. So it's really kind of heartening that, in this temperature-controlled age, the collective thirst for seasonal beers, far from diminishing, is actually growing—and that the number of seasonal beers made by craft brewers (and, lately, by mass-market beer makers eager to exploit the trend) continues to expand.

Newfangled seasonal beers include all manner of FRUIT AND VEGETABLE BEERS (e.g., the **pumpkin ales** made by numerous brewers and now ubiquitous at Thanksgiving time), HARVEST ALES, and the ever-growing number of **winter ales** and **Christmas ales** (usually some spiced variant of the OLD ALE style; see also SPICED AND HERBED BEERS). Other beers covered in this A-to-Z that have a seasonal aspect or that are mostly drunk during a particular season are AMERICAN WHEAT BEER, BARLEY WINE, BERLINER WEISSE, BOCK, GOLDEN ALE, HEFEWEIZEN, and WEIZENBOCK; see also the info on the German seasonal style called Sticke, under ALTBIER.

Session beer, a term that can be used for any beer low enough in alcohol (generally in the 4 to 5 percent ABV range) that one can drink several in one *session* without getting wasted. The term originated in Britain (see BITTER) but is commonly employed by American craft brewers, many of which make a "session beer" in addition to other, higher-strength offerings.

Small beer. See pages 164–65.

Smoke beer, a.k.a. **smoked beer.** See RAUCHBIER.

SOUR BEER

For most beers, sourness is a fault—an off taste, and evidence that something went wrong in the beer-making process. But there are a few kinds of European beer, notably BERLINER WEISSE, FLANDERS RED, LAMBIC (including GUEUZE and KRIEK), and OUD BRUIN, that are intentionally made sour. And, lately, scores of North American craft brewers have been experimenting with sour beers of their own.

Sour beer is a bit of a catchall term rather than an individual style, but most sour beers share this in common: they're fermented with yeasts of the *Brettanomyces* genus rather than (or in addition to) the *Saccharomyces cerevisiae* yeast typically used by brewers. These **"Brett" yeasts** look different from *S. cerevisiae* (they're generally tubular or sausage-shaped, rather than ovoid), and they act different. They're hungrier (eating more of the sugar in a wort), they're longer-lived, and they produce lots of acetic acid and other compounds that convey tartness and other unusual flavors. (Many sour beers have a "funky" smell and taste that's often referred to as **barnyard**. And—for an aficionado of sour beers—that's not a bad thing.)

Most craft sour beer makers inoculate their brew with cultivated strains of *Brettanomyces* yeasts, but a few throw caution to the wind (quite literally) by exposing the wort to the open air, permitting so-called spontaneous fermentation to occur as wild yeasts waft their way into the soup (along with **lactic-acid-producing bacteria**, which also play a role in the fermentation). This is, after all, how the lambic beers of Belgium are fermented, and letting nature rather than nurture do the trick adds, in these makers' minds, to their sour beers' authenticity. Spontaneously fermented North American craft beers, by the way, are sometimes referred to as **American** (or **Canadian**) **wild ales**.

Using *Brettanomyces* yeasts, whether cultivated or naturally occurring, carries some risk. For one thing, the fermentation (and the aging that typically follows, about which more in a sec) can be difficult to control, and the beer that results may travel beyond sour and funky into the territory of *acrid* and *lousy*. And for brewers who make both sour and nonsour beers, the risk is more complex. If *Brettanomyces* yeasts accidentally contaminate equipment used to brew their not-supposed-to-be-sour beers, they can wreak havoc, ruining batches. So great is the risk of *Brettanomyces* contamination that sour beer making is often conducted in what amounts to an on-site quarantine.

> It amounts to an on-site quarantine

The souring of sour beer doesn't end with fermentation, or, to put it more accurately, the fermentation doesn't end in the fermentation vessel. When the initial fermentation has progressed to a certain point, sour beer is usually transferred to unlined oak barrels, where the microorganisms continue to do their business (and contact with the wood itself contributes to the beer's sourness). Different sour beers are aged for different lengths of time—often a year or longer—before bottling. Some are also flavored with fruit (during aging, which, curiously, may intensify the sourness as the fruit sugars themselves ferment) or with fruit essences or syrups (after aging, which sweetens the product).

For the moment, sour beers—imported and domestic—remain a niche market in America, and their enjoyment an acquired taste, although at least one craft brewer has been quoted as claiming that "sour is the new hoppy." Although that's probably overstating sour beers' potential appeal to American beer drinkers at large, they do constitute a trend—or increasingly important trendlet—within the craft-beer community. (Sour beers are, by the way, hopped, but usually with **aged dried hops** that help preserve the beer without adding much, or any, bitterness to the brew.)

The best time to try a sour beer may be a hot summer's day, since these beers are renowned for their ability to refresh the drinker. (This makes good sense: just think of tart lemonade's effect on a heat-parched throat.)

Spezial (pron., SHPETZ-ee-ahl), a German word meaning "special," applied to the brand names of various beers of various German styles (HEFEWEIZENS, KELLERBIERS, PILSNERS, RAUCHBIERS, etc.) and occasionally used in brand-names by North American brewers of German-style beers. *Spezial* is one of those terms (compare EXPORT) that seem to have been devised to drive the beer neophyte nuts. It doesn't mean anything besides that the brewer thinks that beer X is, well, kind of special.

Spiced and herbed beers, ales and lagers flavored with botanical ingredients other than (or in addition to) hops. There are a number of traditional beers that use things besides hops for spicing (see GOSE, GRUIT ALES, SAHTI, and WITBIER), but the variety of spiced and herbed beers created by today's craft brewers has burgeoned beyond reckoning. Some relatively recently invented spiced SEASONAL BEERS (**pumpkin ales** dosed with pumpkin-pie spices, **Christmas ales** infused with mulling spices) have become so common as to feel completely familiar. Other spiced brews, however, clearly belong in the EXTREME BEER class. It sometimes seems there's almost no kind of plant matter that some brewer, somewhere, won't throw into the brew kettle just to see what happens. Spices and herbs now being used in beers include those on this—abridged!—list: allspice, anise, basil, cardamom, cinnamon, cloves, coffee, coriander, fennel, ginger, ginseng, horehound, horseradish, juniper berries, lavender, lemongrass, lime leaves, mint, nutmeg, orange peel, pepper (both peppercorns and jalapeños and other chiles), saffron, spruce, vanilla, and walnut leaves. Drinkology has even heard of (though mercifully not sampled) a beer that's spiced to taste like pizza.

There is, obviously, no generalizing about spiced and herbed beers, which represent an array of styles and strengths. And there are no developed standards for assessing them. A few pointers for evaluating a spiced/herbed beer's success, however, seem very sensible: Is it well balanced? Do the spices/herbs used complement or overwhelm the beer's other tastes? Does the flavor seem natural, or artificial? Does the spicing/herbing seem a good fit with the beer's style? You be the judge. (For info on other unusual ingredients used to flavor beers, see also FRUIT AND VEGETABLE BEERS.)

Starkbier. See BOCK.

Steam beer. See CALIFORNIA COMMON BEER.

Stein beer, beer brewed by adding superheated rocks to the brewkettle. *Stein beer* (the word *Stein* means "stone" in German) does not designate a particular style of beer but rather an ancient brewing method. By adding white-hot stones to their kettles, pre-modern brewers could achieve an instantaneous, roiling boil—sustaining it for whatever length of time they desired by continuing to drop more hot stones into the brew. The method made a lot of sense in the Middle Ages, because it takes a long time (and a *lot* of firewood) to bring a large pot of liquid to a boil and because it's so difficult to sustain a constant boil over a wood fire. With the development of more efficient heating technologies, the method went into eclipse, only to be revived by a few present-day craft brewers. (Craft brewers, as we remark elsewhere, love finding arcane and difficult ways of doing things.) Theoretically, a stein beer could be of virtually any style, ale or lager. Among beer makers that have experimented with stein beers are Sixpoint Craft Ales of Brooklyn, New York (which created its Dr. Klankenstein ale using this ancient method for the Museum of *Modern* Art's restaurant—weird), and the Port Brewing Company of San Marcos, California, which offers its aptly named Hot Rocks dark lager as a springtime release.

Stock ale. See OLD ALE.

STOUT
Before it became a euphemism for "fat," the word *stout* meant "strong." And that's why stout is called stout: it's *strong* ale. Before

the eighteenth century, many sorts of stronger-than-usual British ales—stronger in alcohol content, that is—were referred to as stouts. But modern stouts are all historically related to PORTER, the dark brown ale first brewed in London circa 1720. Stout, in fact, is a kind of porter—alcoholically stronger than other porters and often darker and earthier flavored, as well. You might think of stout as *porter on steroids*.

Brewers have always brewed beers of different strengths to suit the tastes and tolerances of different drinkers, so it was natural that some eighteenth-century British brewers would try their hands at making "stout porters" (which is what stouts were originally called)—and then even stouter porters. The stoutest porters of all, **imperial stouts**, originating in the middle to late 1700s, were developed by British beer companies to satisfy their aristocratic customers in czarist Russia (hence the adjective "imperial"). It wasn't just that Russians *liked* these stronger-than-ordinary beers (although they did—the famous horsewoman Catherine the Great being a particularly passionate admirer), but the beers' high ABV, because of alcohol's preservative nature, helped the brew survive the voyage through the North and Baltic seas over to St. Petersburg and enabled it to be stored, without spoiling, for relatively long periods of time after reaching its destination. (Note that in recent decades craft brewers have sometimes applied the "imperial" moniker to stronger-than-ordinary versions of other kinds of beers—for example, "imperial" INDIA PALE ALES and "imperial" red ales—but this is just a marketing device with no historical justification.)

Catherine was a passionate admirer

Of course, Russia isn't the country most closely associated with stout in the popular mind. That would be Ireland, another land celebrated, scorned, and/or pitied for its inhabitants' abiding thirst for strong drink. Because of British drinkers' shift in taste, over the preceding century and a half, toward lighter beers, stouts (and porters generally) had virtually vanished from Great Britain by the 1960s. In Ireland, by contrast, stout remained very much alive and well. And, of course, the Irish beer maker most closely associated with stout in the popular mind is the Dublin-based concern of Guinness, Ltd., which, founded in 1759, began selling what it then called "extra stout porter" in 1820, and which surely holds the world record for the quantity of stout produced. (And, yes, there was a pun in the preceding sentence.) Though the best known internationally, Guinness isn't the only maker of the variation of stout—black in color, creamy in mouthfeel, and caramel-coffee roasty-toasty in taste—that has come to be known as **Irish stout** (or, alternately, **dry stout**); Murphy's and Beamish stouts, both brewed in the city of Cork, are two other big brands.

Stout's robust maltiness earned it the reputation of being an especially nutritious beer, and stout makers in the past often promoted their products as such—aiming their pitches at, among others, pregnant women and nursing mothers. (Concerns about fetal alcohol syndrome among contemporary moms-to-be would doubtless put the kibosh on such an advertising strategy today.) Its purported nutritional value was a major selling point of so-called **milk stout**, a stout substyle, invented in late nineteenth-century Britain, in which the milk sugar lactose is added to the brew; since yeast can't eat lactose, the sugar remains in the finished beer, making it sweeter and higher in calories than other stouts. (Mackeson

Stout, first brewed in 1907, is a surviving example of the original generation of British milk stouts.) Even Guinness got on the stout-is-healthy bandwagon with a long-lived advertising slogan, first introduced in the 1920s, that claimed "Guinness Is Good for You."

Oatmeal stout—another late nineteenth-century invention—was likewise originally touted as having restorative powers. Oatmeal stouts' grain bills incorporate a smaller or larger amount of malted or flaked (porridge) oats. Used by themselves, oats don't make for great beer—a beer made solely or even largely from oats would be too bitter—but when they constitute a relatively small proportion of a mash, their proteins confer an extra-silky mouthfeel to the resulting stout.

As mentioned, stout had almost disappeared from its birthplace by the mid-twentieth century. But the British Campaign for Real Ale (CAMRA; see pages 98–99) encouraged its revival, as did the craft-brewing movement in North America and elsewhere. Hundreds of stouts are now being commercially brewed, including newfangled substyles such as **coffee stout** (in which coffee is added to the boil) and **chocolate stout** (which may get its chocolaty flavor from so-called chocolate malt or from the addition of actual cocoa to the brew). Drinkology generally loves these immensely satisfying beers, and a British chocolate stout, Young's Double Chocolate Stout, made by the London-based Wells & Young's Brewing Company, Ltd., is one of our absolute favorite beers—not just for drinking by itself, but for mixing with other things (see page 283) and for baking (see page 296).

Stouts are often, and sensibly, paired with strong cheeses and densely flavored desserts, but, somewhat counterintuitively, dry stouts also perform well when served with some seafoods—especially oysters. This is a traditional pairing—oysters' creamy flavor complementing the creaminess of the stout. Back in the day, stouts meant to be served with oysters—a common snack in nineteenth-century taverns—were called **oyster stouts**. But some contemporary brewers have taken that associative term literally, producing oyster stouts that *actually suspend fresh, shucked oysters in the brew kettle.* Yum? Or yuck?

Yum? Or yuck?

Strong ale. For the English style of strong ale, see OLD ALE; for the Belgian styles, see BELGIAN STRONG ALES.

Summer beer. See AMERICAN WHEAT BEER.

Trappist beers, a family of beers brewed by, or under the direct supervision of, Trappist monks in six monasteries in Belgium and one in the Netherlands. *Only* beers brewed by Trappists are allowed to be called "Trappist," and the consortium of Trappist brewers has not been timid about taking violators of this rule to court. (See ABBEY ALES for info on other Belgian beers that have monastic roots or connections.) The following list of the Trappist breweries gives their "brand names," as well as the (translated) full names of the monasteries that operate them:

Achel (Monastery of Our Lady of St. Benedict)

Chimay (Our Lady of Scourmont)

Orval (Our Lady of Orval)

Rochefort (Our Lady of St. Rémy)

Tilburg (Our Lady of Koningshoeven) [This is the Dutch Trappist brewery.]

Westmalle (Our Lady of La Trappe of the Sacred Heart)

Westvleteren (Our Lady of St. Sixtus)

Monkish beer making dates back to medieval times and the founding of the great monastic orders—and the construction, all over Europe, of cloisters to house their members. Outposts of what remained of western civ during the darkest centuries of the Dark Ages, monasteries were also models of self-sufficiency. The monks farmed, raised livestock, wove cloth, built buildings, and made their own wine (wherever the climate was warm enough for the growing of grapes) and their own beer (wherever it wasn't). The humorous figure of the jolly, tipsy monk—tonsured, winking naughtily, and hoisting aloft an overflowing stein—is an iconic image, but beer played a serious role in the life of a monastery. Not only was it nutritious and safe (in the days when water often wasn't), but it was a *liquid* food, which meant that it was not forbidden during periods of compulsory communal fasting at Lent and other times of the religious year. (A number of current beer styles originated as **Lenten beers**; see, for example, the brief history of Doppelbock that appears on page 91.) Monks were innovative beer makers. Monastic brewers are credited by some sources as being the first to use hops to flavor beer, the discoverers of bottom-fermenting yeast, and the inventors of the lagering method. From the breakup of the Roman empire until the late Middle Ages and the rise of commercial brewing, monasteries were just about the only places where large-scale brewing went on and where the brewing was performed by men. Outside these enclaves, the making of beer was an individual household's task—and, like other food preparation, women's work.

The great antiquity of the monastic brewing tradition, however, shouldn't mislead you into thinking that the Trappist beers of Belgium and the Netherlands are themselves of medieval origin. First, the Trappist order is itself relatively new. It was founded in 1664, at the abbey of La Trappe, in Normandy, France. And it was only in the late eighteenth century that Trappists—some fleeing the anticlerical persecutions of the French Revolution— began migrating in large numbers to the Low Countries, where

they either settled into exist- ing monasteries that had been abandoned or built abbeys of their own. Beer-making oper- ations at these monasteries didn't start up until the mid- nineteenth century or later and were interrupted at most of them by one, the other, or both world wars—with the "interruption" at the Achel monastery lasting from 1914 until 1998, when the monks there at long last decided to reestablish an on-site brewery.

As indicated, the term *Trappist beer* does not denote a specific style but rather a range of styles made by the seven monasteries. That said, there are certain commonalities among Trappist brews. For example, with one exception (a BOCK-style lager produced by Tilburg), they are all top-fermented ales. Most are bottle conditioned—the carbonation results from a second, in-bottle fermentation caused by the addition of a little yeast and, often, sugar to the brew before bottling. (Yeast residue can form a sludge or "cake" in the bottle, necessitating slow and careful pouring.) They're aged before release and, as a group, continue to age well in bottle; it's recommended that you hold off drinking some of these beers until two or three years after purchase—assuming you store the bottles properly (and have godlike patience).

An appropriately beatific episode

The most important similarity, however, is that these are *great*, complexly flavored beers. We've liked every one we've tried—and we recall our first sampling of Orval as an appropriately beatific episode. Lest you think this is merely Drinkology's opinion, check out the generally divine ratings Trappist beers receive on websites like ratebeer.com and BeerAdvocate.com.

Categorizing Trappist beers by style is not a simple matter. Not only do the numbers of styles made by the Trappist breweries differ, but the breweries use different systems of identification or nomenclature to distinguish among their brews: Chimay, for example, IDs its beers by color (red, white, and blue bottle caps and labels); Rochefort names them according to a numbering system (6, 8, and 10). Despite the divergences, however, Trappist breweries loosely (emphasis on the *loosely*) adhere to a tripartite system that has also been adopted by Belgian abbey ale brewers. The three levels of this system are (1) a moderately strong golden ale (the old term for this kind of ale is *enkel*—Flemish for "single"—although nowadays it's likelier to be called a blonde; see BLONDE ALES); (2) a stronger, darker ale (often called a DUBBEL, or "double"); and (3) an even stronger, though gold-colored, ale (often called a TRIPEL, or "triple"). For more on the meanings of these terms, consult the relevant entries, but note that a "double" is *not* twice as strong, alcoholically, as a "single," nor is a "triple" three times as strong—rather, the terms indicate a gradation of relative strengths. If you find this confusing, you're in good company.

And, just to magnify your confusion, go back to that crucial word *loosely* in the paragraph above. In truth, only one of the Trappist breweries—Westmalle—follows the three-strengths system religiously. As mentioned, the number of styles produced varies from monastery to monastery. Orval produces just two—one being a lighter, weaker version of its standard brew—while Tilburg produces a full dozen different kinds. Also, some of the Trappist breweries make a *very* strong ale, which they denominate a QUADRUPEL (that is, of course, "quadruple"). And (yes, this does go on) some make "brown" ales, "extra" ales (which can be comparatively weak or comparatively strong, depending on the maker), and yet other beers that don't fit neatly into the 1-2-3 system.

Beyond all their other attributes, Trappist beers are interesting from a mercantile perspective. Although they sell their beers commercially, the monasteries don't do so for profit—or not in the usual sense of "profit." Proceeds from beer sales are used for the monasteries' upkeep (Trappist communities are required by the order to be self-supporting) and to underwrite the monks' charitable enterprises. Drinking a Trappist beer, in other words, can make you feel good in more ways than one. And finding a Trappist beer to drink has become fairly easy. Many U.S. beer retailers carry, at a minimum, one or more of the Chimay beers. (Chimay was the first Trappist brewery to market its beers abroad.) The only Trappist beer you're unlikely to find here is Westvleteren, which is available only at the monastery. (Westvleteren is so esoteric that it doesn't even *label* its bottles—its three beers are identified by their bottle caps alone.)

Tripel (pron., trih-PELL), a designation applied to some strongly alcoholic Belgian TRAPPIST BEERS and ABBEY ALES. The term *tripel*—which means "triple" in Flemish—is used in a beer-naming convention that grades the ales produced by a given brewery by strength; the terms *blonde* (see BLONDE ALES) and DUBBEL designate beers of lesser strength. (For more on this somewhat confusing system, see the entries on dubbel and on Trappist beers.) Although powerfully boozy (ranging from 8 to 12 percent ABV), tripels are surprisingly light in color—usually bright gold in hue. Well-made tripels are complexly flavorful, nicely balancing the bitter and the sweet, and they don't taste as strongly alcoholic as they, in fact, are—so be sure to drink them slowly.

Triple, a designation used by some beer makers to indicate that a beer has a much greater alcoholic strength or hoppiness (or both) than is standard for that style; see DOUBLE for a fuller explanation. Some non-Belgian brewers may use the word *triple* in brand names of beers that emulate the Belgian TRIPEL style.

Vegetable beers. See FRUIT AND VEGETABLE BEERS.

Vienna lager, a crisp, clean-tasting amber or copper-tinged lager that gets its color from a mixture of malts, including pale malts, the slightly darker Vienna and Munich malts, and (in small proportions) dark-roasted malts. Well-made Vienna lagers are exercises in subtlety and balance: softly malty, usually mildly hopped (though American craft-brewed versions may be more bitter), moderately carbonated (though often with persistent heads), and moderately alcoholic (generally in the 4.5 to 6 percent ABV range). They may be perfectly dry or slightly sweet (especially on the finish). Vienna lager is, obviously, named for the Austrian capital, where it was first created in the mid-nineteenth century, but its popularity has long since peaked in Europe, and such Vienna lagers as are still made in Austria are rarely exported. Interestingly, however, the style migrated to Mexico, and Vienna lagers made by Mexican brewers (e.g., Dos Equis Amber, Negra Modelo) are the brands best known to American beer drinkers. Numerous U.S. craft brewers offer their own takes on the Vienna lager style.

Note that there is a great deal of overlap, in appearance and taste, between Vienna lagers and other darker lager styles, such as AMBER LAGER, DUNKEL, and MÄRZEN/Oktoberfest.

Wee heavy. See SCOTCH ALE.

Weissbier (pron., VICE-beer), a southern German (Bavarian) style of WHEAT BEER. *Weissbier* means "white beer," but Weissbiers, like "white" people, aren't really white; they're just comparatively pale. Weissbier—spelled *Weißbier* in German, if you want to get all *Eszett*-y about it—is exactly the same thing as Weizenbier

(= wheat beer); some brewers prefer one term; some, the other. There are several different substyles of Weissbier (substyles with entries in this A-to-Z follow), but all have a few things in common: They're all top-fermented ales. The grist always contains a high proportion of malted wheat. (German law requires that any wheat beer be made from at least 50 percent wheat, and most Weissbiers pump it higher than that—up to 70 percent.) They all have formidable, dense, long-lasting heads—a function of wheat's high protein content. They're not terrifically hoppy. And they all have distinctive, "phenolic" flavor notes—banana, clove, vanilla, "bubblegum"—that betray the use of wheat yeasts in their fermentation. (See WHEAT BEER for a fuller explanation of these attributes.)

Wheat beer has a long history in Bavaria (there's archaeological evidence for its having been brewed there for at least 2,800 years), and some of today's Weissbeer breweries can trace their own lineages back to the late Middle Ages. Over the centuries, however, the popularity of Weissbier has waxed and waned—waning to the point of Weissbier's virtual extinction during the first half of the twentieth century. The past fifty years have seen a huge revival, however. More than a thousand different Weissbiers are now brewed in Bavaria, and it's lately become Bavarians' favorite beer, accounting for more than a third of all the beer drunk in that beer-soaked region. (It's also gained an international following, and a good selection of Bavarian Weissbiers is usually available at better beer retailers in the United States.)

In Bavaria, Weissbier is universally served in tall, narrow glasses that grow bulbous near the mouth—to accentuate the beer's usually spectacular head. Some *Ausländer* ("foreigners") believe that this already-refreshing beer is improved by adding a slice of lemon, but for most German Weissbier drinkers, that amounts to sacrilege.

For more on Weissbier, have a look at the entries on substyles of the brew: DUNKELWEIZEN, HEFEWEIZEN, KRISTALLWEIZEN, and WEIZENBOCK. Do note that Weissbier—a specifically *southern* German style—is *not* to be confused with the very different, *northern* German style known as BERLINER WEISSE. Note, too, that a number of American craft breweries produce beers that they call "Weissbier" or "Weizenbier"; some of these resemble their German cousins, while others— which may use a significantly smaller proportion of wheat and/or a lot more hops—don't much. (See AMERICAN WHEAT BEER for more on these differences.)

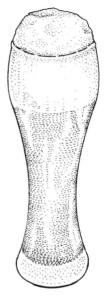

A WEISSBIER GLASS

Weizenbier (pron., VITES-zen-beer). Same as WEISSBIER, above.

Weizenbock (pron., VITES-zen-bock), a Bavarian WEISSBIER that stretches the definition of "Weissbier" beyond its usual limit. Yes, Weizenbock is a WHEAT BEER—the name means "wheat bock"— but, unlike other German wheat beers, it's truly *dark* in color, chocolaty dark. It's also much higher in alcohol than other German wheats, generally in the 7 to 10 percent ABV range. It's the alcohol content that earns it the suffix *-bock*; it differs from other BOCK beers in that it's a top-fermented ale, whereas other bocks are lagers. The dark-roasted barley malts that constitute a portion of Weizenbock's grist can give it stewed-fruit flavors (think prunes and raisins), in addition to the banana/clove/vanilla notes usually discernible in Weissbiers. And whereas other Weissbiers (especially HEFEWEIZEN and KRISTALLWEIZEN) are often viewed as summertime thirst terminators, Weizenbock has an autumnal character—it's a beer to sip and to brood over as the leaves fall and the days shorten and chill.

If Weizenbock isn't broody enough for you, you might try **Weizen Eisbock** (= wheat ice bock; pron., VITES-zen ICE-bock), which is even stronger, darker, and more densely flavored. That's because it's subjected to **freeze distillation**: a batch of Weizenbock is chilled to the point where some of the water in the brew freezes, and then the ice crystals are removed, yielding a more concentrated, higher-alcohol beer (in the 12 percent ABV range). Despite their divergences from other German wheat beers, however, Weizenbocks and Weizen Eisbocks have a smooth and creamy mouthfeel; they're not syrupy. Aventinus Weizenbock and Aventinus Weizen-Eisbock, both made by the Schneider brewery of Kilheim, Germany, are extremely highly regarded versions of these beers; both are fairly widely available.

WHEAT BEER

Wheat beer is (you guessed it) beer that's made from wheat. But there's a catch. Few wheat beers are made *entirely* from wheat. The grain bills for almost all wheat beers include a smaller or larger measure of barley malt—anywhere from 30 to 70 percent of the total grist. The wheat in most wheat beers is malted, but there are a few wheat beers—for example, LAMBIC—whose recipes employ raw, unmalted wheat.

From the brewer's point of view, there's very good reason for including a fair amount of barley in the mix: wheat, unlike barley, is a "naked" grain—the kernels are not encased in hulls. And, as we learned in part 1 (see page 13), barley hulls play an important role in the first stage of beer making—the mash—where they keep the kernels of malted grain separate, allowing the mash water to circulate through the grain, extracting sugars (and becoming wort in the process). Hull-less wheat kernels, by contrast, are liable to glom together in the mash tun, producing a gloppy mass and leading to what's called a stuck, or set, mash.

There are so many different styles of wheat beer that it doesn't make sense to discuss them all in detail here. (A list of wheat-beer styles covered in this chapter appears at the end of this entry.) But we can note a couple of things about wheat beers in general—just so long as you promise to remember that there are exceptions to virtually everything we say!

The ancestral home of today's wheat beers is southern Germany—specifically Bavaria, where several wheat beer styles remain popular. That Bavaria is historically identified with wheat beer is, however, somewhat ironic, because it was in Bavaria that the *Reinheitsgebot*, the famous German Beer Purity Law, was first promulgated in the early sixteenth century—and it forbade the making of beer from any other grain but barley. (For more on the German Beer Purity Law, see pages 68–70.) Wheat beer managed to survive the purity law for one simple reason: Bavaria's monarchs and nobles really liked the stuff, and so an exception to the regulation was carved out to permit the making of wheat beer to continue in the local *Burgen* (castles) and *Schlößer* (palaces).

How depressingly familiar. The swells get to drink (and to do) whatever they want, while the ordinary saps . . . well, you know. (The law was later amended to allow the brewing of wheat beer more widely.)

Beers whose recipes combined wheat and barley doubtless antedate German beer making by several millennia, however. People who go around scraping the ancient residues off the insides of ancient vats and jugs and then analyzing them to find out what the heck ancient brewers made their ancient beer out of have at several ancient sites discovered that ancient mashes contained both barley and wheat (of ancient varieties, natch). So there.

But back to the present. The terms *wheat beer* and *white beer* are sort of, but not quite, synonymous. So-called white beers always incorporate some measure of wheat in their recipes, but not all wheat beers are "white"—meaning pale gold in color and often (not always) cloudy or hazy in appearance. The "whiteness" of white beers results partly from the use of wheat, which makes for a lighter-colored brew, but also from the use of pale (barley) malts. And the haziness typical of many white beers is also partly a by-product of wheat's use, in that wheat is significantly higher in protein than barley, and the wheat proteins—*if* they are not filtered out—remain suspended in the finished brew, giving it a cloudy appearance. But there's another factor behind the haziness of some wheat beers: yeast. In many traditionally made, unfiltered German wheat beers, yeast sediment remains in the bottle, thickening the haze. Having grasped all this, however, you should note the following: (1) You can make a wheat beer that incorporates darker barley malts, in which case the beer will not be "white" (pale) in color, and/or (2) you can filter out the residual proteins and yeast, in which case your white beer will not be hazy. (See the entries for DUNKELWEIZEN and KRISTALLWEIZEN, respectively, for more on such arcana.) Note, too, that just as *wheat* and *white* sound alike in English, their German-language equivalents are near homophones: *Weizen* (pron., VITES-zen) is the German word for wheat; *weiss* (pron., vice) is the German word for white.

In and of itself, wheat adds virtually no flavor to a beer. What it does add—and this is typical of wheat beers generally—is a silky mouthfeel. That smoothness, coupled with the facts that wheat beers are often brewed using pale barley malts and are often comparatively low in alcohol, is what makes many wheat beers so refreshing. Wheat beers are *not* lagers—they're top-fermented ales—but many have an appearance and a refreshing character very, very close to

All whites are wheats, but not all wheats are white

those of PILSNER-style lagers. That said, there are notable differences in taste. Wheat beers (especially non-American wheat beers) are generally less hoppy in flavor and less bitter than pale lagers, and wheat beers (especially German wheat beers) often have distinctive flavor notes contributed by the special wheat yeasts used in their making. During fermentation, these yeasts produce **esters**—organic compounds associated with various flavors—that our noses and tongues "read" as banana, clove, and vanilla.

Another characteristic that distinguishes wheat beers, generally: many have formidable heads and good **head retention**. Wheat, unlike barley, contains a lot of gluten—the gluelike proteins responsible for the internal "architectural" structure of a loaf of bread. (It's the presence of so much gluten that makes wheat a better grain for baking than barley.) Well, glutens contribute to the "architecture" of a wheat beer's head, as well, allowing the CO_2 bubbles to pile up, one atop another, and keeping that bubbly structure in place for a longer time than in most nonwheat beers.

To get a handle on the wide variety of wheat beers, you might begin by grouping them geographically, in terms of where the styles originated:

First, there are the *southern German* wheat beers, which include WEISSBIER and its substyles DUNKELWEIZEN, HEFEWEIZEN, KRISTALLWEIZEN, and WEIZENBOCK. Then there's the highly unusual *northern German* wheat beer called BERLINER WEISSE.

Next come the *Belgian* wheat beers, divisible into two major styles: LAMBIC and WITBIER.

And then there are the AMERICAN WHEAT BEERS, some of which pay homage to European styles, while others chart new New World territory. Wheat beers are also produced, nowadays, in Britain, though wheat beer is not a traditional British style.

Finally, it bears mentioning that some wheat beers do well when flavored or mixed with fruit. Lambics are often fruit flavored; Berliner Weisse is often drunk with a bit of fruit syrup mixed in; and Bavarian Weissbier is sometimes served in a fifty-fifty mixture with lemonade. American wheat-beer brewers have often experimented with fruit flavorings. During the 1990s, raspberry-flavored wheat beer was an American brewpub staple, and although its popularity has declined somewhat, there are still numerous berry-flavored American wheat beers on the market.

Whisky ale. See SCOTTISH ALE AND SCOTCH ALE.

White beer. See BERLINER WEISSE, WEISSBIER, WHEAT BEER, WITBIER.

Wild ales. See SOUR BEER.

Winter ales. See SEASONAL BEERS.

Winter warmer. See OLD ALE.

Witbier (pron., VEET-beer), a Belgian or Belgian-style WHEAT BEER. The name, in Flemish, means "white beer"; in French, Belgium's other major language, it is known as *bière blanche*. Pale gold in color, witbiers are moderately alcoholic and often slightly sour, but their most salient characteristic is that their primary spicing is provided *not* by hops but by a combination of coriander and orange peel (and/or other botanical flavorings). Although contemporary witbiers are lightly hopped, the style is a throwback to a much earlier era of beer making, in which lots of things *other than* hops were used to flavor beer. (Such combinations of herbs, spices, and fruits go by the general name of *gruit*; see GRUIT ALES.)

Like many other region specific beer styles trounced by PILSNER's world conquest, witbier all but disappeared during the twentieth century. Its revival was fathered in the 1960s when a milkman named Pierre Celis, living in the Belgian town of Hoegaarden (a center, historically, of witbier brewing), decided to brew his own, using a traditional recipe. His cottage industry proved very successful, and the Hoegaarden brand he established (which has long since passed from the Celis family's ownership) is now the best-known witbier in the world, though it has many emulator-competitors, especially among

North American craft brewers. (Celis himself moved to America, where he founded the Celis Brewery in Austin, Texas, and continued to brew witbier; he later sold the Celis brand name and product lines to the Michigan Brewing Company, which today makes Celis White and a number of other Belgian-style beers that Celis formulated.)

Witbiers' grain bills typically consist of about 50 percent unmalted wheat, mixed with barley malt and (sometimes) a small proportion of unmalted oats; they often have the haze or cloudiness associated with wheat beers generally. Their fruitiness, lactic-acid tang, and relatively light body earn them their reputation as summertime refreshers. Drinkology just loves Hoegaarden; it may be our favorite wheat beer of all. We're also partial to the coriander-and-orange-peel-spiced Witte, made by the Ommegang Brewery of Cooperstown, New York.

Zoiglbier. See KELLERBIER.

Zwickelbier. See KELLERBIER.

PART 3

Beer and Culture

(AND BEER CULTURE)

I F BEER IS "THE NEW WINE," IT'S GOT A LOT OF CATCHING UP to do, culturally. If that sounds like a putdown, it isn't—just an observation, and, Drinkology thinks, an accurate and interesting one. It can be reasonably argued that beer, historically, has been every bit as important a beverage as wine—even more important, if you focus squarely on the sustenance beer has provided human beings since ancient times. It's curious, then, that wine is so densely threaded into our cultural traditions—literature, art, music, religion—in a way that beer is not.

Drinkology's no statistician, but numbers can be revealing. Take Shakespeare's works, for example. In the whole Shakespearian corpus, the word *wine* makes eighty-six appearances—and this doesn't count mentions of specific kinds of wine (like *sack,* which is the word Shakespeare uses for sherry). By contrast, *beer* and *ale* together (including related words, like *alehouse* and *alewife*), receive fewer than thirty mentions, total, from the Bard. (Given that beer was every bit as vital to life as wine in Elizabethan England, we find this very strange.)

Or have a look at *Bartlett's Familiar Quotations*: Drinkology's copy lists 102 quotable quotes containing the word *wine* or related words (*winepress, wines,* etc.), whereas quotes containing either *beer* or *ale* (or related words) number just twenty-one—and the number doesn't make it to thirty even if you add in the quotations containing *brew, brewer,* and *brewery.*

Drinkology wondered whether this kind of differential would show up on Google, and, somewhat to our surprise, it did. A search performed one afternoon in the late summer of 2010 found that "wine" got 312 million hits; "beer," meanwhile, got 136 million. Drawing meaningful inferences from such numeric comparisons can, of course, be an imbecilic endeavor. Just for the hell of it, we then also Googled "Lindsay Lohan" and "Katharine Hepburn"—and discovered that Ms. Lohan got 35 million hits to Ms. Hepburn's paltry 870,000. Only a cretin (or someone unspeakably young) would interpret that difference as indicative of their relative greatness. Obviously, you've got to look beyond the numbers.

Try this experiment

So let's do. Try this experiment: Think for a moment of all the phrases—whether attributable quotations or just common, time-worn clichés—that you know that refer in some way to wine. Putting ourself to this test, Drinkology immediately came up with "days of wine and roses," "in vino veritas," "new wine in old wineskins," "kisses sweeter than wine," "it's the wine talking," "wine, women, and song," and, of course, "trampling out the vintage where the grapes of wrath are stored." Now, think of all the familiar phrases you can that have to do, somehow, with beer. In several minutes of mulling this over, we came up with two: "champagne taste on a beer budget" (which, of course, mentions wine, too) and "it smells like a brewery in here."

At this point, we can hear you saying, "*What is going on here? I thought this was supposed to be a book about beer.* Where in God's name is the *beer*?" Which, dear reader, is exactly Drinkology's question.

Frankly, we don't really know why, *comparatively speaking,* there's so much about wine and so little about beer in western culture and in the "products" of western culture that have been handed down to us. We have some speculations, which appear in the section on beer in art, below, but they're just that—speculations. What we do know for certain is that there *is* this remarkable difference—there just *is*. So beer, if it's truly to be the new wine, has the whole wine-dark sea of our culture to emerge from.

And there are other dimensions, too, to the "cultural" problem facing beer—ones that have to do not with western culture writ large but with what we'll call *beer culture*. One dimension, to put it dangerously bluntly, is that beer culture is, generally speaking, *low* culture—or is often perceived as such, which has the same effect in terms of beer's being taken seriously by some people. Let's face facts. Although there's undoubtedly some (cheap) wine

Beer culture is *low* culture

consumed at tailgate parties, it was beer drinkers, not oenophiles, who invented the phenomenon.

And the other dimension—about which we'll be just as riskily straightforward—involves the way that beer is "gendered" in our society, which is a fancy-assed way of talking about sex. In America, at least, beer culture is masculine culture, and sometimes and in some respects it's masculin*ist* culture—culture that not only excludes or disparages women but that simultaneously celebrates some of the less charming aspects of American man/boyhood.

Okay, okay, we know that these are extremely sweeping statements that can be undermined by thousands of counterexamples. And, yes, we also know that beer culture has changed and is continuing to change, ever more rapidly. We can trot out some of those counterexamples and some of that evidence of change, ranging from the minor (the writer of the *New York Times* "wine" column devotes an ever-increasing number of inches talking to beer) to the major (an ever-increasing number of women are entering the brewing profession, becoming beer connoisseurs, beer writers and bloggers, etc.). And yet . . . well, just have a look at the sections on beer songs and beer movies and beer games in the pages that follow, and then let us know how much you think beer culture has *really* changed.

Throwing all caution to the winds, we want to toss one other observation into this kettle—an observation that might seem to contradict what's been said so far in this chapter (and in much of this book). In fact, it *is* contradictory, but then Drinkology always thinks that it's smarter to be of two minds rather than merely one. The observation: as beer gets culturally "upgraded"—as craft breweries and brewpubs proliferate across the land, as beer sophisticates install beer cellars and start obsessing about just when the Belgian ales they've laid in will reach their "peak," as ordinary middle-class folk begin to dither about which porter to pair with which artisanal cheese, that is, as beer culture (in certain quarters) grows more and more to resemble "high" wine culture—something important is in danger of getting lost, or at least obscured.

And that something is beer's simplicity. The homely and homey plainness of much of the world's beer. After all, when most beer drinkers crack open a brewski, what they're usually looking for—and what they usually get—is the comfort of the unchallengingly familiar. When they "pair" their beer, the accompaniment they choose is likely to be on the order of pretzels, or peanuts, or pizza. And there's a virtue in this. Drinkology would **Simplicity** wager that, for many, many people, "having a beer" **is a virtue** carries a different set of meanings—much less heavily freighted—than "having a glass of wine" or "having a cocktail." And, in a way, that's how it should be. (Which won't, however, stop us from showing a lot of attitude about the idiocy of much beer culture in the sections that follow!)

BOTTLES OF BEER ON THE WALL? (BEER IN ART)

Every two years, the city of Venice, Italy, hosts its Biennale—an enormous art festival that brings together artists representing countries around the world. For the 2009 Biennale, the nation of Iceland was represented by a guy named Ragnar Kjartansson—a painter and former musician—whose contribution to the festival was a performance piece called *The End*. The Biennale lasts for nearly six months—from early June till late November—and Kjartansson stayed on site the whole while, holed up with a friend (named Pall Haukur Bjornsson) in a decrepit palazzo on the Grand Canal. Every day, Kjartansson painted a picture of Bjornsson, who, for the daily sitting, wore only a Speedo bathing suit (oh, and a scarf and shoes when the weather turned cold). By the festival's end, Kjartansson had produced 144 portraits* in all—paintings that were exhibited, the following year, at the Luhring Augustine Gallery in New York, which is where Drinkology saw them.

So what's *this* got to do with beer? Well, during the months that Kjartansson was painting Bjornsson, they both drank a lot of beer, and—how do you say "total slob" in Icelandic?—they let the empty bottles accumulate in the broken-down palazzo. On the furniture, on the floor, *everywhere*. And groups of those empty beer bottles (some Beck's bottles, but mostly Italian brands like Castello, Moretti, and Peroni) figure importantly in the paintings. It's fair to say that the beer bottles are *the* major props in the pictures—their ubiquity, along with the repeated depictions of Bjornsson's skinny, seminude figure, are what tie the series together.

For works that were executed so quickly, Kjartansson's *The End* pictures are pretty interesting, but it's all those beer bottles that truly make them unusual. And the reason for that is that, in the whole history of art, there are relatively few depictions of beer or beer-related stuff. In fact, it's easy to make a list—a very brief list—of virtually all the beer-related visual art that's been made since the beginning of time:

1. Ancient art, including some Mesopotamian depictions of people drinking beer and some Egyptian wall paintings and statuettes of people making and serving beer (see pages 3 and 5 for illustrator Glenn Wolff's interpretations of a few of these images).

---

* Drinkology realizes that the math doesn't work. Nearly six months of painting a picture every day ought to result in more than 144 pieces. So maybe Kjartansson took the weekends off, or maybe he destroyed some of the works, or maybe he was just too hung over to paint on some days; the press releases don't say.

2. Flemish and Dutch paintings from the sixteenth and seventeenth centuries, showing either (a) peasants engaged in peasant-type activities, including beer-drinking (for example, Pieter Bruegel the Elder's *The Corn Harvest,* 1565, and Peter Paul Rubens's *The Village Fête,* 1635–38), or (b) still lifes that include beer glasses (or tankards or jugs) among the objects depicted (for example, Pieter Claesz's *Still Life with Overturned Jug,* 1635). Oh, yeah, and there's Rembrandt's remarkable 1635 picture *Portrait of the Artist with his Wife Saskia,* in which an impish Rembrandt, outfitted as a cavalier, seems to be toasting the viewer, hoisting an absurdly tall beer flute.

3. Some French paintings from the mid-nineteenth through the early twentieth century showing either (a) café/nightclub scenes (for example, Édouard Manet's inexpressibly great picture *The Bar at the Folies-Bergère,* 1882, which shows, among the bottles arrayed on the bar, a couple of bottles of Bass Ale, with Bass's instantly recognizable red-triangle logo on their labels), or (b) still lifes that include beer glasses (or mugs or pitchers) among the objects depicted (Vincent van Gogh, Fernand Léger, and Juan Gris were among the painters who made such still lifes).

4. A few works by the American post-Expressionist artist Jasper Johns, including, most famously, his *Painted Bronze* (1960), which is a painted cast (in, yes, bronze)

(APOLOGIES TO JASPER JOHNS)

of two Ballantine Ale cans. The cans are not quite identical: one has been opened (you can see the church-key holes), the other hasn't.

That's not quite it, actually. There are some medieval manuscript illuminations, a lot of anonymous prints showing beer barrels and pub signs and the like, some English tavern scenes, a couple of great American social realist pictures (John Sloan's 1912 *McSorley's Bar*; Thomas Hart Benton's 1948 *Poker Night [from "A Streetcar Named Desire"]*), and, of course, a helluva lot of advertising art from the 1800s on. And, if you look on the Internet, you'll find lots of recent, kitschy beer-related images that hardly merit the name *art*. But, all told, beer-themed fine art doesn't amount to all that much, at least in terms of quantity. (To be fair, we should mention that quite a few contemporary craft breweries spend a lot of effort on creating superbly well-designed art programs for their packaging and paraphernalia.)

So, anyway, why this dearth of fine art about beer—as compared, for example, to art about wine, of which there's a whole lot more? Well, off the top of our head, Drinkology can think of at least five possible reasons:

1. There's no unambiguous mention of beer in the Bible—whose stories were the inspiration for much of western art up until the last couple of centuries. The Hebrew word *shekhar*, which is usually translated as "strong drink" and which some scholars interpret as meaning "beer," occurs in several places in the biblical record—but even if "strong drink" does equal "beer," there's too little there to build an iconography on. (Wine, by contrast, appears hundreds of times in the Bible, and it's centrally important in both Jewish and Christian ritual.)

2. The ancient Greeks didn't like beer. They had no beer god or goddess equivalent to Dionysus (the Greek god of wine), they didn't drink beer, and they looked down their aquiline noses at those "barbarous" peoples who did drink it. Now, just like biblical stories, scenes from Greek mythology are a great source of western visual imagery. But since there's no beer in the Greek myths, there's no beer in the art that takes its cue from them.

3. Italians aren't all that keen on beer and never have been. Sure, Italians make and drink beer—witness those Italian lagers with which Kjartansson and his model wiled away their Venetian sojourn—but Italian culture and cuisine, from time immemorial, have been identified with wine, not beer. (And, frankly, Italian beer isn't generally very good—though, to be fair, there is now a nascent craft-beer movement in Italy.) Now, think about all the art you know, and then think of how very much of that art was made by Italians—and you've landed on another possible reason for the relative paucity of art about beer.

4. Beer has a reputation—sustained to this day—as a drink of *ordinary* people. In the grand scheme of art history, it was only very recently that artists began depicting ordinary people (and their surroundings and belongings) with any frequency or respect. Beer does make appearances in images—for instance, the Dutch and Flemish genre paintings and American realist works mentioned above—made by artists interested in portraying the lives and environments of everyday folk, but it's absent from depictions of the high and mighty, of which, historically speaking, there are many, many more.

5. Beer's ingredients and the beer-making process aren't especially picturesque. A stalk of barley isn't nearly so pretty as a grape cluster, and, in terms of visual appeal, there's no beer-making equivalent to a peasant stomping around barefoot in a vat of grapes. Beer making, no doubt, is a highly interesting process—but it's not so very *visually* interesting (which is why brewery tours become tedious after you've taken a few; see pages 43–45).

A concluding observation: Drinkology does do a few other things with our life besides drink and write about drinking, and we've taken a fair number of art studio classes—drawing and painting, mostly. In many of those classes, students have been required to bring in objects from home to use in composing still lifes, and, whenever this has happened, at least a few students have included a wine bottle or bottles among the objects they've toted to the studio. They never, however, bring in *beer* bottles to paint. *Never.* Which is odd, really, because a beer bottle is every bit as inherently interesting (or not) as a wine bottle—plus, beer bottles are mostly smaller and lighter and would thus be easier to carry to class. Drinkology thinks that this phenomenon has something to do with what people, in general, think of as appropriate subject matter for art. Wine, yes; beer, nuh-uh.

And that, finally, is why Kjartansson's beer-bottle-strewn images are, in their understated way, rather shocking. When it comes to the artist's palette, the grape and the grain are apparently not to be mixed.

ALEHOUSE ROCK (SONGS ABOUT BEER)

As a musical and lyrical muse, beer is kind of . . . well . . . it's kind of *limited*. There are hundreds of songs about beer, maybe hundreds and hundreds, but, with few exceptions, beer songs fall into one or another of the following three thematic categories:

1. Beer is great—let's have a beer!

2. I feel like crap—think I'll have a beer.

3. My woman done gone and left me, and I feel like crap (think I'll have a beer).

There are of course subcategories, such as the "Beer is great—let's have a whole lot of beers and get really wasted!" subgenre and the "My woman done gone and left me, and everything else in my shitty life is totally wrong, too, and I feel like crap (think I'll have a beer)" subgenre.

Until very recently, almost all beer songs have been written and sung by men. That's beginning to change, what with all the beer-slinging young ladies around, but it's still true that getting plastered (on beer) and crying into one's beer remain, at least artistically, mostly male-gender pursuits.* Past exceptions to the boys-only rule

---

* The 2007 song "Restorative Beer," by the Fiery Furnaces, represents a rare instance of a woman—singer Eleanor Friedburger—crooning about crying into *her* beer. By the way, Drinkology did take the time to read every line of every song by Amy Winehouse, who, of course, often sang about drinking (and smoking dope, etc.) during her seemingly brief career. (Come back to us, Amy!) To our surprise, there appears to be only *one* direct reference to beer in Amy's oeuvre: the line "Take your Stella [Artois?] and fly," in the song "You Know I'm No Good."

include "Beer Bottle Boogie," as recorded by the great blueswoman Koko Taylor; "Gimme a Pigfoot and a Bottle of Beer," by the equally great blueswoman Bessie Smith; and "I Spent My Last $10 (on Birth Control and Beer)," by the lesbian country-rock ensemble Two Nice Girls. And, of course, there are old standards like "Beer Barrel Polka" and "Im München Steht ein Hofbräuhaus," which were written by who-knows-who and have been lustily sung by guys and gals alike. Both of those last two songs, by the way, belong to the "Beer is great—let's have a beer!" category. Drinkology learned the "Im München" song—whose title and main lyric roughly translate as "In Munich There's a Beer Pub"—when we took a German class in high school. Public education has changed considerably since then.

Not only are beer songs written and sung (mostly) by men, but they're written and sung (mostly) by *certain kinds* of men. Sinatra didn't sing beer songs (he sang songs about drinking, but that's a different thing). Dean Martin didn't sing beer songs (though he, too, frequently sang about drinking). Paul McCartney? No beer songs. David Bowie? No beer songs. Antony Hegarty (of Antony and the Johnsons)? Are you kidding?

No. Generally speaking, beer songs are the province of rough, tough, heterosexual-type* men. Used-to-hard-times, down-on-their luck-but-full-of-macho-attitude kind of dudes. Like, for example, *Irish*men; Irishmen sing beer songs (viz., the Clancy Brothers' "Beer, Beer, Beer"). As do C&W/rockabilly types (viz., Webb Pierce's heart-piercing "There Stands the Glass" and Bob Wills's "Bubbles in My

---

* Beer is homoerotically mentioned in the song "Papa Was a Rodeo," by unapologetically gay singer-songwriter Stephin Merritt, of the Magnetic Fields— but we can't think of any other exceptions.

Beer"). And punk-slacker-thug types, in both their American and British avatars (viz., PsychoStick's "Beer!!!!" and Bad Manners' "Lager Delirium," respectively). And also bluesy rocker types (viz., John Lee Hooker and George Thorogood, whose 1966 and 1977 covers, respectively, of Rudy Toombs's "One Bourbon, One Scotch, and One Beer" are equally masterful). And, of course, Tom Waits, who remains in a class all by himself. (Give a listen to Waits's "Warm Beer and Cold Women," from his 1975 album *Nighthawks at the Diner*.)

Now to the exceptions to the thematic categories. Drinkology can think, off the top of our head, of four. First, there's the beer song *everybody from the age of two up* knows: "100 Bottles of Beer on the Wall" (a.k.a. "99 Bottles of Beer on the Wall"). This song—which isn't quite a *song*, really, and which used to keep kids entertained on long, boring drives in the days before the invention of electronic devices for keeping kids anesthetized—is *almost* a "Beer is great—let's have a beer!" song. The thing is, it doesn't really speak to beer's *pleasures* per se. It more or less says, "We've got a bunch of beer, so let's have one, and then another, and then another, etc., until we've drunk the whole damned lot of them." Which strikes Drinkology as the hardest-core beer message of all.

The second exception is represented by several songs that distinguish themselves by being *against* beer. Actually, the kind of beer in question is malt liquor, which may make the negative sentiment somewhat easier to comprehend (see pages 163–71 for more on why this is so). Musical putdowns of malt liquor range from politically charged tirades (e.g., rap group Public Enemy's 1991 "1 Million Bottlebags," which castigates African-American malt-liquor drinkers for participating in their own "genocide") to more personal

BEER BELLIES AND BEER JUGS

Now Drinkology will answer a question so important, of such burning concern, that you'll feel justified in having spent your hard-earned cash to buy this book.

Q: Are beer bellies caused by drinking beer?

A: Yes. . . . And no.

See? Drinkology is so generous, we give you two answers for the price of one. Here's the reason for the (seemingly) contradictory response:

Beer bellies—*abdominal obesity*, to get all technical about it—can certainly result from drinking too much beer. But that's because beer is highly caloric and loaded with carbohydrates (well, except for light and low-carb beers*). Beer, in other words, is a high-cal, high-carb *food*. Which means that you can develop the visceral fat that outwardly manifests itself as a "beer" belly even if you're a teetotaler. The culprit is too much food, no matter whether that food is porter or porterhouse. (Genetic predisposition toward obesity also appears to play a role.)

Note, however, that you're much more likely to grow a classic beer belly—that peculiarly "pregnant" profile—if you are a *man*. That's because men tend to first gain weight in their abdomens, whereas women tend to first put on the pounds in their hips, breasts, and arms. (Of course, if you continue to eat—or drink—much too much, you'll eventually get fat all over, no matter your gender.)

---

* FYI: A typical twelve-ounce mass-market beer (of the nonlight variety) will tip in at 150-plus calories and probably contain at least 10 grams of carbohydrate. Light beers average 103 calories per 12 ounces. Note, however, that low cal doesn't necessarily translate into low carbs; some light beers are relatively low carb, while others have nearly as many carb grams per serving as "regular" beers.

While pursuing the formidable research that it took to compile this sidebar, Drinkology also happened upon the following, possibly alarming, information: there's some evidence that drinking too much beer, besides causing beer bellies, can lead to the growth of what are politely termed "man boobs." In this case, the culprit isn't calories or carbs; it's *hops*. It appears, you see, that hops are *estrogenic*—they contain estrogen-like compounds that can affect a man's hormonal balance, constricting the flow of testosterone and causing him to develop those "primary sexual characteristics" known as *breasts*. Moreover, long-term exposure to hops can (purportedly) lead to impotence—or "brewer's droop" as old British slang charmingly put it. There are even Internet conspiracy theorists who believe that the *Reinheitsgebot,* the German Beer Purity Act of 1516—about which you can read more on pages 68–70—specified that hops *and hops only* could be used to flavor and bitter beer because those who promulgated it wanted to keep the populace "feminized" and therefore docile. Jeesh.

Drinkology knows we're supposed to be all scientific and everything when reporting such info. But, in fact, we're (1) confused and (2) amused. Confused: if hops "feminize" male beer drinkers (and if male and female behaviors are really as stereotypical as these theorists seem to believe), then you'd think there would be no such thing as a *bar fight* involving beer-drinking men. Amused: in contemporary craft-beer-drinking culture, ultra-hoppy beers seem such an emblem of masculine identity that we can't help finding it ironic that such beers might promote the development of what we can't help but refer to as "beer jugs."

eruptions of alcoholic pathos (e.g., the late indie singer-songwriter Elliott Smith's 1995 "St. Ides Heaven," which *almost* belongs in the "I feel like crap—think I'll have a beer" category except that it's even more depressed and depressing).

The third thematic exception is Traffic's classic "John Barleycorn," from the group's 1970 album *John Barleycorn Must Die*. This song—an arrangement by lead singer/keyboardist Steve Winwood of a traditional English ballad—is lovely, haunting, melancholic, poetic, beautiful, moving, and strange: a set of qualities that distinguishes it from *every other* beer song. (For more on the "John Barleycorn" ballad, see page 12.)

Not that there aren't other, *just plain strange* beer songs, and what must be the strangest ever represents our fourth exception: Frank Zappa's "Titties and Beer," which first appeared on the record *Zappa in New York* (1978). In a way, this audacious number resembles a "My woman done gone and left me" beer song, except that the woman in question, a big-chested skank named Chrissy, disappears when she is *eaten by the Devil*. (The Devil later vomits her back up, no worse for wear.) This is a song that it's impossible to really like *and* impossible not to be awed by.

SAD TRUTHS—AND SADDEST MUSIC (BEER IN FILM AND TELEVISION)

Back in 2004, a small-budget romantic comedy/drama featuring an ensemble of little-known actors became a huge, multi-award-winning international hit. The film, *Sideways,* focused on two men—former college buddies now in their forties—and the two women they get involved with while on a road trip to southern California's wine country. Wine—the characters' love of it, their knowledge about it, their issues with it—is central to the story. The characters are portrayed sympathetically even when they behave badly (as the two men most certainly do).

Their problems—with alcohol, money, careers, friendship, and, yes, sex—are treated seriously even as they provide the

Wake up and smell the pinot noir

material for the movie's uproariest moments. It's a film that, in the words of the reviewer for *Time Out London,* is "intelligent, funny, and moving." It is, in short, a movie for *adults.*

There has never been a film like this made about beer. Which is a crying shame. Maybe that's why one Internet list maker included *Sideways* on his list of "The 10 Best *Beer* Movies of All Time," writing that, in *Sideways,* "People get drunk, people have sex, and people [he means 'men'] love their alcohol like their women. Finally a beer movie (under clever disguise) made it to the Academy Awards!" To which Drinkology replies, *Wake up and smell the pinot noir, buster. No amount of wishful thinking can make what you say true.*

PUERILE CINEMATIC IDIOTS
The sad (well, depending on your point of view, we guess) truth about movies "about" beer—we're talking about *fictional* stories that give beer a starring role—is that most of them are gross-out comedies in which young men (often traveling in packs) get insanely drunk; try to hook up with babes (sometimes successfully, often not); throw up, piss themselves, etc.; and suffer the social and physiological consequences of their misbehavior, at least briefly.

They're morality tales, of a sort, in which the moral is something like, "That was really stupid, but, dude, you know what? We'll be doing it again." Some of these films are brilliant—e.g., *Animal House*, the 1978 farce (and the granddaddy of all the films in this "fratire" genre) that underscored John Belushi's comic genius and launched Kevin Bacon's movie career. Some are unbrilliant—e.g., *I Hope They Serve Beer in Hell*, a 2009 flick based on blogger and best-selling "memoirist" (we use the term loosely) Tucker Max's monumentally cocksure accounts of his adventures with booze and boobs. And some are apparently so unbrilliant that they go directly to DVD (which, with films of this genre, is really some kind of achievement)—e.g., *Road Trip: Beer Pong*, a 2009 movie about which Drinkology would prefer to know *nothing*.

There is a veritable pantload of such dimwitted fare out there. Between the time this paragraph is being written and the time you're reading it, several new beer-soaked fratires will probably have besmirched the screens of your local multiplex. And—you know what?—Drinkology doesn't give a flying you-know-what. It's not that we're *against* young men's burning desires to carry on, get laid, etc. (we were, after all, once a young man ourself). We're just not very *interested* in it anymore.

(Yawn. We are getting *old*.) Anyway, having said all that, we've got to admit that there've been quite a number of good movies about *drinking*—movies, that is, in which beer may or may not share the spotlight with other forms of hooch. The thing about most of these films, though, is that what they're really about is the *perils* of alcohol. That's true of classics like *The Lost Weekend* (1945) and *Days of Wine and Roses* (1962). It's a little less true (but not much less) of *Leaving Las Vegas,* the 1995 Nicolas Cage vehicle that, though it turns a gimlet eye on alcoholism, does leave the question open as to whether it might not be existentially, metaphysically okay to drink oneself to death. About the only film we can think of that (sort of) celebrates inebriation as a lifestyle is *Barfly,* the 1987 adaptation of the late poet, novelist, and famed lowlife Charles Bukowski's semi-autobiographical writings. (Bukowski wrote the screenplay; Mickey Rourke and Faye Dunaway starred.)

And we can't think, really, of a single fictional film that celebrates the pleasures of beer per se in a nonidiotic, nonpuerile way. For all its moral complexity, *Sideways* evidenced an abiding love of wine and wine culture, and, as we said, there just isn't any beer *Sideways.* For filmic celebrations of beer, beer making, and beer drinking, you've got to turn to documentaries. There've been a handful of beer-boosting documentaries in recent years, including *The American Brew* (2007), about the history of beer in this country (paying special attention to the craft-brewing movement); *Beer Wars* (2009), about competition within the contemporary American beer industry (and paying special attention to the craft-brewing movement); and *The Beer Hunter* (2010—though not yet released as of this writing), about the late, great beer (and whiskey) writer Michael Jackson (and paying special attention to Jackson's influence on and championing of the craft-brewing movement). We don't know about you, but we kind of detect a running theme here.

"Beer in Film" is a slender topic, but we can't let it go without mentioning a couple of other flicks. Drinkology much prefers the Three Stooges to latter-day puerile cinematic idiots; we like the Stooges now just about as much as we did when we were, say, seven.

Well, there's a highly watchable 1935 Three Stooges short called *The Three Little Beers*, in which Larry, Moe, and Curly get themselves hired as brewery deliverymen. Despite its title and the setup, there's not too much about beer in this movie—most of the eighteen-minute-long romp takes place on a golf course that the Stooges invade (no, this doesn't make much sense, but you can view the film online if you want to find out why)—but it does contain an LOL sequence in which our heroes are chased downhill, uphill, and down again by beer kegs that have rolled off their delivery truck. They also, of course, get bonked in the head by beer barrels that have somehow become airborne.

To go from the ridiculous to the sublimely ridiculous, let us mention what must be the strangest beer-related movie ever made: *The Saddest Music in the World*, released in 2003 and directed by Guy Maddin. The good news is that it stars Isabella Rossellini, and Drinkology sort of likes Isabella Rossellini. The other news is that Ms. Rossellini plays a Canadian beer magnate (the film is set in Winnipeg in the 1930s) who, to boost sales, announces her brewery's sponsorship of an international competition to find the saddest music in the world. The *other* other news is that (1) the character played by Ms. Rossellini is legless—she lost both lower limbs in an auto accident years before the film opens—but, during the course of the movie, she is given a set of prosthetic limbs *made of glass and filled with beer*, and (2) another of the film's characters is a musician whose young son has passed away and who *carries his dead son's heart around in a jar*. And the *other other* other news is that this film is a musical *comedy*. Put it on your Netflix queue, immediately.

Film, generally speaking, is a beer desert. TV, while not a beer oasis, has at least provided a couple of diverting watering holes, notably the long-running (1982–1993) NBC sitcom *Cheers* and the even longer-running (1989–?) Fox cartoon sitcom *The Simpsons.*

Beer permeated the atmosphere of *Cheers*—set in a Boston bar and starring Ted Danson and Shelley Long and, later in its run, Woody Harrelson and Kirstie Alley, along with a sizeable crew of other regulars—though in only a few of its episodes was beer a plot-turning narrative device. The relationship between one of the *Cheers* barflies—Norm Peterson, played by actor George Wendt—and his beloved beer was, however, a constant theme in the series and the source of many gags. There's even a 1992 episode, "The King of Beers," in which Norm almost—but not quite—lands his dream job: being a professional beer taster at a brewery.

The Simpsons, though only sporadically set in a barroom, is a much more beer-soaked program. The adoration of beer evinced by pater-familias Homer Simpson is, Drinkology would guess, unparalleled on television or in any other art form since the beginning of time.

It is no overstatement to say that Homer lives to drink beer, and it isn't pretty when he's deprived of the brew—as, for example, in episode 16 of season 4, when Homer's slapped with a DUI charge and his wife, Marge, endeavors to persuade him to give up drinking for a month. The title of that episode, "Duffless," makes reference to one of *The Simpsons*' enduring contributions to American pop culture: the fictional beer, called Duff, that's the hometown brew of Homer's hometown, Springfield. (In another memorable episode, "Selma's Choice" [season 4, episode 13], the Simpson kids, Bart and Lisa, are taken by their Aunt Selma on a visit to "Duff Gardens"—a beer-themed amusement park that parodies the Busch Gardens parks originally established by the Anheuser-Busch company.)

Other notable *Simpsons* episodes whose plots hinge on beer include "So It's Come to This" (season 4, episode 18), in which Bart mischievously—and with disastrous results for Homer—uses a hardware store's paint-can shaker to shake up a can of his father's beer; "Homer vs. the 18th Amendment" (season 8, episode 18), in which Springfield enacts a prohibition ordinance and Homer, in response, takes up bootlegging; and the "Treehouse of Horror XX" Halloween episode of 2009, when Homer becomes impaled on the microbrewing apparatus at Moe's bar—the Springfield tavern where Homer spends a good many of his off hours. The ghoulish joke is that the barflies at Moe's—Homer's cronies—*love* the taste of the brew flavored by Homer's blood. *The Simpsons* is also famous for its writers' creation of numerous comical beer songs, including some that parody pop standards (including a twist on the Sinatra classic "It Was a Very Good Year").

We could go on. But let's end with this note, intended to tickle the fancy of beer-trivia/TV history buffs alike. There was a moment when the universes of *Cheers* and *The Simpsons* briefly collided. In a *Simpsons* episode called "Fear of Flying" (season 6, episode 11), Homer gets banned from Moe's and, looking for another spot wherein to quench his thirst, wanders into a bar called Cheers—which is populated by cartoon versions of the *Cheers* characters, voiced by the actors who originally played them. Television has rarely been so ingenious—and beer rarely such a spur to ingenuity.

MADE FROM BEER

Our section on beer and film and TV unfairly excludes the one filmic genre in which works about beer are legion and in which beer-related works of genius are not rare. We speak, of course, of the television commercial—the only great art form, writer Gore Vidal famously quipped, that America ever created.*

Beer commercials date back to television's earliest years—you can find plenty of early examples on YouTube. In the 1950s and early '60s, some featured cartoon characters (e.g., Mr. Magoo, who appeared in spots for Stag Beer) or flesh-and-blood entertainers (e.g., Hank Thompson, who crooned a tune for the Falstaff brand) or semi-celebs (e.g., Ed MacMahon, who shilled for Budweiser); others depicted suburban party scenes, at which well-dressed white people (men and women) politely socialized over beers; others featured working-class men quenching their working-class-manly thirsts; yet others capitalized on the connection between beer drinking and sports (including not just baseball, football, hunting, and fishing but also improbable—in context—sports like archery; we've even seen one old commercial, for the Stroh's brand, set at a logrolling contest). And there were lots of commercials, of course, that focused forthrightly if rather prosaically on the quality of the beers they promoted (or, more frequently, of those beers' ingredients).

Things started changing sometime during the mid-'60s, and a harbinger of that transformation was the ad campaign mounted

---

* We bet you didn't know that there's been a movie—a comedy—about the making of beer commercials: the aptly titled 1985 film *Beer*, starring Loretta Swit (of the *M*A*S*H* TV series fame) and Rip Torn. We didn't either, till we discovered it while looking at our cable provider's "on-demand" options one evening. We were able to stand about six minutes of it.

MADE FROM BEER

(from about 1967 into the 1970s) by the Colt 45 Malt Liquor brand. Colt 45's early one-minute spots were mini dramas of the absurd. Each opened with a handsome, suited, bored-looking guy sitting patiently at a bistro table placed in an inappropriate location: on a beach, in a bullring, on an airplane runway. He continues to wait, affectlessly, while various goings-on happen around and to him (in the bullring spot, he and the table get knocked over by a charging bull; he dusts himself off, sets the table upright, and goes on waiting). At some point in each ad, a comely young woman passes by and gives him a come-hither once-over, to which he reacts with indifference. Finally, a waiter carrying a tray that holds a can of Colt 45 and a glass arrives in some unexpected fashion—in the beach commercial, via surfboard; in the runway spot, via parachute. The waiter sets the can and glass down on the table, and the heretofore affectless guy smiles and pours himself a beer, while a voiceover announces, "In the dull and commonplace experiences of day-to-day living, one thing stands out as a completely unique experience: Colt 45 Malt Liquor." Although these commercials today look primitive and more than a little dated, it's clear when you compare them with the older beer ads that something revolutionary was going on.

Today's beer commercials—the clever ones and the stupid—are the heirs of that revolution. On the dumb side of the divide are the ads that mindlessly stroke the urges and exploit the anxieties of the young men they're mostly (solely?) aimed at. Sex—a matter of subtext and innuendo in those early Colt 45 spots—long ago moved to full-frontal position in most beer advertising. (Colt 45 was a pusher of the envelope in this regard, too, with a series of racy spots featuring actor Billy Dee Williams back in the 1980s.) You probably don't need a primer in the plots of these commercials; suffice it to say that beer's the vehicle enabling some young dude to hook up with some hot babe—or babes—or, sometimes, for him to escape the clutches of his wife or girlfriend and flee into the friendlier precincts of his beer-drinking buddies. (The heterosexual and the homosocial are two sides of the same coin in these adolescent narratives, where girls are things to have sex with and boys are people to *romance*.)

But there's a lot of beer advertising that's a lot more interesting than this—including many beer commercials that parody the stock storylines of the genre. Trouble is, describing the best of these commercials would spoil the fun. So let Drinkology direct you (again) to YouTube, where you'll find masterpieces like "A Big Beer" and "Flashdance"—both commercials for the Australian brand Carlton Draught, whose brilliant slogan is "Made from Beer." If you haven't seen them, also look for the Bud Light spots called "Swear Jar," "Dude," and—maybe the best— "Tongue in Cheeks." A warning, though. Once you've started, you'll find it all too easy to waste an entire afternoon searching YouTube for favorites of your own.

One last observation: the beer commercial has, it seems, real potential as a folk-art form. Every year, the Midwestern beer Grain Belt (made by the August Schell Brewing Company of New Ulm, Minnesota) sponsors a competition for the best homemade commercial advertising its Premium and Premium Light brands. You can check out the most recent field of prizewinning and runner-up entries by going to Grain Belt's website, www.grainbelt.com. Most are failures—or at best gems in the production-values rough. But there are a few that give Madison Avenue a run for its money.

Losing Is Winning, or Is It the Other Way Around? (Beer Games)

The goal of some beer games is to get your opponent or opponents as drunk as they can be as quickly as possible. The goal of other beer games is to get *all* the players as drunk as they can be as quickly as possible. But the spirit in which most (all?) of these games is played means that that first goal will soon slide down that beer-slicked slope into the second.

Drinkology is a tired old crank for whom beer games hold little appeal. (We don't need to play a game to justify getting drunk. The pain and sorrow of daily life provide rationale aplenty.) Nevertheless, we remember fondly the first—and only—beer game we ever played, which is called the Birkenstock-Wearing Lesbian Game. We're a bit tentative about introducing you to it, of course, because it could be construed as homophobic and mean-spirited. Our only defense is that we were taught it by a lesbian and that we played it, to general hilarity, in a mixed gay-and-straight crowd. Also, it's kind of a great game.

It can be played by any size group (though six to eight people would probably be ideal), and it goes like this: The players sit in a circle. The first player says, "Birkenstock-wearing lesbian." The second player (to the first player's right or left—doesn't matter) must come up with another present-participial adjectival phrase (got that? it just means a descriptive phrase using an "-ing" verb) to add to "Birkenstock-wearing lesbian." The phrase may be simple or complex (complex is definitely better), but it *must* conform to stereotyped ideas about what lesbians are like. For example, the second person might say, "k.d.-lang-fan-club-belonging, Birkenstock-wearing lesbian" or "Margaret-Cho-Comedy-Central-special-watching, Birkenstock-wearing lesbian."

You're undoubtedly already getting the idea. The third player must, in turn, come up with another stereotypically descriptive "-ing" phrase to add to the string: "organic-produce-purchasing, k.d.-lang-fan-club-belonging, Birkenstock-wearing lesbian" would work nicely. The catch, obviously, is that when making your own contribution, you must also remember and accurately repeat, in order, all the descriptive phrases that have preceded yours—a task that quickly becomes extremely difficult. If you flub it, you must drink (the amount you must drink should be set in advance), and the challenge passes to the next player. Play goes round and round the circle, and the game ends when nobody can remember the whole string of phrases, or when the players have passed out, drifted off, or just don't care anymore.

The Birkenstock-Wearing Lesbian Game belongs to a whole wide category of verbal beer games that challenge players to remember strings of phrases or to perform other mnemonic feats—which, given alcohol's impairment of memory, becomes an increasingly losing proposition. Which is, of course, the point.

"HI, BOB!" (DRINK.)

Verbal games are just one category of beer games. There are also, for example, movie games—theoretically Drinkology's favorite category, though we've never played any and don't much want to. The movie games are all exactly the same, conceptually, though the specific rules depend on the film—Drinkology has seen versions that use the 1959 swords-and-sandals epic *Ben-Hur,* the 1974 Mel Brooks cowpoke farce *Blazing Saddles,* the 2004 comedy *Napoleon Dynamite*, and even the 2005–2009 TV series *My Name Is Earl*. Episodes of TV series lend themselves just as well as movies to this kind of game—maybe even better, 'cause they're generally shorter. In fact, it's likely that the first-ever game of this kind, invented back in the '80s, was one called Hi, Bob!—played while watching reruns of *The Bob Newhart Show.* (The game's one rule was that all players had to drink whenever any character said, "Hi, Bob!")

The movie beer game setup: Make sure you have tons of beer on hand. Gather everybody around the television to watch a DVD of a movie or program that everyone has at least a passing familiarity with—or, preferably, one that's a cult favorite among the crowd. Specify the rules—which you can write yourself—in advance. These should require the viewers/players to drink certain amounts of beer when certain things happen on screen. The amount to be drunk should vary according to the frequency with which something—the appearance of a particular actor, the speaking of a particular line of dialogue, or an event (a gun being shot, a car blowing up, a car chase, a sex scene)—occurs during the course of the movie or show. Things that happen more frequently (like repeated lines of dialogue) require that the players drink *smaller* amounts of beer; things that happen less frequently (say, the appearance of a famous actor who has just one brief cameo) require that the players drink more.

Beer Frames, Etc.

It needs no saying that the drinking of beer has been associated with games for a long, long time. The Egyptians probably engaged in beer-drinking contests while playing Hounds and Jackals. Casual rules for time-honored barroom games—darts, shuffleboard, pool—often impose beer-related penalties for losing a shot or a game. (Usually, the losing player must buy a beer or beers for the winner.) And games and sports besides those ordinarily played in bars have also been inoculated with beer. Take bowling, where a **beer frame** is a frame in which all the bowlers except one roll a strike—and the low roller has to buy a round for all the others. (We assume the poor klutz may treat him- or herself to one, as well.) Or the **beer mile**, a mile-long race (run on a quarter-mile loop) in which each runner must drink a twelve-ounce can of beer at the end of each lap.

Beer has even insinuated itself into bridge—the card game—although not, of course, into its official rules. The *un*official rule regarding what's called the **beer card** (the Seven of Diamonds), according to the bridge glossary on the Bridgeguys.com website, is as follows:

> [I]f the declarer succeeds in making the contract and wins the last trick with the Seven of Diamonds, dummy must buy the declarer a beer. [I]f the opponents defeat the contract and one of them wins the last trick with the Seven of Diamonds, the opponent who wins the last trick is bought a beer by the other opponent.

Drinkology used to play bridge years ago, but we've drunk so much since that we've forgotten all the rules, so we have only the dimmest idea what this means.

So beer and games have forever and will forever be linked. What's notable, though, is how fecund our own boozy-woozy era has been when it comes to the invention of new beer-related parlor entertainments. Google "beer games" (or "drinking games"), and you'll get thousands of hits, some to sites that provide rules for hundreds of different beer games: not just verbal and movie games but also card games, games of skill, games of endurance, and "classic" games—ranging from chess to Monopoly to Twister—whose rules have been modified to include the drinking of beer as reward and/or punishment. (We think beer chess sounds like a really bad idea.) Moreover, rules for beer games are fungible. Any particular game is likely to exist in several different variations, and some versions (many, actually) invite players to make up new rules as they go along—including rules about who may take bathroom breaks and when they may do so, and about what to do if any of the players pukes.

COIN TOSSES AND RELAY RACES

The well-known game of skill called **Quarters** seems to require the greatest amount of actual mental acuity and physical dexterity. There are numerous variations, but all involve each player's trying to bounce a quarter on a flat surface (tabletop or bar) and up into an open vessel (beer cup, beer glass, pitcher, pail) from a given distance. Make the toss and you get to demand that your opponent(s) drink(s). Drinkology sort of lied, earlier, when we said that we'd only ever played one beer game; our friend Fritz Kenemer tried to teach us the version of Quarters that he used to play, in the younger day, in the bars of Kansas City. Anyway, the lesson didn't take. Fritz proved to be still quite good at Quarters, while Drinkology was discouragingly lousy (even for a beginner) and resolved never to try *that* again.

Endurance games, by contrast, demand little skill, or none at all—unless you regard the ability to drink a lot of beer in a short amount of time while remaining reasonably compos mentis as a skill. **Boat Race** is one of the best-known endurance-type games (it was featured, for example, in the 2009 "bromance" comedy *I Love You, Man*). As usual, there are many variants of the rules, but a simple version goes like this: Divide an even number of people into two equal teams (teams of four to six people work best). The teams' members stand opposite one another along the long sides of a table or counter. A plastic cup filled with beer is placed on the table in front of each player. At the word *go*—announced by somebody who's not playing the game—the two opponents facing each other at one end of the table pick up their cups and begin drinking. When each finishes, he or she sets down his cup—and it is only at that instant that the next player in the line may pick up his or her cup and begin drinking. The principle is that of a relay race. You must wait for the teammate in front of you to finish before you can begin your "leg." The team that drinks all its beers first wins. Multiple rounds may, of course, be played—and there will, we'd wager, soon be no criterion for distinguishing between winners and losers. Variations include, for instance, a version in which each player, on finishing the beer, must invert the empty cup and place it on his or her head—where it must remain until the race is over. This is surely much more fun in the playing than in the telling.

KING PONG

But of all the beer games created over the past few decades, one game—a skill-endurance hybrid—trumps all the rest: **Beer Pong**, which according to some accounts was invented by students at Dartmouth College in the 1950s or '60s. (Other colleges and universities also lay claim to being Beer Pong's birthplace.) Numberless Internet sources will inform you that Beer Pong is also called **Beirut**, but no one seems to know why—and Drinkology is doubtful that many people actually refer to it as Beirut, at least not nowadays. The *Pong* in *Beer Pong* comes from the Ping- Pong balls with which it's played—and from the fact that it was originally played on Ping-Pong tables. (The "official" Beer Pong tables now manufactured by several companies are longer and narrower than standard Ping-Pong tables.) Whether it was originally also played with Ping-Pong paddles is a matter of some dispute. In any case, it no longer is. What Drinkology finds fascinating about all this is that Beer Pong's origin—which goes back only fifty or so years—is as beclouded by historical fog as that of, say, baseball, whose beginnings date back centuries.

Now, there's not enough space in this little book to explain in any detail how Beer Pong—which began as an ad hoc college drinking game but transmuted into an international cultural phenomenon—is played. Rules vary widely, anyway, and tournament rules can be somewhat elaborate. (You can find an example of such at www.bpong.com, the website of the World Series of Beer Pong, which sponsors a big competition, held in Las Vegas each January, that in 2010 drew more than a thousand contestants.) In essence, though, the game is pretty simple:

Two teams (generally of two players each, but sometimes of four) face off across a Ping-Pong or other, similar table. Atop the table, two groups of ten 16-ounce plastic cups are arranged, one group at each end. The cups are "racked" in triangular formation—like billiard balls at the start of a game of pool—and beer is poured into them. (The level to which the cups are filled differs according to the particular rules being followed, and, often, two other cups—filled with water—are also placed on the tabletop, for rinsing off Ping-Pong balls that skitter to the floor during play.) Play proceeds by turns, with each team tossing its Ping-Pong balls at the opposing team's cups; if a ball lands in one of the opponents' cups, an opponent must drink all the beer in the cup and remove the empty cup from the rack. The game ends when one team—that would be the losing team—has been forced to drink the contents of all the cups and has removed them from play.

These "essentials," however, hardly cover everything—it's as if we'd just "explained" baseball without discussing how to distinguish a strike from a ball, or how bases may be stolen, or what a bunt or a balk is. Complete rules for Beer Pong—of whichever variation—may also specify the distance from the table at which a throwing player may stand; the manner(s) of throwing allowed (e.g., is it legit to bounce the ball into an opponent's cup?); the kinds of interference, if any, that a defensive team may employ (e.g., may one try to swat an incoming ball away?); the manner in which a losing team, on the brink of disaster, may "redeem" itself; and on and on. The World Series of Beer Pong's rules even lay down dicta concerning the tactics that teams (and their partisans among tournament spectators) may use to try to distract opponents. Abusive language, apparently, is very much okay, so long as you're not right up against the player screaming your abuse into his or her face.

Abusive language is permitted

The elaboration of Beer Pong rules covering various contingencies, the rules' codification by "official" bodies, and the proliferation of competitions at which champions receive cash prizes all lend credence to the claim, oft-heard from Beer Pong players, that "You know, dude, this isn't just about drinking or getting drunk or whatever. Beer Pong is a *real sport*, man!" To which Drinkology responds, Well, yeah, okay . . . maybe. Certainly, Beer Pong's history, however brief, does seem like a case study in how casual games can go on to become bona fide professional sports. But, you know, dude, you can't just, like, *ignore* the beer, man. 'Cause, let's face it, a big part of what Beer Pong's *about* is getting your opponents hammered so that they can't aim as well as you. If Beer Pong's a sport, then it's a sport in which a drug—a performance *un*enhancing drug, so to speak—is centrally important.

PENT-UP DEMAND
BY TONY MOORE

[Editor's note: Beer festivals range from mammoth, days-long events like Munich's Oktoberfest, which draws more than six million visitors each year, and Denver's Great American Beer Festival, which in 2010 showcased some 2,200 craft beers, to the hundreds of smaller regional and local festivals mounted around the country (and a good deal of the world) each year. Which means that you can probably find one, at some point during the year, being held within driving distance of your house. Having attained the hoary age at which we cannot think of anything we'd like to do less than plunk down in the middle of a huge crowd of drunk people, however, Drinkology was overjoyed when our young(er), less cranky friend Tony Moore offered to file a report from the field. Here's his eyewitness account of his first beer fest.]

So when you think of Harrisburg, PA, or Central PA to broaden it a bit, you might not think of handcrafted, small-batch, craft-brewed, microbrewed, craft beer or any other such string of piled-up catchalls to describe this nebulously named phenomenon that beer drinkers in the United States find themselves stumbling through (in a good way) these days. You probably don't think of beer at all. And that's a mistake. Because what we have in Central PA is Tröegs and Victory and Stoudt's and Weyerbacher. We have Yuengling (well, they're in Pottsville, which is just east of what is properly Central PA). Apart from these, we have either too many or too few others for me to name. But prowl around BeerAdvocate.com and you'll see that the beer brewed here is often ranked high up the ladder—for instance, Tröegs Nugget Nectar, which I lie in bed thinking about at night when I should be thinking about what presents I'm supposed to buy tomorrow for my daughter's birthday, is ranked number thirteen on BeerAdvocate's "Top Beers on Planet Earth" list. *Of all the beers in the world*, it's ranked *number thirteen*.

So it makes a good amount of sense to have a beer festival here in Central PA. The particular fest at hand, the Harrisburg Brewers Festival, is put on by the above-named Tröegs to benefit the Cystic

A windshield-shattering burp

Fibrosis Foundation. No one needs an excuse to get together and drink all that good beer, but it's nice to have one. In 2010, thirty-nine full-scale breweries and two pubs that brew their own beer participated. (The inclusion of the two pubs makes me wonder a little bit. Do the guys at Stone or Dogfish Head or Sierra Nevada think, *Who the hell is Market Cross Pub?* Maybe, but MCP's Olde Yeller IPA and Excalibur Imperial Stout are damn good.)

Going in, I knew the names or beers of all but twelve breweries on the list, so I hoped to try those twelve for sure and work from there. Some other things I knew: (1) It was going to be 90 degrees and (2) outdoors, and (3) I'd be standing around drinking beer for three hours. Thinking about this setting led me back to the one more-than-anecdotal anecdote I had heard about this particular fest before going in: A friend of mine had attended the year before. Following the event, she had (1) demanded during the car ride home that her husband take her to the hospital for a flaring heart attack (subsequently relieved by a windshield-shattering burp), (2) peed in the middle of her street twenty feet from her front door, and (3) told her seven-year-old daughter, while tucking her in that night, that Sleeping Beauty was a "pussy," when asked if she liked that particular princess. She sat this year's beer fest out.

So with these six things in mind, I was expecting something like . . . trouble.

There was suddenly a shortage of babysitters the day before the festival, so our wives (naturally) had to take the bullet for the team and back out. It was just me and my friend Fowler, along with two other guys I don't have room to introduce, who ended up going. Fowler and I had already (instantly!) arranged to sell our wives' tickets to some guy on Craigslist. (Here's something odd. You know how a concert gets sold out and then you go looking for scalped tickets and they're all, like, twice as much as face value? And you're, like, "This is why scalping is illegal!" So I heard there was a hot market on Craigslist for these brewers fest tickets, and I got online and looked around. There were plenty of people looking for the tickets, true enough, but every one of them was listing the face value of the ticket [forty dollars] as what they were willing to pay.)

"ANY WAY YOU WANT IT"
(AND A UKULELE PLAYER)

Fowler's wife dropped the four of us off near the entrance to the site in downtown Harrisburg, and we surveyed the area. This was at five PM, when the event officially started, and the pavement was hotter than a Wal-Mart parking lot in Morocco. (I don't do well in heat; it probably wasn't that hot.) We could see the tent where the ticket takers were lurking, and the line of people stretched from there back a block, around the corner, down another block, and, as we found out, several blocks around the corner again. There was a bar near the entrance tent with its front door open and people sitting there already drinking cold beer. They felt pity and ridicule for all of us standing in this massive line. You could just tell. Journey's "Any Way You Want It" was blasting from the bar's stereo, so . . . we moved quickly away.

Contemplating this seven-block-long line, I decided to take my friend Amy up on an offer she'd made the day before—"I'll be working the gate. Come find me."—so that my team of beer drinkers and I wouldn't have to wait. These things always sound good, but inside connections never quite work out for me. And of course I went and looked for her and couldn't find her. I sort of felt bad cutting in front of three thousand (est.) other people sweating it out in the sun anyhow, so I wasn't all that disappointed. (When I was sixteen or so, I got to cut in front of a lengthy line at an INXS concert [let's just skip any other details]. I could feel everyone's hostile eyes on me and felt like a turd, instead of like a cool insider, which I think is how you're supposed to feel.) So we found the back of the line, got ID'd and stamped, and were ready to go.

The line really moved. I'll say that much for that damn line. In the end, I bet it only took us fifteen minutes to get from where we started just across the Ohio border to the tent where our tickets were collected. Along the way were scalpers selling tickets (unsuccessfully, from what I could see) and, oddly, cars coming up the street. There were three thousand people in that street (*in the street!*), and motorists thought it would be a good idea to drive through us all. But the key takeaway from the Long March was a homeless (I'm assuming) guy playing ukulele and singing this weird song in this weird, warbling falsetto that made me not want to give him money but just hope that the line didn't stall out right in front of him and leave me there looking self-consciously away while he sort of brayed his way through whatever it was (indecipherable) he was crooning.

"My Sharona"
(and Whatever That Band Was Playing)

We segued from that guy's song to The Knack's "My Sharona," now the song of choice at the bar near the festival entrance with the smug drinkers. And then we went through the tent and were issued our tasting cups and proceeded inside.

"Inside" was two city blocks closed to traffic and cordoned off with snow-drift fencing. As we went in, on our right was a two-block-long, ten-foot-deep white tent with lots of people under it mechanically pulling taps. On our left was the stream of people squeezing past the mob of drinkers already fifteen deep waiting for the beer being served under that long tent. (I noticed later that every guy in this sardine-can crowd seemed to be constantly squeezing his girlfriend's/wife's butt. It was an ongoing feature of the festival.) This was the setup the entire two blocks: people jammed together waiting to fill their three-ounce cups with beer and more people trying to get past them to where it was (hopefully) less crowded. Along the way, we had to pass a band that played throughout, but I swear I never heard them until after the fest was over. The crowd noise was so dense—not loud exactly, but thick and unavoidable—that you just couldn't hear the music. (If you were five blocks away in your apartment trying to read the *Wall Street Journal* and listen to Bach, the band would probably have sounded like it was playing next door.)

#1: Flying Dog, Raging Bitch Belgian IPA, 8.3% ABV

The MO of the drinkers became apparent very quickly. Get in line, fill your cup, and drink that beer while you get in the next line. By the time you get to the head of that line

#2: Pennsylvania Brewing Company, Penn Pilsner, 4% ABV

you'd fill your cup again. The beauty of this process, like the line outside, was that it didn't take any time at all to get your cup filled. The lines looked torturously long and annoying, but then you had a new beer

#3: Springhouse Atomic Raygun Imperial Red Amber, 8.3% ABV

in literally two minutes, every single time.

And there was never some guy trying to get in front of you or someone accusing you of cutting in line. It was cool, and it just worked. Things were bizarrely quick and friendly. So quick, in fact, that I constantly found myself suddenly at the head of the line with half a cup of beer left over from the previous line and had to dump it down my throat

#4: Clipper City Brewing Company, Heavy Seas—Loose Cannon IPA Hop³ Ale, 7.25% ABV

to fill my cup with the next beer.

I'm not going to comment on the beers I drank except for this one, this Loose Cannon. This is a beer I had had several years ago, thought was good, and forgot about (too many to keep track of). Then suddenly Fowler is all into it recently, and I'd had a few here and there. It is very good beer. But on tap, at this festival, it was supernaturally good. It tasted just like hops smell when you take them out of a vacuum-packed bag and give them that good old fiendishly deep inhale (see page 315). Turns out the beer was only four days old, which means it was likely the freshest it can be unless you're drinking it out of a shiny vat at the brewery. Wow.

#5: Great Divide Titan IPA, 7.1% ABV

And then I ran into Tom Warren, the guy who cofounded this whole festival and was running his share of it with nothing but a yellow festival T-shirt and a Bluetooth I never quite saw. (Another guy standing there had to tell me, "He isn't talking to you right now.") Tom is the kind of high-energy guy you might expect to organize and run a beer fest in his spare time. He has the same kind of manic, somehow businesslike exuberance Tom Arnold has in *True Lies*, which in Tom Arnold's case must have stemmed from his being in this Schwarzenegger/Cameron volcanic eruption of a movie instead of . . . whatever else he was in before it to support his habits. In Tom Warren's case, he just seems to be doing something he loves and is happy as hell about it.

Tom pointed to something over the top of everyone and then beer splashed from somewhere onto my leg. It came from nowhere, somehow sourceless. But who really got it was this guy who turned out to be my beer fest nemesis—this guy in a wife-beater and mirrored fake Ray-Ban aviators who was swearing aggressively at his friends the entire time (I saw this guy everywhere I went) and just sort of being the tool that doesn't need to be at these things but is always there in some form. He got the bulk of this flying beer right in the chest, all over his precious, ribbed, a-little-too-tight, snow-white tank top. The best part of it was, he thought that Tom had done it, and he started to look to me for an answer (swearing under his breath, of course), like he thought I was associated with Tom (I was, obviously) and needed to alert Tom that Tom had spilled a beer (which Tom didn't have) on this guy so that this guy could . . . do something about it. He wanted to turn hostile. I told him Tom was running this thing, didn't have a beer, and that it must have come from somewhere else.

And then Tom turned to lead me off (somewhere; wherever it was, we never got there), unaware of any of this stuff with wife-beater guy, and I followed. But

#6· Market Cross Pub Red Courage Ale (home-brew contest winner), ~5% ABV

the people were clumping fiercely, clogging everything, and I lost him right away. And then my phone rang (on vibrate; there was no way to hear it, and at that very moment a loud cheer went up from the crowd at the other end of the block; the crowd did this every now and then, I soon saw, just to make some noise and show their excitement about all the beer they were drinking), and it was the guy I was selling the spare tickets to—the Buyer. He was not on site yet and was waiting for a cab. So he promised to call me back when he got there, and we'd do the exchange. I hung up and grabbed another beer.

#7: Stone Arrogant Bastard Ale, 7.2% ABV

I told the Stone guy how much I loved pretty much all their beer, and he gave me his card and a couple of stickers (one of which went on my mountain bike the next day: FIZZY YELLOW BEER IS FOR WUSSIES).

#8: Weyerbacher Double Simcoe IPA, 9% ABV

#9: Weyerbacher Double Simcoe IPA, 9% ABV

And then my phone rang again and it was Fowler asking me where the hell I was (we had all gotten separated the moment we entered the site) and telling me that he had found a secret keg of 90 Minute IPA at the Dogfish Head booth. I told him there were 2,390 people between me and the DFH booth but I'd work my way down there. I hung up but noticed on my (new) phone (which I didn't know how to work yet) that I had a "missed event." I tapped the icon with my fingertip and saw the Buyer's number. So I punched his number and called him back. He answered and said he hadn't called, wasn't there yet, and he'd be in touch when he got there. I felt stupid and hung up. (I also started to get paranoid that we would never meet up with this guy and would have to eat the tickets.)

#10: New Holland El Mole Ocho, 8% ABV

#11: Bethlehem Brew Works Hop Explosion, 5.5 % ABV

When I got back out of the crowd to start moving toward the DFH booth, I saw a bunch of Harrisburg police hanging around outside the fencing. I looked over the huge crowd and then turned to the cops and asked them if anything at one of these events had ever required their intervention.

#12: Voodoo Wynona's Big Brown Ale, 7.3% ABV

Not once.

#13: Bethlehem Brew Works Hop'solutely Triple IPA, 11.5% ABV

Not once in seven years had the police had to act. I thought that was pretty damn impressive and said a lot about the people attending this thing. (What was less than impressive was when I started asking the people attending this thing what cystic fibrosis was. Not one person I asked knew. I didn't know either, which was why I was asking, but still.) So I turned away from the police and hit one of the food trailers and grabbed a cheeseburger and some water. There was, thankfully, lots of food and jugs of water everywhere. I know for a fact, though, that I was the only one of our foursome to eat anything,

#14: Smuttynose IPA, 6.6% ABV

which probably explains why I could still read most of my notes the next day and why everyone else either couldn't stop talking to the cab driver or never said a word to anyone during the cab ride home.

And then the Buyer called for real. It was 6:21 PM, nearly an hour and a half into the festival. I told him to meet me "under the bridge" and suddenly had these brief and idiotic notions of being in a bad spy/ drug dealer movie. But he and his friends met me under the bridge (an iron footbridge that arched over the festival), and we swapped tickets for money over the fence and that was that. It was a big relief. Bigger than you'd think. (The next day, my phone rang and it was his number. When I picked it up, no one was there. There was something unsettling about it.)

#15: Swashbuckler Plank Walker IPA, 6.4% ABV

At around this point, I found Fowler and the Dogfish Head booth and the hidden 90 Minute keg. Fowler was pointing to this long-haired guy, this insider—button-down shirt opened to the waist, standing on the sidewalk behind the booth—and said he was back there pouring his own beer. So I filled my cup

#16: Dogfish Head 90 Minute Imperial IPA, 9% ABV

on the normal side of the booth and went back there and started talking to him (simply holding a notebook and pen lets you pretty much go wherever you feel like—in general, not just here). His wife was there with him, a woman with a perfect French pedicure just inches from a horribly swol-

Incident at the Port-a-Potty

len and road-rashed ankle. He told me that his wife's cousin's fiancé(e?) was someone at DFH and that this somehow allowed him to go back there and pour his own 90 Minute

all day long. He was vague about how all this worked (or I just didn't get it), but somehow someone's past job at Rogue out in Oregon had made it all happen. But anyhow, we stood there with him shooting the shit for nearly a half an hour, and he did in fact pour his own beer.

#17: Dogfish Head 90 Minute Imperial IPA, 9% ABV

#18: Dogfish Head 90 Minute Imperial IPA, 9% ABV

#19: Dogfish Head 90 Minute Imperial IPA, 9% ABV

But it became clear that his story was not going to get any more lucid or interesting, so I decided to hit the bathroom. Unfortunately, the Port-a-Potties were all grouped at the other end of the event, and when you have to go, getting through three thousand people to do so can really be a trick. So I filed into the stream of people going that way and followed along.

There were about fifty Port-a-Potties, and they were marked with symbols for Male, Female, and Both (this last type actually seemed *un*marked, which led to what happened next). So I went to one of the unmarked units and opened the door to the graphic, gynecologic sight of some girl finishing up. I shut the door and got into the next open one as quickly as possible. (The only thing I'll say about the Port-a-Potty in general is that it didn't smell as bad as you might think.)

"LET IT BLEED" (AND THE CICADAS)
When I came out, Fowler and the other guys were standing there, as though magically. Everyone was just drenched with

#20: Lancaster Co Congrtage PA Same Gadles IPA (This is my handwriting; I have no idea what beer this was.)

beer sweat and humidity and fatigue (usually there'd be shame mixed in with a description like this, but not this time, although it was close), red-faced with hair doing stuff it doesn't ordinarily do, dripping like Shaquille O'Neal. I doubt I looked any better.

"It's eight-thirty," one of them said, and I noticed that the blocks-long keg tent was powering down, the festival-goers already moving toward the other end of the festival area to head out. The time had gone very fast, and the suddenness of the festival's ending felt like the last scene of *Monty Python and the Holy Grail*. We all looked at each other, not sure if we should be relieved or disappointed.

So instead of figuring it out, we immediately (but slowly) went into find the-last-beer-stations-open-and-fill-up mode. It wasn't easy. There were maybe ten still open, but everyone was onto them and the lines were backed up to the third circle of Hell.

#21: Union Barrel Works Mindblock Maibock, 9% ABV

When we got separated again—naturally—I headed to the exit to wait and drink that last beer. A girl held up her hand for me to high-five. "Great game!" she said, and I high-fived her (normal, right?). I must have either stopped or doubled back, because about five minutes later, I passed her again. This time she looked at my T-shirt and said, "BP Oil!" (it said "Chevron Gasolines," so either she couldn't read or was just a big fan of BP and its recent Gulf spill) and high-fived me again. And then I sat on the curb waiting for my friends and sweating and drinking that last beer and looking at people:

There was the ninety-year-old man staggering out, blind drunk and probably heading into traffic. There was the couple holding each other up and then suddenly holding each other down on the sidewalk. (When I saw these two fall onto the pavement together, I finally heard the band. They were playing the Stones' "Let It Bleed" ("We all need someone we can lean on . . ."); the timing was uncanny. And there was my festival nemesis, just still being generally annoying/aggressive, punching his friends, and scowling around.

But the weird thing was, besides these few people (and me, apparently), no one seemed especially drunk. (Although in a nearby bar afterward, I saw something to make me rethink this a little. A guy at a urinal next to his buddy: "I'm gonna Ghostbuster your ass!" and he proceeded to jump away from his own urinal and piss on his friend, who loved it and ran out laughing. Huh?) Keeping the average ABV and the size of the cups (3 ounces) in mind, I'd had roughly nine normal-size, normal-ABV beers in those three hours, which pretty soundly accounts for how I was feeling.

So when enough was enough—but with the streets still full of people—we found our way into a cab. It was dark, so I didn't take any notes; I don't know what the hell went on during our ride home. Everyone else wanted to drink a few more beers (and we did go back to Fowler's garage briefly to do this), but I was spent and hot and wet with sweat and just feeling sort of grotesque all around and needed to go home.

My wife said, "You stink"

My house was nice and cool and dark and quiet, and I went upstairs to see what was what. I poked my head into our room and saw my wife lying there, TV on, sleeping. I kissed her on the forehead and she woke up (sort of), opened one eye, looked at me, and said, "You stink." And then she closed her eye and rolled away, and I shut the TV off and went to check on the kids. They were all sleeping, rustling under the covers or as still as the moon. I didn't say much to any of them.

Outside their rooms, I stood there, not knowing what to do. Shower? Go to bed? Watch TV? None of it sounded right. I was a little amped up, although exhausted, and it was still too damn early. So I went down to the mini fridge in the basement, opened a beer,

Bear Republic Brewing Hop Rod Rye, 8% ABV

and went out to the backyard and sat down. It had been a full, full night, and I closed my eyes and sat out there with the cicadas and the bats and just sat there.

PART 4

Beer Bash

S O FAR, *DRINKOLOGY BEER* HAS BEEN LONG ON WHAT BEER IS, short on what you should do with it—beyond drinking it, of course. This fourth and final part is a hodgepodgey collection of stuff not covered so far: things like beer obsessions, beer faults (things that can go wrong with beer), growlers (those jugs of draft beer you can carry home from a brewpub), and the trick to properly tapping a keg. Here's also where we throw in some recipes for making mixed drinks with beer and for cooking with beer, and, finally, where we take on the topic of home brewing.

But let's begin with the presumably simple topic of how to pour a beer from a bottle (or can) into a glass. Are we going to make it complicated? No. All we're going to advise is that you tilt the glass at a forty-five-degree angle, and that you pour slowly, letting the beer gently slide down the inside wall of the glass.

The obvious result of a slow, gentle, angled pour is that, with most beers, it won't produce much of a head. And that's a good thing. A snowy head thickly blanketing a golden or darker brew can be a lovely thing—but there are two or possibly three problems with creating a big head: (1) All that foam makes it more difficult for your mouth to get to the beer, which is annoying, and (2) it'll cause the beer in your glass to go flat more quickly. A big head means that much of the carbon dioxide in the beer is being released immediately; avoid creating one when you pour, and your beer is more likely to remain fizzy until you've finished drinking it. And then (3), if the beer is one with lots of hops aroma, a big head may cause that aroma to dissipate quickly—not good, if savoring the hops aroma is a big part of your beer-drinking pleasure.

OBSESSION 1: SERVING TEMPERATURE

Just how obsessive about beer do you want to get? For example, do you want to take pains to ensure that the beer you serve yourself and your friends is poured within the "ideal" temperature range for that style? If so, you may want to consult the table on the next page, which gives what are purportedly the ideal temperature ranges for serving many of the beer styles discussed in part 2.

Frankly, though, Drinkology doesn't share your obsession. And—if you're just drinking bottled beer at home and don't have multiple refrigerators set at different temperatures—we're not sure how you'd go about getting the temperature just right. Would you use some algorithm to calculate the amount of time it will take a beer pulled from the fridge and allowed to remain at a certain

Ideal Temperature Range	Beer Styles
Very cold (32–39°F)	Mass-market beers: cream ale, golden ale, pilsner-style lager and light beer, malt liquor
Cold (39–45°F)	Berliner Weisse, Hefeweizen, Kristallweizen, Kölsch, witbier
Cool (45–54°F)	Abbey and Trappist ales, Altbier, amber ale, California common beer (steam beer), Dortmunder, Dunkel, Dunkelweizen, gueuze, Irish red ale, lambic, pale ale (American), porter, Rauchbier, Schwarzbier, Vienna lager
"Cellar" (54–57°F)	Belgian strong ale, bière de garde, bitter and other English pale ales, bock, brown ale, India pale ale, Kellerbier, old ale, saison, Scottish and Scotch ales, stout, Weizenbock
Warm (57–61°F)	Barley wine, Doppelbock, Eisbock, imperial stout, imperial IPA

ambient temperature to achieve the desired degree of warmth? Would you plunge a thermometer into an opened bottle? We consider life too short for such fetishism. So let the beer cognoscenti go ahead and scoff at us as we recommend the following, vastly simpler procedures—albeit ones that are based on the same principles that lie behind our "authoritative" temperature table.

First, if you're drinking a mass-market beer, drink it straight from the fridge. Chilling beer (or any other beverage or food) suppresses flavor, which is probably *just what you want to do* with a mass-market pilsner-style lager or similar beer. Drinking it ice-cold will let you enjoy its refreshment, and your nose and tongue won't have to deal with the unpleasant "off" smells and tastes that so often reveal themselves as these adjunct-laden beers warm up.

Second, if you study our table, you'll see that, in general, paler and less-alcoholic beers are better when served at cooler temperatures, while darker, stronger beers are better if drunk somewhat warmer. Drinkology's pitifully inexact method for achieving a vaguely correct serving temp—assuming we're drinking a good beer—is to take the bottle from the fridge and let it sit, unopened, for a while before pouring: maybe twenty minutes for a light-colored wheat beer, maybe half an hour or longer for something darker and stronger.

The thing is—and here's where we really don't get the "ideal temperature" business—is that the beer's going to continue warming up as you drink it. And the beer's flavor is going to alter—to "open up" (or possibly shut down!)—over that period of time. It may get better as it warms, it may get worse, or it may just change. To us, that ineluctable experience is much more interesting than fretting over whether your Doppelbock or porter or imperial IPA is just the "right" temperature at the moment it's poured.

OBSESSION 2: DRAFT BEER AT HOME

Virtually all serious beer drinkers agree that draft beer—beer drawn from a keg—is better, in most cases, than bottled beer. The reason's simple: a keg, with its pressurized, airtight, light-tight interior environment, is much better than a bottle at preserving the beer inside. But for most of us, the draft-beer experience is limited to the time we spend drinking at a brewpub or other bar or restaurant—places that have the room to store kegs and the equipment to keep them properly chilled, and places (or so it's to be hoped) that sell enough draft beer quickly enough that the beer in their kegs doesn't have the chance to go stale. Devotees of draft beer may tote home the occasional growler (see pages 272–74) from their local brewpub; if they're hosting a small get-together and have the refrigerator space, they might pick up a five-liter **mini keg** from the beer store.*

But there's a small but growing contingent of beer enthusiasts who won't settle for anything less than having a steady supply of real draft beer at home. And, mercy be, Drinkology even knows someone belonging to this elite set: our very own editorial consultant, Danielle Casavant. According to Danielle, she and her husband, the equally beer-crazy Rod Lambert, buy their craft beer by the keg for two reasons. They drink a lot of beer, and draft beer is much cheaper than bottled beer when you calculate the cost on a per-glass basis. Much more important, though, is the taste. Danielle's rather a hops fiend—we don't think she'll mind that characterization—

---

* In this section we're ignoring bottled and canned beers marketed as draft beers. A "bottled draft beer" is a contradiction in terms. A beer can't be bottled *and* be a draft beer. Mass-market bottled "draft" beers differ from other mass-market bottled beers in that they're not pasteurized, but to ensure a lengthy shelf-life they're subjected to an additional filtration that strips away flavor. "Canned draft beer" isn't quite so oxymoronic, in that such beers—canned Guinness Draught is an example—are packaged in special pressurized cans (containing the little plastic balls called *widgets*; see page 55) that do have the effect of emulating real draft beer.

and she insists that kegs, beyond their other virtues, are immensely better than bottles at keeping delicate hops aromas intact.

To keep draft beer on tap at home, however, requires space, equipment, muscle (picking up a keg is not like picking up a six-pack), and maybe a substantial cash investment. Rod's a handy guy, so he converted an old refrigerator in his and Danielle's basement into a **kegerator** (a fridge for chilling kegs), installing appropriate shelving and drilling holes in the box's side through which tap lines could be run. If you're not the handy type, you'll have to lay down some serious money for a purpose-built kegerator. Commercial models—readily available on the Internet—start at several hundred bucks and go soaring up into the thousands of dollars.

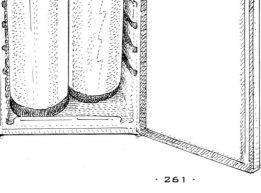

A COMMERCIAL KEGERATOR DESIGNED FOR HOME USE. THE SPOKE RISING FROM THE TOP OF THE BOX IS A TOWER ENCLOS-ING THE TAP LINES.

Buttered Beer?
(Beer Faults)

If you've read part 1 of this book, you've no doubt begun to comprehend what a complicated process brewing can be. Many things can go wrong—and missteps on the brewer's part may result in a finished product that doesn't look, smell, or taste as it should. But even after it's been brewed and packaged, a perfectly good beer can be damaged in ways that irreparably affect its appearance, aroma, or flavor. When something's wrong with a beer, it's said to have a **fault**. In some cases, faults are divergences from the standards for a particular style. For example, a sour flavor would be considered a fault in a porter but not in a lambic (which is supposed to be sour). But there are some faults that transcend style categories. No beer should smell of wet, moldy cardboard—a fault widespread enough that, if you drink enough beer, you're almost certain to experience it at some point.

Just because you don't care for a particular beer doesn't mean that it's faulty. A fault isn't a matter of preference; it's a sign of something having gone *objectively* wrong. Here are a few common faults—their names, attributes, and probable origins. We've divided them into two sets: those that usually originate in the brewery and those that are more probably the result of something that happened during shipping, handling, or storage.

Infectious (and Other) Diseases
Beer faults originating during brewing often come from contamination of the wort by microbes other than yeast or from some other fermentation-related issue—for example, fermenting at the wrong temperature or the brewer's choosing a yeast that's inappropriate for a given style.

"Infected" beers taste *sour*—like vinegar or lemon juice or sour milk. As we mention above (and explain in more detail in the sections of part 2 on lambic and sour beers, pages 136 and 185, respectively), sourness isn't always a fault—but it *mostly* is. As many home brewers learn, it's all too easy for a beer to get infected and turn sour, which is why home-brewing guidebooks and websites are full of stern warnings not to forgo any of their recommended sanitary measures. Modern commercial brewers are scrupulous about cleanliness and sanitation, which means it's fairly rare, these days, to encounter a commercial beer that's spoiled.

Other sorts of "off" flavors you might possibly run into include **diacetyl**—named for a chemical compound that, in the words of our editorial adviser Danielle Casavant, makes beer taste "like movie-theater buttered popcorn." Again, the presence of a buttery flavor in a beer isn't always a fault; low levels of diacetyl are acceptable or even desirable in some darker ales. But this butteriness (which can result from a number of different causes) has no legitimate place in a lager or pale ale.

Yeast-related afflictions include "off" smells and tastes that are rubbery, cabbagey, or medicinal. However, the presence of *some* flavors produced as fermentation by-products by certain strains of yeast—for instance, the banana- or clovelike tastes caused by the esters associated with so-called wheat yeasts (see page 26)—may or may not be a fault; yet again, it all depends on whether the style of beer is *supposed* to have those flavors or not.

One of Drinkology's favorites in the blame-the-brewer category of faults, at least as regards its name, is the "Band-Aid" flavor that can result from using overly chlorinated water in the brew—and that therefore is much more likely to appear in a home-brewed beer, since commercial brewers are so meticulous about controlling and adjusting their water's chemical content.

BUTTERED BEER?
(BEER FAULTS)

The number of possible brewing-related faults is legion, and we can't provide an exhaustive list. But let us mention just a coupla-three others. An improperly made beer might taste strongly of **fusel oils**—a catchall term for alcohols other than ethanol produced by yeast during fermentation. Fusel oils are present in many beers; that presence rises to the level of a fault when the beer has a solventlike taste or gives you a harsh, burning sensation in your throat. And there are faults of over- and under-carbonation. If a beer's a **gusher**—flying out of the bottle as if you'd shaken it before opening—it may be a sign of bacterial infection. Don't drink it. If it's flat when poured, something else is wrong: in the case of a bottle-conditioned beer, flatness probably means that the beer was **primed** with too little sugar to reactivate the residual yeast in the bottled brew. And, finally, **cloudiness** is a fault in beers that aren't meant to be cloudy, and it may be a signal that something went awry when the beer was clarified. (Cloudiness is the rare fault, however, that usually has no effect on the beer's taste.)

AILMENTS DUE TO ACCIDENT OR AGE
Drinkology adores sunshine; we love to fill our lungs with air—so rich in life-giving oxygen; and we hope, God willing, to live to a ripe and healthy old age. Beer would beg to differ with us on all three scores. For beer, light and oxygen are enemies, and most beers—especially beers that aren't very alcoholic or hoppy—are destined to die young. (For information on beers that can be successfully aged, see the section on cellaring, beginning on page 267.)

If a bottled beer is improperly exposed to light (possibly during brewing but much more probably during shipping or storage) it might get **light struck**—a fault that's immediately identifiable when smelling the beer, because it will have a skunky odor resulting from light-induced deterioration of the aromatic compounds in the hop oils in the beer. Trust your nose, and toss the beer.

Likewise trust your nose if, when smelling a just-opened beer, you catch a whiff of something like cardboard or old wet newspapers. That musty smell's a definite indication of **oxidation**—in all probability the result of the beer's being too old. It's nigh unto impossible to prevent a beer from being exposed to at least a little bit of air (just think of the air space in the neck of a beer bottle), and the oxygen in that air will have begun slowly working its deleterious effect on the beer from the moment the beer was brewed. The effect grows worse over time—till the beer becomes undrinkable. Because kegs are pressurized and airtight, draft beer is safer from oxygen's depredations than bottled beer—but that protection lasts only as long as the keg remains untapped. Once that seal's been violated, oxygen in the air pumped into the keg will do its dirty work very quickly, causing the beer to go stale within just a couple of days. (But see page 266 for a method of preserving kegged beer's freshness.)

Staleness—not so technical a term but just dandy for describing the over-the-hill qualities that old beer accrues—can also be perceived in a general flattening or washing-out of aroma and flavor. A stale beer is one that's lost its pizzazz. It might also have lost its ability to form a head (though a weak head is not, depending on the style, necessarily a sign of a stale beer).

There's also the issue of how to keep the beer from staling once the keg's been tapped. The **party pumps** typically used to tap kegs keep the beer flowing by forcing ordinary, well-oxygenated air into the keg—and the beer's exposure to that oxygen will cause it to go stale within a couple of days, at most. So unless you're having a beer bash attended by dozens of people, there's no way you'll be able to drink all the beer in a **full keg** (which, at fifteen and a half gallons, holds 124 sixteen-ounce servings) before it goes bad. Danielle and Rod solve this too-much-beer-too-little-time problem in two ways. First, they're lucky enough to have a group of friends who are as beer-obsessed as themselves. Various members of this group often share the cost of a keg, immediately divvying up the beer by transferring it into three smaller kegs of the type known as **Corney kegs**.* But even these "small" canisters hold too much beer—five gallons—for a couple of people to work their way through before the oxygen-imposed deadline.

So Danielle and Rod employ a strategy like that used by bars and restaurants to keep their draft beers fresher longer. They connect a tapped keg, via tubing, to a canister of CO_2 equipped with a regulator. As beer is removed from the keg, the empty space is filled with carbon dioxide that's under just enough pressure to keep the beer under a tight, stabilizing blanket of gas without causing the liquid to absorb any extra CO_2.

---

* Corney kegs, more properly known as **Cornelius kegs** after their original manufacturer, the IMI Cornelius Company, were long used to contain the soda dispensed at soda fountains. In recent years, they've become popular among home brewers who prefer to keg rather than bottle the beer they make.

Drinkology is impressed and thinks this is all very nifty, but we can't imagine summoning the dedication and energy needed to sustain such a hobby, even if we didn't live in a tiny little house with no room for kegerators and CO_2 canisters and such. As we're quick to confess, we're awfully *lazy*.

OBSESSION 3: CELLARING BEER

We've so far talked a lot about the importance of freshness to most beers. But there *are* beers—quite a few, actually—that can be successfully aged in bottle, and the hobby of **cellaring** beer is burgeoning

HOW NOT TO MAKE A FOOL
OF YOURSELF AT A KEG PARTY

A beer keg has a single opening in the center of the keg's top. The seal protecting the keg's contents from the external environment is a simple ball valve: a ball is socketed into the opening and held in place by the pressure within. When you tap a keg, you're pressing down on this ball, dislodging it and allowing the beer to flow out.

Tapping a keg with a party pump is actually a pretty simple maneuver. Remove the plastic cap covering the keg's opening, position the coupling fitting at the bottom of the pump's shaft above the ball valve, and then simultaneously *press down* on the fitting and *twist it* to lock the pump into place. Beer will immediately flow into the **tap line**—the snake of plastic tubing connected to the pump—and can be dispensed by using your thumb to press down on the little trigger on the **faucet**. The pump works exactly like a bicycle pump.

It's that easy—which doesn't mean, however, that people don't run into all sorts of trouble when tapping kegs. Here are just a few notes on avoiding common problems:

1. *Make sure you've got the proper pump.* Most American kegs use the same kind of pump, but pumps for European kegs are calibrated differently. Use the wrong pump, and the beer will spray everywhere. To avoid any possibility of this happening, get your pump from the retailer selling you the keg. (You'll have to leave a small deposit and return the pump with the empty keg when you're done.)

2. After bringing the keg home, *let it rest for a while,* and *chill it thoroughly* before tapping. The keg will get shaken up while being transported, so it's got to settle down for a few hours, or you'll end up tapping beer that's way too foamy. Besides cooling it, chilling

will also help calm the beer down. If you haven't got a kegerator, chill the keg by putting it into a (very) large garbage can and surrounding it with ice. (This may take five or six big bags' worth of ice cubes.)

3. When you first tap the keg—even if the beer's had time to settle—you'll get lots of foam. The first pitcher's worth or so won't be drinkable, so just discard it or set it aside to give the head a chance to dissipate.

4. When dispensing the beer, press down firmly on the faucet's trigger to ensure that the nozzle is fully open and the beer flows strongly and evenly. If the flow is weak, the beer will be too sudsy.

Be aware, too, that there's no need to keep pumping and pumping. When you first tap the keg, the beer will flow out under its own initiative. Use the pump only when the flow slows down. When you pump, pump vigorously—but only as often as needed to keep the beer flowing forcefully and smoothly.

A PARTY PUMP, SHOWING
THE PUMP SHAFT (A),
COUPLING FITTING (B),
TAP LINE (C), AND FAUCET (D).

among ultra-devoted beer enthusiasts. Cellaring, at least in the precise sense, is out of the question for Drinkology for the simple reason that we haven't got a cellar. But here are some tips we've picked up to guide you, in case you want to raise (or lower?) your beer obsession to a whole new level:

First, remember everything that's been said over the course of this book about the *preservative* role of alcohol and hops. The beers that are likeliest to age well are those that are higher in alcohol—generally 8 percent ABV and above—and those with more potent hops character. An imperial IPA—strongly alcoholic and overloaded with hops—will, if kept under the proper conditions, probably survive for years; a 4 or 5 percent ABV, mildly hopped Hefeweizen probably won't. (In fact, there's no chance it will, so don't even try it.) There are exceptions to this rule. For example, Belgian lambics—especially gueuzes (see page 118)—may endure a good long rest rather beautifully, despite their relatively low ABV. But such exceptions are rare.

Second, cellaring is largely an *experimental* process. There's no guarantee that a particular beer will age well, nor is there much in the way of available literature on the amount of time that this or that beer ought to be left to age. So if you're going to do this, you've got to *embrace* the experimental aspect of your undertaking. And, like the experimental "scientist" you'll be becoming, you'll want to establish controls and keep records. Buy several bottles of the same beer, drink one immediately (and take notes on your impressions), then drink the others at intervals over the next few years, each time taking notes on color, smell, flavor, and so on. Serious wine lovers—those with cellars—have long kept journals (called cellar books) chronicling their encounters, over time, with the bottles they've laid down for keeping. You'll want to do the same.

Third, regarding proper storage conditions: Cellared beer keeps best at what, no surprise, is called **cellar temperature**—an unvarying temperature in the range of 50 to 55 degrees Fahrenheit. It also does best under slightly *humid* conditions, which makes refrigerators (which dehumidify the air inside) unsuitable for long-term storage, especially for bottles stoppered with corks, since cork tends to shrink as it dries out. The best place to cellar a beer, in other words, is a cellar, whose below-ground location keeps temperatures from fluctuating and whose dankness is, in this case, a plus. Although a good beer cellar resembles a good wine cellar on these scores, there is one important difference in the manner in which wines and beers should be stored. Nearly everyone agrees that beer bottles, unlike wine bottles, should be set upright rather than laid on their sides during years-long storage.

How will a beer taste after it's been cellared for a while? You won't know till you try it, but people who pursue this hobby report that the flavors of ageable beers generally both mellow *and* grow more complex. A high-alcohol, hoppy beer will lose some of its alcohol sting, and its hops bite will relax, allowing other, subtler flavors—malty, chocolaty, fruity, sherry-like—to come to the fore. Carbonation may diminish. Some degree of oxidation will inevitably occur, but this isn't necessarily a bad thing—until, of course, it *is* a bad thing. Kept properly, a beer that's capable of long in-bottle aging may last, and even improve, for years or perhaps decades—but at some point, it'll be past its prime. And at some later point, it'll just give up the ghost.

Over the past few years, **growlers**—large glass jugs filled with beer direct from a brewpub's or tavern's tap—have become the beer container of choice for the hipster-hopster set. One Internet ad we saw describes growlers as the "classy" way of transporting beer home. That description would have amused, or maybe angered, Drinkology's grandmother.

Grandmom Gussie (short for Augusta) had a childhood that could aptly be called Dickensian. Born in a Baltimore slum known as Pig Town (because pigs were driven to slaughter through its streets), Gussie was the child of recent German immigrants, both of whom died before she was six. As was a common custom then, she was "taken in" by a neighbor family. Although the family saved her from the streets and provided minimal care, their rationale for rescuing the orphan wasn't what you'd call altruistic. After just a few years of school, she was put to work, and one of the daily chores she was forced to perform throughout her childhood was to carry empty pails to a nearby saloon, have them filled with beer, and tote those heavy buckets back to her "foster" home. It was hard and miserable work for a six-, seven-, and eight-year-old girl, and God help her if any of that nickel's worth of beer spilled along the way. She hated having to do it, and she never forgot the experience.

Such beer buckets, often made of the mottled-enamel-coated metal called graniteware and usually with a capacity of half a gallon, were called *growlers*, purportedly because of the growling noise the buckets made as the CO_2 escaped the sloshing beer inside. (Frankly, this etymology strikes us as a little suspicious; the *Oxford English Dictionary,* which dates the earliest published use of the term to 1888, gives no derivation.)

When Drinkology, as a child during the 1950s and 1960s, listened to Gussie recounting her childhood woes, the practice of fetching "loose" beer from local saloons—"rushing the growler," as an old slang expression put it—seemed unimaginably long ago and far away. Beer, after all, was a commodity packaged in bottles and cans and delivered weekly to our house by a local liquor store. (And we latter-day children, of course, weren't expected to do such grueling work.) What little Drinkology didn't know was that, even then, growlers, now in the form of glass jugs rather than metal buckets, were still in common use in some of Baltimore's other neighborhoods—and kids were still "rushing" them, presumably illegally. We learned this just recently from an old friend, who as an enterprising boy in East Baltimore during the fifties ran his own growler business, running jugs between neighbors' houses and local taverns and collecting a tip for each delivery.

But Baltimore was a late holdout, it appears. After the repeal of Prohibition, most breweries began bottling and canning their own beers, and growlers eventually disappeared (a process aided, in several states, by laws prohibiting their use).

For the craft-beer movement, however, everything old is new again. Back in the 1980s, although some start-up craft breweries did bottle their beers (often by hand), many smaller brewpub operations had no way of letting their customers carry their brews home. And so glass-jug growlers were resurrected. Sources disagree as to which brewpub was the first to revive the growler, although the Yakima Brewing & Malting Co., of Yakima, Washington, has a credible claim to the glory, since photos of the brewpub from the early eighties show bartenders filling jugs—

recycled gallon-size wine jugs, they were—with Yakima's signature Grant's Ales.

Nowadays, glass-jug growlers (more or less standardized at a sixty-four-ounce capacity) are ubiquitous. A recent *New York Times* piece noted that the beer cognoscenti of Brooklyn sometimes tote them home in strollers—giving, it must be said, a whole new meaning to the term *baby bottle.*

Although Grandmom Gussie would doubtless disagree, growlers *are* appealing. Because they're refillable, they present an option that's more sustainable than bottles or cans, so many of which get discarded despite recycling programs. And growlers are retro (*really* retro), which ever-nostalgic Drinkology always finds an attractive trait. Plus—and most important—they enable beer drinkers to enjoy absolutely fresh beer at home without having to buy and tap a keg. As Drinkology friend and growler devotee Tom Gubanich put it to us, "As to why I like beer from a growler, it just tastes better. I will always prefer draft beer, then bottles, never cans. Growlers give me draft at home."

A couple of cautions are, however, in order. If you buy beer by the growler, make sure that the person dispensing the beer fills the jug properly—if it isn't filled to the very top, the air remaining inside the neck will cause the beer to go flat very quickly. Refrigerated, an unopened, properly filled growler will keep beer fresh for a week or, at the very longest, two. But once the growler's been uncapped, you have to drink all the beer within four to six hours. (Of course, if some does go flat, you can always use it for cooking.)

BEER AND WHAT? (BEER COCKTAILS)

Since this is a Drinkology book, we felt compelled to include some recipes for beer-based mixed drinks. We realize, of course, that mixing beer with other stuff—like orange juice, and Coke, and gin—will repel some readers, but Drinkology isn't at all opposed to doing so.* After all, mixed beverages combining beer and other ingredients, including fruit juices and syrups, are not some trendy innovation. Several traditional styles of beer—including, for example, Hefeweizen (page 120) and Berliner Weisse (page 79)—are sometimes or always mixed with fruit beverages or syrups before serving, and some other styles—Belgian witbier (page 207) and kriek (page 134) and other fruit-flavored lambics—amount, really, to premixed mixed drinks.

A Google search for "beer cocktails" yields hundreds of recipes—most for concoctions that, in their simplicity, hardly merit the name *cocktail*. The very simplest involve the addition of a shot of fruit syrup or liqueur to a glass of beer (example: the **Liverpool Kiss**, made by dumping an ounce or so of crème de cassis into a pint glass of stout). Slightly more complicated, at least logistically, are the many beer shooter-chaser combos that involve pouring a glass of beer and a shot glass of liquor and then either downing the shot and immediately "chasing" it with the beer *or* dropping the full shot glass (yes, the glass itself) into the glass of beer and, taking care not to damage your front teeth, drinking both together.

The best-known shooter-chaser combo is, of course, the **Boilermaker** (shot of whiskey, glass of beer). You'll find a recipe

---

* We *are* opposed to "cute" neologisms like *beertail* and *beertini*, which hurt our eyes, ears, and sensibility.

for it—though it's not much of a recipe, really—in the first book in this series, *Drinkology: The Art and Science of the Cocktail* (updated and revised edition, 2010). That first Drinkology book also contains recipes for several other well-known beer-based mixed drinks that won't be repeated here. These include the **Black and Tan** (stout and pale ale), the **Black Velvet** (stout and champagne), the **Shandy** (beer and lemonade), and the **Shandygaff** (beer and ginger beer).

ABBEY STING

 Drinkology's variation on the Bee Sting—a bee-belly-ish yellow-and-brown-striped layered drink consisting of half orange juice and half dark beer—uses a Belgian Trappist ale rather than the usual porter or stout. (And there's almost too much wordplay in the name we've given it, since *abbey* is a near homonym of *abeille*—which means "bee" in French, one of Belgium's three official languages.) The combination sounds just *dreadful*, but it turns out to be wonderfully tasty. We also use Tropicana Original (no pulp) orange juice, whose smooth consistency makes it, we think, better for this drink than pulpy fresh-squeezed OJ.

about 6 ounces pulp-free orange juice
about 6 ounces Trappistes Rochefort no. 6 Belgian ale

Pour the orange juice into a 12-ounce tumbler. Float the ale on top by positioning the back of a spoon directly above the surface of the juice and very slowly and gently pouring the ale onto it.

FLAMING DR. PEPPAR

 Readers who care about such things may notice that the "Dr. Peppar" part of this drink's name is a misspelling. It's an *intentional* misspelling, however—one that's often used (1) because the drink does not contain the famous soft drink to which its moniker alludes, and (2) to avoid trademark-infringement litigation. That said, this odd concoction—which is popular among people who are a lot younger than Drinkology—tastes astonishingly like that famous soft drink. Because Drinkology doesn't want to get sued—by anybody!—we should also warn you to exercise proper care and caution when making this or any other flamed drink. Alcohol burns at a fairly low temperature, but playing with fire always carries some risk. So make sure there's a working fire extinguisher nearby, and *please* blow out the flame on the shot glass before dropping it into the beer.

about ¾ ounce amaretto
about ¼ ounce 151-proof rum
a good pilsner-style lager

Fill a 1-ounce shot glass three-quarters full with amaretto, and carefully float the rum on top. (Do not allow the rum to mix with the amaretto, since that will make the liquid difficult or impossible to ignite.) Pour the lager into a highball glass, leaving about an inch and a half of room at the top. Using a kitchen match, carefully light the rum, and let it burn for about a minute before blowing out the flame. When the flame's out, drop the shot glass into the glass of beer. (Do be careful when drinking not to chip your teeth!)

MICHELADA/CHELADA

Ai yai yai. The Latin American beer-based mixed drink called the Michelada, or sometimes the Chelada (or sometimes the Cerveza Preparada), can make you feel like a confused, woebegone tourist who just doesn't understand the local lingo. That's because the names *Michelada* (literally, "my little cold one"), *Chelada* ("little cold one"), and *Cerveza Preparada* ("prepared beer") are used relatively loosely and somewhat interchangeably.

At its most basic, this drink—whatever you call it—combines beer and lime juice in a salt-rimmed glass. It was probably originally concocted in that simplest form in Jamaica sometime in the early twentieth century and then, in the 1940s, migrated westward to Mexico, where it got its Spanish-language name(s)—and where it got a lot livelier, with the typical addition of hot chile sauce to the mix. Shortly thereafter, it crossed the border into the southwestern United States. And wherever it landed, the Little Cold One adapted to the local customs.

That is, it changed. In Mexico, Clamato juice was (and is) sometimes mixed with the beer, and the drink is often spiced with Worcestershire sauce and Maggi-brand seasoning sauce (Maggi Jugo Sazonodar) in addition to the hot chile sauce. Drinkology's friend (and well-traveled booze-hound) Christine Sismondo reports that, in the parts of Mexico she's visited, the name *Chelada* is usually—though not always—used for this more complicated version of the drink, while *Michelada* is reserved for the simpler salt-lime-beer combo.

In the U.S., soy sauce is sometimes included among the Michelada/Chelada's ingredients. In fact, a quick Internet search turns up scores if not hundreds of Michelada/Chelada recipes, many of which lay claim to being *the* absolutely authentic version of the drink. Don't you believe any of these claimants—and, please, don't fret about your Michelada's authenticity or lack thereof. In Drinkology's view, immigration = diversity, and diversity is to be embraced and celebrated. In that welcoming spirit, we provide three Michelada/Chelada variations here.

What's *not* to be celebrated (or drunk!), however, is any of the pre-mixed, canned and bottled Chelada-like beverages now on offer from several of the large commercial beer-makers. Why bother with such artificial-tasting fakery when you can so easily stir up a zesty, fresh Chelada (or Michelada, or Cerveza Preparada) of your own?

VARIATION #1

kosher salt
lime wedge
juice of ½ lime
2 or 3 ice cubes (optional)
12-ounce bottle cold Mexican lager (e.g., Corona, Dos Equis, Tecate)

Spread a layer of salt on a small plate. Rim a highball glass with the lime wedge. (Reserve the wedge for garnish.) Upend the glass onto the salt-covered plate and turn it until the lip is thoroughly coated with salt. Pour the lime juice into the glass, drop in the ice cubes (if desired), and then carefully pour in the beer. Stir very briefly, and drop the lime wedge into the glass.

VARIATION #2

kosher salt

lime wedge

juice of 1 lime

dash Maggi Jugo Sazonodar or soy sauce

dash Tabasco or other hot chile sauce

dash Worcestershire sauce

pinch of freshly ground black pepper

2 or 3 ice cubes (optional)

12-ounce bottle cold Mexican lager (e.g., Corona, Dos Equis, Tecate)

Spread a layer of salt on a small plate. Rim a highball glass with the lime wedge. (Reserve the wedge for garnish.) Upend the glass onto the salt-covered plate and turn it until the lip is thoroughly coated with salt. Pour the lime juice into the glass, add the Maggi (or soy sauce), Tabasco, Worcestershire, and pepper, and stir. Drop in the ice cubes (if desired), and then carefully pour in the beer. Stir again very briefly, and drop the lime wedge into the glass.

Variation #3

celery seed
kosher salt
lime wedge
6 ounces Clamato juice
juice of 1 lime
2 dashes Tabasco or other hot chile sauce
2 dashes Worcestershire sauce
pinch freshly ground black pepper
3 or 4 ice cubes (optional)
12-ounce bottle cold Mexican lager (e.g., Corona, Dos
    Equis, Tecate)
♂ celery stalk

*Important: Use a pilsner glass or other large (22-ounce) glass
for this variation. Pour equal amounts of celery seed and salt
onto a small plate, mixing the two with your fingers. Rim
the glass with the lime wedge. (Discard the wedge.) Upend
the glass onto the plate and turn it until the lip is thoroughly
coated with the celery seed–salt mixture. Pour the Clamato
and lime juice into the glass, add the Tabasco, Worcestershire,
and pepper, and stir. Drop in the ice cubes (if desired) into the
glass, and carefully pour in the beer. Garnish with the celery
stalk, using it to gently stir the drink.*

SKIP AND GO NAKED

Also known as the Hop, Skip, and Go Naked, this supposedly exercise-and-nudism-inspiring libation has countless
variations—many of them combining beer with frozen lemonade and vodka. Drinkology's version is . . . well, it's
classier—basically a Tom Collins topped with beer rather
than club soda.

lemon wedge
ice cubes
1½ ounces Plymouth gin
1 ounce fresh lemon juice
½ ounce simple syrup
dash of grenadine (optional)
a good pilsner-style lager
♻ lemon slice

*Rim a highball glass or Collins glass with the lemon wedge.
Discard the wedge, and fill the glass with ice cubes. In a cocktail shaker filled with more ice cubes, combine the gin, lemon
juice, simple syrup, and (if desired) grenadine. Shake well,
and strain into the prepared glass. Carefully top with the
lager, stir briefly, and garnish with the lemon wedge.*

SNAKEBITE

This simple antidote-to-thirst doesn't deserve its poisonous name. You may use any sort of beer you like, though Drinkology recommends something that's light in color and body and not overly hoppy—perhaps a golden ale.

about 8 ounces hard cider
about 8 ounces golden ale or other beer

Pour the cider into a 16-ounce glass, then carefully add the beer.

WEST END

This is Drinkology's anglophilic twist on a drink called the Broadway—a fifty-fifty mix of pilsner-style lager and Coke. At first, the thought of mixing cola and beer filled us with— let's confess it—revulsion. And then we screwed up our nerve and tried such a combo, but using Young's Double Chocolate Stout—a dark and toothsome British beer whose ingredients include chocolate malt and actual chocolate—and Mexican Coca-Cola (superior to American Coke, because it's made with cane sugar rather than corn syrup). And, surprisingly, we *loved* it. (There's also a German variation on this drink, called the Cola-weizen, which marries cola and Hefeweizen—a yeasty wheat-based ale—in equal parts.)

about 8 ounces cold Young's Double Chocolate Stout
about 8 ounces cold Coca-Cola

Carefully pour the stout and then the cola into a 16-ounce glass. (When mixed, the beer and cola form quite a head, so pour this one especially slowly.)

Eat Your Beer

From this book's opening pages, we've stressed the fact that beer *is* food. Now it's time to talk about the fact that beer is also an amazingly versatile ingredient in cooking and baking. Or rather—since the pudding's proof is in the eating—to *demonstrate* that fact by presenting you with a selection of recipes using beer. The nine recipes included here represent only the most minuscule corner of

Washing with Beer

If you were to wash yourself with beer, you'd . . . well, you'd stink.

And getting stinky is exactly the point of **beer-washed cheese**. Beer-washed cheeses are a subset of the class of cheeses known as *washed rind cheeses*—so called because their rinds are given periodic (sometimes daily) baths while the cheeses are maturing. Well-known washed rind cheeses, which are typically stiff on the outside (the rind) but soft or semisoft on the inside when ripe, include Brie and Taleggio. Most often, the "bathwater" used to bathe such cheeses is brine. And, as you know if you've had a good, ripe Brie, washed rind cheeses usually stink.

Well, substitute beer for brine, and the cheese will stink even worse. (Or *better*, if you're like Drinkology and think that the unwashed-socks smell of such cheese is the very Odor of Heaven.) That's because beer's even better at fostering the growth, on the rind, of a bacterium called *Brevibacterium linens,* the malefactor (or benefactor) causing the unholy (or holy) stench. In fact, scientists at a British university have determined, or so they claim, that one beer-washed cheese, a French cheese called Vieux-Boulogne, is *the* stinkiest cheese in the world.

the wide world of beer-based cuisine, but, together, they do show that beer can be used in the making of snacks, appetizers, soups, main courses, and desserts. If they leave you hungry for more, there are a number of good beer cookery books on the market; we especially recommend Lucy Saunders's *The Best of American Beer and Food: Pairing & Cooking with Craft Beer* (Brewers Publications, 2007).

If you like cheese (and beer) but aren't particularly partial to the stinkier cheese varieties, you'll be happy to know that beer can be used in other ways in the cheese-making process. For instance, an exceptional, semi-hard, and not very stinky goat's-milk cheese called Pondhopper, made by Tumalo Farms, of central Oregon, is made by steeping the curds in a beer produced by a local microbrewer. That particular beer is potently hopped with Cascade hops (named for the nearby Cascade Range)—and the flavor imbues the cheese, growing more lemony as the Pondhopper ripens. Drinkology is hardly a hophead, but we *love* this cheese. Somehow, the hops' tang and the tang of the goat's milk strike an extremely melodious chord.

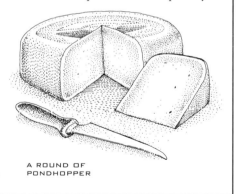

A ROUND OF
PONDHOPPER

Maple-Stout Glazed Pecans

What could be better than a beer-drinking snack made with beer? These pecans, coated in a maple-syrup-and-stout reduction and then baked, have a spicy, Cracker Jack flavor.

unsalted butter for pan (about 1 tablespoon)
1 cup stout or porter
1 cup maple syrup
8 ounces (about 2 cups) pecan halves
2 tablespoons sugar
1½ teaspoons table salt
⅛ teaspoon cayenne pepper

Set the oven to 350°F. Lightly butter a jelly-roll pan.

Combine stout and maple syrup in a small saucepan. Bring to a boil over high heat, then reduce heat to medium, letting the mixture boil gently until reduced by two-thirds (to 2/3 cup of syrupy liquid), about 35 minutes. Watch the pan carefully during the final 10 minutes, reducing the heat if necessary to prevent the syrup from boiling over.

Place the pecans, sugar, salt, and cayenne in a medium-size metal bowl, pour hot syrup into the bowl, and mix until the nuts are thoroughly coated.

Spread the nuts in a single, even layer on the jelly-roll pan and bake for 10 minutes.

Allow them to cool on the pan. Break them apart and store in a wax paper–lined container.

Yield: About 2 cups

Kentucky Beer Cheese

Native to Kentucky, this spread/dip is incredibly popular in the state, where numerous cottage-kitchen industries produce their own variations. Here's Drinkology's (nonnative) take. It's important that you use *flat* beer in this recipe.

4 ounces mild cheddar, grated
4 ounces sharp cheddar, grated
2 ounces cream cheese, softened
1 large clove garlic, minced
1 tablespoon minced onion
½ teaspoon dry mustard
⅛ teaspoon Tabasco
⅛ teaspoon Worcestershire sauce
⅛ teaspoon freshly ground black pepper
pinch of table salt
pinch of cayenne
about ½ cup golden ale or amber lager, warm and flat

Place all ingredients except the ale in a food processor and pulse three or four times to mix. Turn the processor on and slowly—very slowly—pour the beer through the food chute. The mixture should have the consistency of hummus; if it is too thick, add more beer, tablespoon by tablespoon, until the desired consistency is achieved. Transfer the spread to a plastic tub, cover, and refrigerate for one or two days. Remove it from the fridge an hour before serving. Spread it on crackers or use it as a dip for pretzels.

Yield: About 1 cup

BROWN ALE/WHOLE WHEAT QUICKBREAD

Beer is liquid bread; bread is solid beer. So why not put the two together? This quickbread has a dense crumb and nubbly crust. A hoppy brown ale will give it a bitter tang, which Drinkology likes—a nice counterpoint to the butter you're going to slather on every slice.

2 tablespoons unsalted butter
1½ cups all-purpose flour
1½ cups whole wheat flour
4½ teaspoons baking powder
1½ teaspoons salt
12 ounces brown ale, room temperature
⅓ cup dark brown sugar, packed

Set the oven to 350°F. Grease a 9-by-5-inch loaf pan using 1 tablespoon of the butter. Melt the remaining 1 tablespoon butter and set it aside.

In a large mixing bowl, whisk together the flours, baking powder, and salt. Pour the ale into a 2-cup measuring cup, carefully add the sugar (the ale will foam up), and stir briefly. Add the liquid to the flour mixture and stir until you have a thoroughly mixed, wet, somewhat stiff dough. Use a spatula to transfer the dough to the pan. Drizzle the melted butter on the dough. Bake for 50 minutes to 1 hour, until a toothpick inserted in the center of the loaf comes out clean.

CHEDDAR-CAULIFLOWER-BEER SOUP

Wisconsin is famous for (1) beer and (2) cheese. Hopheads and "cheeseheads" alike will cheer—and be cheered by—this traditional beer-based soup from the Upper Midwest.

1 small head cauliflower, broken into florets
6 tablespoons unsalted butter
1 large onion, diced
2 cups pale ale
1 (14.5-ounce) can chicken broth
1 tablespoon Worcestershire sauce
1 cup milk
1 cup half-and-half
¼ cup cornstarch
3 cups (about 8 ounces) shredded sharp cheddar cheese
1 cup (about 4 ounces) shredded yellow American cheese
freshly ground black pepper
hot paprika

Steam the cauliflower florets until tender, about 8 minutes. Immediately transfer the florets to a colander and spray with cold water to stop the cooking. Drain and set aside.

In a soup pot, melt 2 tablespoons of the butter over medium heat, then add the onion and sauté until translucent, about 5 minutes. Add the ale, chicken broth, and Worcestershire, raise the heat and bring the liquid to a boil, then immediately reduce the heat and allow the broth to gently simmer.

In a large saucepan, heat the milk, half-and-half, and the remaining 4 tablespoons butter over medium heat until the butter begins to melt. Gradually add the cornstarch, whisking quickly and constantly until the sauce begins to thicken. Do *not* allow to boil. When the sauce has thickened, add the cheeses, stirring constantly, until they are completely incorporated.

Pour the cheese sauce into the simmering broth. Add the cauliflower florets and stir. Raise the heat to medium and heat the soup thoroughly, but do not allow it to boil. When the soup begins to steam, remove it from the heat and ladle it into bowls, adding a pinch of black pepper and lightly dusting each portion with paprika before serving.

Yield: 4 large servings

MUSSELS STEAMED IN BEER

A simple variation on *moules marinières*—the classic Belgian preparation in which mussels are steamed in their own juices—this dish can be served either as an appetizer (in which case two pounds of mussels will be sufficient for four people) or as a main course, served with *frites* (Belgian-style French fries). If it's the main course, use at least one pound of mussels per person and multiply the other ingredients accordingly.

The mussels you'll find at your supermarket or seafood shop will probably already have been cleaned, in which case all you have to do before cooking them is to rinse them in cold water and discard any whose shells have opened. If they have not been cleaned, you'll have to remove their "beards" by pulling them off with your fingers, or cutting them off with a sharp paring knife, while running cold water over the shells.

We use a Belgian blonde ale for steaming the mussels, though any good, pale-colored ale or lager will work well, so long as it's not too hoppy. (A very hoppy beer will make the sauce bitter.) The beer should be at room temperature.

Serve this dish with generous slices of buttered bread, to sop up the sauce.

1 tablespoon extra-virgin olive oil
3 cloves garlic, minced
1 large shallot, minced
4–6 whole sprigs fresh thyme
⅓ teaspoon kosher or other coarse-grained salt
pinch freshly ground black pepper
8 ounces ale
2 pounds mussels, in shells (cleaned)
3 tablespoons unsalted butter
1 tablespoon fresh flat-leaf parsley, chopped
1 teaspoon Dijon mustard

Heat the oil over medium heat in a large Dutch oven. Add the garlic, shallot, thyme, salt, and pepper, and sauté until the garlic and shallot become fragrant and begin to soften, about 1 minute. Add the ale and stir, raising the heat to medium-high. When the liquid begins to boil, add the mussels to the pot and cover tightly. Steam until the mussels have opened, about 5 minutes.

Using a slotted spoon, transfer the mussels to large serving bowls, keeping the heat on under the liquid in the pot. Cover each bowl with a plate to retain the heat. Add the butter, parsley, and mustard to the Dutch oven and whisk until blended and hot. Remove the covers from the serving bowls and ladle the sauce over the mussels. Serve immediately.

BEER-BRAISED CHICKEN

This variation on the Belgian stew called carbonnade uses chicken rather than the more traditional beef. You're basically throwing a whole bunch of stuff into a pot along with some beer and letting it cook, covered, in the oven. It's amazing how delicious the result is.

2 strips thick-sliced hickory-smoked bacon
1 tablespoon extra-virgin olive oil
8 chicken thighs
½ cup all-purpose flour
¼ cup dark brown sugar, packed
1½ teaspoons kosher or other coarse-grained salt
1 teaspoon smoked paprika
1 teaspoon fresh or dried thyme leaves
12-ounce bottle amber lager or Belgian blonde ale
1½ cups beef broth
12–18 very small white onions
4 carrots
2 medium red-jacket potatoes
2 tablespoons cornstarch
5 ounces (½ box) frozen peas
2 tablespoons fresh flat-leaf parsley, chopped

Set the oven to 350°F.

Fry the bacon until it is cooked but not crispy, drain it on paper towels, and cut or break into 1-inch pieces. Set aside.

Heat the oil in a large Dutch oven (or other large pot with tight, ovenproof lid) on the stovetop over medium-high heat. Dredge the chicken thighs in flour and place them in the pot, browning them on each side (about 3 minutes per side). Turn off the burner and add the bacon, sugar, salt, paprika, and thyme to the pot. Pour in the beer and beef broth and stir. Cover the pot with its lid and place it in the oven for 45 minutes.

During this initial period of braising, prepare the onions: drop them into boiling water for 1 minute, remove them from the water with tongs or a slotted spoon, and allow them to cool for a few minutes before peeling (the skins should slide off easily). Peel the carrots and cut each one crosswise into 3 pieces. During the final few minutes before you remove the pot from the oven, cut the potatoes into about 12 pieces each.

Remove the pot from the oven and add the vegetables, stirring briefly. Re-cover the pot and return it to the oven for another 45 minutes.

After this second period of braising, remove the pot from the oven and turn the oven off. Using a slotted spoon, transfer the chicken and vegetables to a large bowl. Place the pot back on the stovetop and heat the sauce over medium heat. Whisk the cornstarch into the sauce and continue whisking until the sauce thickens, about 1 minute. Turn off the burner. Return the chicken thighs and vegetables to the pot, add the peas and parsley, and stir. Cover the pot and let it sit for 5 minutes.

Serve in soup bowls, with a crusty bread for sopping up the sauce.

Yield: 4 servings

Lamb Chili with Hominy

This stupendous chili has evolved over decades (we're not kidding) of experimentation and refinement. The mix of ancho chile powder (mild) and ground red chipotle (hot) produces just the right level of spiciness.

Shopping and cooking tips: Ground lamb tends to be fatty; try to select meat that is as lean as possible. You may use any reasonably robust beer or ale, but Drinkology chose the Mexican dark lager Negra Modelo—not because it's especially good (it isn't) but because its caramel flavor complements other flavors in the dish and because, hey, it's Mexican.

About hominy: Hominy is *not* hominy grits. Rather, it is whole corn kernels that have been soaked in lye-water (yes, *lye*-water) to remove their hulls. The canned hominy that Drinkology uses is the Manning's brand, which emerges from the can in a solid, gelatinous lump that must be broken apart in the saucepan before being heated. If you cannot find it, use about one and a half 15.5-ounce cans of Goya brand hominy (Spanish, *posole*) instead, but note that Goya's product consists of separate hominy kernels packed in water and must be drained before using; it does not need to be broken apart in the pan.

FOR THE CHILI:

3 generous tablespoons ancho chile powder

1 generous tablespoon ground red chipotle

2 generous teaspoons ground cumin seed

1½ teaspoons kosher or other coarse-grained salt

1 teaspoon celery seed

½ teaspoon cayenne pepper

2 bay leaves

2 cubes demerara sugar

1-inch square dark chocolate

2 or 3 tablespoons extra-virgin olive oil

1 large onion, diced

6 cloves garlic, minced

2 pounds ground lamb

2 (12-ounce) bottles Mexican dark beer, warm

1 (14.5-ounce) can diced tomatoes, drained

1 cup canned red kidney beans, drained (about half a 15.5-ounce can)

FOR THE HOMINY:

1 (20-ounce) can hominy

½ cup milk

2 tablespoons unsalted butter

crema (Mexican sour cream), for garnish

Prepare the spices and flavorings by combining the chile powders, cumin, salt, celery seed, cayenne, bay leaves, sugar, and chocolate in a small bowl. Set aside.

Heat the olive oil in a 5-quart Dutch oven over medium-high heat. Add the onion and stir with a wooden spoon until the pieces are translucent and just beginning to brown, about 4 minutes. Add the garlic and continue stirring until aromatic, about 30 seconds. Add the ground lamb in chunks, stirring and chopping with the wooden spoon until thoroughly browned, about 10 minutes.

Add the beer—pouring carefully—as well as the tomatoes and all the spices and flavorings, stirring until combined. The liquid should just cover the meat; if it does not, add just enough water to cover. Bring the mixture to a boil and then immediately reduce the heat. Simmer, uncovered, for at least 1½ hours, stirring every 15 to

20 minutes. If the chili becomes too thick or seems in danger of burning, add small amounts of water as necessary. About 20 minutes before serving, add the kidney beans and stir.

(Because the chili's flavor will improve with longer cooking, you may allow it to remain simmering on the stovetop for up to three hours. If you do so, remember to continue stirring every 15 to 20 minutes and to add small amounts of water as necessary to keep the chili from becoming too thick or burning.)

About 10 minutes before serving, open the can of hominy, drain it if necessary, and empty it into a small saucepan over medium-low heat. (If the hominy is a solid mass, break it apart with a wooden spoon.) Add the milk and butter, and stir. Heat, stirring occasionally, until the butter has melted and the milk begins to steam, about 5 minutes. Do not allow it to boil.

Spoon the hominy into soup bowls, ladle chili over the top, and garnish each bowl with a dollop of crema. Serve with guacamole and corn chips or with a simple salad of sliced tomatoes, red-onion rounds, and ripe avocado slices dressed with extra-virgin olive oil and salt.

Yield: 4 to 6 servings

DOUBLE CHOCOLATE STOUT CHOCOLATE CAKE

This is a magnificent cake. The only problem—aside from one's desire to eat much too much of it—is that the cake tends to settle in the middle. Drinkology tried and tried to solve this, adjusting the ingredient amounts and baking the cake in a variety of pans of different sizes and types (springform and regular)—and finally we just gave up. (Though the permutation of the recipe given here does seem to work best.) If your cake does sink slightly in the center, just fill the depression with extra frosting. You'll have lots to work with. The object of so thickly frosting the cake is to make it look like a dark stout crowned by a massive, creamy head.

FOR THE CAKE:

8 tablespoons (1 stick) unsalted butter, plus enough for the pan

2 cups all-purpose flour

2½ teaspoons baking soda

1 cup Young's Double Chocolate Stout

½ cup unsweetened cocoa

2 cups sugar

2 large eggs

¼ cup sour cream

1½ teaspoons double vanilla extract

FOR THE FROSTING:

2 (8-ounce) packages cream cheese, softened

8 tablespoons (1 stick) unsalted butter, softened

½ teaspoon double vanilla extract

2½ cups confectioners' sugar, sifted

Make the cake: Set the oven to 350°F. Butter the *bottom only* of a 9-inch cake pan with high (3-inch) sides. Place a 9-inch round of parchment paper on the buttered bottom of the pan.

In a bowl, whisk together the flour and baking soda. Set aside.

Combine the stout and the stick of butter in a large saucepan and heat over medium heat until the butter melts. Remove the pan from the stove, add the cocoa and sugar, and whisk until blended.

In a bowl, combine the eggs, sour cream, and vanilla, beating with a fork until blended. Add to the stout mixture in the saucepan. Gradually add the flour and baking soda to the saucepan, whisking constantly until the batter is smooth. Pour it into the prepared cake pan and bake for 45 minutes to 1 hour, until a toothpick inserted in the center comes out clean. Transfer the pan to a rack, and allow the cake to cool in the pan. When it is no longer warm, carefully run a sharp knife around the sides of the pan to free the cake and invert it onto a plate.

Make the frosting: Combine the cream cheese, butter, and vanilla in a large bowl and beat with an electric hand mixer until fluffy, about 2 minutes. Gradually add the confectioners' sugar, continuing to beat until the frosting is smooth.

Spread the frosting in a thick, even layer across the top of the cake but *not* on the sides. (If the cake has settled in the center, fill the depression with extra frosting.)

Yield: about 12 servings

STOUT FLOAT

Say you're mad about strong, dark beer. Say you're also mad about ice cream. Say you decide to indulge your addictions at the same time—in the same glass. Who's to tell you not to? (Note that the number of scoops required depends on the size of your dipper.)

3 to 5 scoops vanilla ice cream
12-ounce bottle or can stout

Load the scoops of ice cream into a pint glass. Very carefully pour in the stout. Serve with a long-handled spoon and a straw.

Yield: 1 serving

MATCH 'N' MIX (PAIRING BEER AND FOOD)

Pairing beer and food isn't a science. It's a game, and one you can have endless fun playing once you learn a few basic rules—and then even more fun, when you feel confident enough to begin tossing those rules aside.

Rule #1: Pair like with like, color- and strengthwise. If you're used to pairing wine with food, you're aware of the age-old dictum that declares that red wines should be drunk with heavier, more deeply flavorful (and often darker) foods and white wines with dishes that are lighter, less rich, and more delicately flavored. Well, a similar color- and strength-based rule applies *in general* to beer-and-food pairings. Darker, heavier, higher-alcohol, "chewier" beers make good sparring partners for richer, more robustly flavored foods, whereas paler beers—which are usually crisper, drier, lighter-bodied, and less alcoholically strong—tend to go better with lighter fare. These kinds of "like with like" pairings make intuitive sense. Steaks and roasts call out for the husbandry of strong dark ales, as do stinky, moldy cheeses; white-fleshed fish want to swim in, or rather *with,* pilsner or some light, innocuous, pilsner-like ale.

Rule #2: Achieve balance through contrast. This rule might seem like a contradiction to the first, and in a way it is. It acknowledges, though, that there's more to a given beer than color, body, and alcoholic strength. Some beers are bitter, others sweet, others sour—and pairing a beer with a food that has an *opposite* character (a sour beer with a sweet dessert, for example) can sometimes enhance the taste of both. This rule, we think, comes in especially handy when deciding on foods to pair with IPAs and other well-hopped beers. Roast chicken and duck—fatty and succulent—contend well with such beers' bitterness; the sugar in a dense, rich cake gives the bitterness something to hammer its head against.

Rule #3: Think seasonally. This is a variation, really, on rule #1. Certain beers, like certain foods, are best consumed during the warm months; others, when it turns cold. And, as it happens, seasonal beers often marry well with seasonal foods. Think Hefeweizen or another, similarly summery white/wheat beer with salad, or seafood, or hot dogs from the grill. Think winter-warming Scottish ale with a beef or lamb stew laden with root vegetables.

Rule #4: Ratchet up the flavor. This only-sometimes-applicable rule says, in effect, that it's a good idea to partner beers and foods that *have similar flavors or sensory effects.* Drinkology thinks it best to follow this go-over-the-top rule mostly with desserts, for example, by pairing a pumpkin ale with a pumpkin mousse, or a lemony gueuze with a lemon tart, or a kriek (cherry-flavored lambic) with a slice of cherry pie, or a chocolate stout with a piece of—what else?—chocolate cake. But applying the rule can also work when pairing beers and cheeses. For instance, accompanying a very sharp cheddar with a bitterly hoppy IPA can deliver a double-whammy punch that'll knock you out (in the good sense). And who could argue with the logic of putting together a Chimay Trappist ale with a beer-washed Chimay cheese produced by the same Belgian monastic brewers?

Rule #5: But watch out *for those hops.* There are very few no-no's when it comes to matching beer with food, but here's one you definitely ought to take into account: unless torturing your tongue gives you a sort of S/M pleasure, don't pair extremely hoppy beers (e.g., double or triple IPAs, some American pale ales) with very hot, chile-pepper-spiced food.

How come? Well, the bitterness of the well-hopped beer will likely exacerbate the effect of the capsaicin in the chiles, denying you the refreshment that beer accompanying a spicy-hot meal should provide.

Rule #6: Find a multipurpose, "house" beer. Many meals consist, of course, of multiple dishes of varying flavors. If you don't want to serve a different beer with each course—and, really, who would have the energy to put on that kind of show more than once in a while?—it's a good idea to find a beer that, in your opinion, goes more or less well with *everything.* Drinkology's multipurpose, "house" beer is Yuengling Amber Lager, but we think that any good non-pilsner lager that's moderately dark and medium-bodied (a bock, maybe?) would do just fine. Such beers are light enough not to obliterate light fare, substantial enough to hold their own against the likes of red meat, and not so hoppy as to present any danger when served with spicy food.

We've barely begun to set the table when it comes to pairing beer and food. There are a number of good books on the topic, including *The Brewmaster's Table: Discovering the Pleasures of Real Beer with Real Food,* by Brooklyn Brewery brewmaster Garrett Oliver (Ecco, 2005), and *He Said Beer, She Said Wine,* by Dogfish Head maestro Sam Calagione and sommelier Marnie Old (DK Publications, 2009). You'll also find advice and ideas at websites like Craftbeer.com and Brewersassociation.org.

Rule #7: Forget the rules. Most important, though, is that you learn to adopt a freewheeling attitude—straying from the rules whenever you think that something *might* work. After all, there are some time-honored combinations—for example, dry stout with raw oysters—that a devoted rule follower might find absurd but that are, in fact, just right. Experiment bravely, and you'll find others.

Home Run (Or, How I Brewed My Own Beer and Drank It, Too)

BY TONY MOORE

> Many a man who thinks to found a home discovers
> that he has merely opened a tavern for his friends.
>> —NORMAN DOUGLAS

[Editor's note: Drinkology is temperamentally unsuited to home brewing. We're not terribly patient (and brewing your own beer requires some patience), and, more important, we kinda like it that there are professional, commercial brewers who do what they do better than we could ever do what they do. Plus, we tell ourself that we're a little short on space to accommodate a home-brewing operation.* Also, it scares us. But we really did want to include something on home brewing in this book, so we couldn't have been happier when our friend Tony Moore offered to write a firsthand report for us of his first-ever home-brewing experience. Note to the unwary: Tony's account is not *a set of instructions. If that's what you're after, get yourself a big, fat book on the subject. Many experienced home brewers recommend John J. Palmer's* How to Brew: Everything You Need to Know to Brew Beer Right the First Time *(Brewers Publications, 3rd ed., 2006); the first edition of the book is available online, in its entirety, at Palmer's website,* Howtobrew.com.*]*

---

* We're lying to ourself. It's perfectly possible to brew your own beer even if you live in a small apartment; suitably petite one- and five-gallon home-brewing kits are available from the likes of BrooklynBrewShop.com. So if you're determined to home brew, do so—no matter how small your lodging.

My friend Fowler got me into good beer (*good* to be defined soon below) in his garage, week by week, while we played Ping-Pong with a bunch of other married-with-children guys from the neighborhood and listened to reggae songs that I grew to hate a little more each week.

When I first started going to those weekly games, I'd bring along beer that I thought was drinkable enough, while also being cheap enough for Ping-Pong nights in a garage. Beer that was socially acceptable but that didn't make me dip into the kids' college fund. I'd bring stuff like the local favorite, Yuengling (I live in Carlisle, Pennsylvania), or Heineken or Molson or some others that I've since given up on. (I still don't know a hell of a lot about beer, but I am now a beer snob.)

And then one night, Fowler—who led me to this process, and this essay, in a roundabout way—extracted something from the fridge in the corner of his garage. Maybe it was a Stoudt's Double IPA. Or maybe a Weyerbacher Double Simcoe IPA. Or a Dogfish Head 90 Minute IPA. Whatever it was, it was a "big" beer, with an ABV around 9 percent, about twice what "normal" beer throws at you. And, to judge from my list of possible contenders, it was an IPA, which would be the first kind of beer I'd attempt to brew myself.

Whatever it was, that beer came at me with a lot more than just that liver-twisting ABV. It had *flavor*. Piles on top of piles of flavor. Flavor of a size and shape you might associate with an absurdly fat and rare filet mignon—a filet that somehow involved the deaths of three cows instead of just one. Something obscene and irresistible. The kind of flavor that makes you hold the glass out in front of you, look at the foam clinging to it, and say, "Damn, that is some good %#@&✳ beer!" The kind of flavor that makes you glance over at Fowler to see him doing the exact same thing—staring at his glass of beer with admiration. With deep respect. Maybe with a tear in his eye.

So, yeah, it was delicious, and it stayed that good all the way across my tongue, all the way down, and long after the fact. It was *good beer*, as I now define it.

If you want *good beer* defined more fully, there are places you can go. You can get on websites like BeerAdvocate.com and ratebeer.com and read beer reviews by writers who make wine writers sound like one-dimensional dimwits. Maybe that's overstating the case, but these guys know good beer, and they know why it's good, and they know how to write about it. I don't. I know what I like and why I like it, and it may have everything in the world to do with the beer's smell or its appearance or its mouthfeel—that's right, the way it feels in your mouth—but I can't explain it in those terms, and I wouldn't even want to try. Those guys can pull it off with flair, but I would just feel kind of silly. When Fowler showed me a review that said a beer had "great legs," we started joking about its other anatomical features, and it quickly became clear that neither of us was mature enough for those sorts of metaphors.

So once my love for good beer became a real, breathing thing, I signed up at BeerAdvocate.com. What BeerAdvocate and the other sites do is expose you to lots of great beers that maybe you've never heard about before. They get your appetite whetted for better and better beer. They let you read exchanges among beer enthusiasts, whose exuberance is contagious. And it was probably that enthusiasm that led us—Fowler and me—to want to brew our own beer.

In a moment of idiotic and epic hubris, we thought, The only way to drink beer better than this—better than Victory's or Stone's or Stoudt's or Bell's or Dogfish Head's—would be to brew our own! It was Fowler who first said it out loud: "You know, we should totally brew our own beer!" And so we totally decided to do just that.

HOME-BREW AND FIRE-PROTECTION EQUIPMENT

Fowler and I *knew* that we could brew our own *great* beer. We could do it with a starter kit. We could do it in my basement. I mean, why the hell not?

So I went to Smitty's Homebrew in Carlisle to buy the kit and any other supplies we might need. Now, there is a larger home-brew store about fifteen minutes outside town, but since Smitty's is a two-minute drive from my house, I thought I'd check it out first.

Smitty's occupies the front room of a larger business called Fire Protection & Safety Equipment. You walk in the front door and see the beer-making supplies lining the walls. In the back room are dozens of fire extinguishers and various related items. The owner, Steve Franciscus, got up when I came in, and I told him what I was up to and why. I asked him what I'd need to brew up some beer, and he pointed to the kits on the wall behind me: LD Carlson Company's Brewer's Best Equipment Kit. It was the only brand he had, which was sort of a relief. (On the other hand, he only had two of the kits. Remaining? Or generally in stock? I wondered how much business this place did. . . .)

"Are they easy? As in *as easy as I hope they are*?" I asked.

"They're completely idiotproof," he said. I laughed and thought, We'll see about that.

"So, everything I need to brew is in this box?"

"Everything. Plus you need one of those boxes underneath." He came around from behind the counter and picked one up. These were the ingredient kits, which determined what kind of beer you'd make—anything from Irish stout to India pale ale to German Oktoberfest to robust porter to Scottish ale to whatever else you might want. This was the true idiotproof element, it seemed. Here's what was in the little box of IPA ingredients I chose:

6.6 pounds (liquid) light malt extract (LME)

1 pound crushed Crystal malt

8 ounces crushed Victory malt

2 ounces Cascade hops pellets (for bittering)

1 ounce Cascade hops pellets (for finishing)

dry ale yeast

mesh bag

priming sugar

instructions

The ingredient kits were about $45 each. The starter kit was $110. But I should mention that when I'd first walked in I'd said to Steve that I was going to be writing about home brewing for a book about beer, and he immediately filled out a slip that gave me 20 percent off my next purchase. (Every time I go into a store now, I try to think of a way I might use that "I'm writing a book" line.)

"And what about all these hops?" I asked. When I'd first entered the store, I'd noticed a counter holding lots of bags of what looked like freeze-dried, high-end marijuana. These were, of course, hops: Cascade and Argentinian Cascade and Chinook and Liberty and Nugget and Warrior and Simcoe. That Steve had Simcoe was a real thrill, because my favorite beer right then was Double Simcoe IPA (the unfiltered, especially) by Weyerbacher (Easton, Penn.), and Fowler and I are both a little obsessed with the idea of Simcoe hops.

"Can't really tell you much about them or what to do with them. I only drink the stuff— I don't make it," Steve said. As he went back behind the counter, I had to ask, "So, what **Like an atheist starting a church** would make you open a home-brew store if you don't brew your own beer?" (It seemed a little like an atheist starting a church.)

He said, "There used to be another home-brew shop in town, and"—he gestured to all the fire extinguishers behind him—"you need CO_2 to home brew, and I had it for the fire-protection business, so I sold them the CO_2. And then they went out of business, and—" The phone rang, and he stopped and turned, and that was the end of that. I never did follow up on the CO_2 thing, and I guess Fowler and I haven't evolved far enough to need CO_2 canisters in our home brewing.

By the time Steve got off the phone, I'd forgotten what we had been talking about, so I asked him how business was in terms of home-brew sales. He told me that, the previous year, he did over a million dollars in fire-protection gear and about twelve thousand in home brew. The way he put it was that he'd be on the phone taking a $100,000 fire-equipment order, and some guy would come in and need him to get off the phone to buy a $1.50 bag of yeast. He laughed when he said it, because *I* was that guy.

So, anyway, I bought the starter kit and an ingredients kit and some extra hops. As soon as I got home, I sent Fowler an e-mail:

> well, it can all begin now. i bought the kits, the IPA malt (or whatever it is), and a bag of Simcoe hops pellets (i guess pellets aren't really the way to go, but it was all they had for Simcoe*). when can you get a minute to check it out?

Fowler e-mailed back, saying he'd be over that night, so I went down to the basement to unpack the kit. (As good timing would have it, my wife and I had just had our basement redone, new bar and all, so we now had the nice new side to drink beer in and the old creepy side to brew beer in.) My kids were in the basement, TV on, and I sat at the bar and cracked open the brew kit. Here's what was inside—supposedly everything you'd need to brew batch after batch of delicious beer:

6-gallon plastic fermenter with lid

6-gallon bottling bucket with spigot

hydrometer

"peel and stick" thermometer

airlock and stopper

bottle filler . . .

I'd gotten about this far when I was distracted. My daughter had cranked up the volume on the Hannah Montana movie she was watching. Meanwhile, my boys were wrestling, and one of them

---

* My naiveté shows here. As it turns out, pellets *are* pretty much the way to go.

had banged the other's head into a steel support pole. Once I got things settled down, I went back to the inventory:

siphon/hand pump

racking cane (which I could never remember the name of and called the "caning tube," the "racking glass," or the "caning rod," the last of which misnomers led Fowler and me to crack increasingly stupid jokes about being caned in a Singapore prison for riding a bike in bare feet or whatever else you might get caned for there)

5-plus feet of rubber tubing

bucket clip

bottle brush

several dozen bottle caps

sanitizer

bottle capper (Italian wing-lever type)

home-brewing instruction booklet

I got a pen and started checking off the items on this list against the equipment list on the recipe that had come with the ingredients kit. They differed, but not by much. We seemed to be lacking only two things (which I thought was pretty good): a 14-quart stainless steel pot and a floating thermometer, both of which Fowler picked up at a restaurant-supply store later that day.

ACTS OF GOD AND MEN

It was a miracle that Fowler and I had finally nailed a night down to begin our beer making, because we're as busy as most adults with kids and jobs, and during the previous few weeks I'd always felt a small amount of relief when we'd planned on brewing and then ended up putting it off. But it wasn't just a scheduling thing. There was something psychological about it. Each time, I felt like I'd escaped an inevitable, soul-crushing failure. So when we agreed on that particular Wednesday night, I got nervous.

From what I'd read about home brewing, you could mess up a batch of beer in about a hundred different ways, and just one wrong move could be enough to make the beer undrinkable—or could make it into something that *isn't even beer*. And of course Fowler and I had been telling everybody we knew that we were making

Turn it over to a higher power

this damned beer, so when it all went south we would have to figure out how to lie about what happened so that it would seem that the reason the beer got ruined was more like an act of God than like me accidentally putting my hand into it as I stirred it as it cooled in the sink. I mean, I'd rather tell people that the power went off in the middle of the boil and ruined the beer than that Fowler snipped open the yeast packet over the brewpot and the clipped end fell right in and contaminated the liquid with some rancid bacterium.

And then there was the possibility that even if *none of those things happened*, the beer might still end up tasting like something you should clean your garbage disposal with.

I mean, was I really supposed to buy a bunch of preboxed ingredients and make beer that people would actually want to drink? This began to make no sense to me. But then what happened is that Fowler started to read more and more about the brewing process online and in John J. Palmer's *How to Brew*. He started to look at discussion boards about troubleshooting and cold breaks and hot breaks and trub and dry-hopping and every other topic you might need to know about if you didn't want to end up with a batch of garbage-disposal cleaner. So I started to feel like I would be saved from my own inadequacies by Fowler's ambition to brew a good goddamn beer. I guess I knew when we started that he would have a greater gift for absorbing all this information. It was like when a contractor tells you how he is going to somehow turn a wall into a closet and run wires everywhere and you're just not getting it, but then you realize you don't have to get it. *He* gets it, and so you turn off your worries and turn the process over to that higher power.

So that night Fowler showed up at nine, ready to brew. He came straight from his kung fu class, and I was lying on the couch in the (new!) basement watching the Yankees embarrass some West Coast team on the big plasma TV. We opened a couple of beers—Sierra Nevada's Torpedo Extra IPA (7.2% ABV) and Weyerbacher's Double Simcoe IPA (9% ABV)—and I got the sanitizer ready while Fowler unpacked the new steel pot he'd bought.

Sanitizer is this white powder that you mix with water and wash everything with. The kind that came with our kit was no-rinse, but we rinsed all the sanitized items with purified water anyhow because everything felt slippery and weird if we didn't, and we just didn't believe that this stuff wouldn't somehow affect the taste of the beer. In retrospect, we should have established two things before undertaking the sanitizing process, which we didn't: (1) How long does the sanitizing solution have to stay in contact with the implement you're sanitizing? And (2) do you have to let the sanitized equipment dry before proceeding? The booklet included in our starter kit was surprisingly vague on these points (i.e., they were not addressed at all). We trusted our kit to know what it was doing, and when the booklet didn't mention things like this, we didn't *know* it wasn't mentioning them.

TOIL AND TROUBLE

To begin brewing, you need to pour two gallons of water into the stainless-steel pot. For some reason, I'd bought two two-and-a-half-gallon jugs of purified water, so the first real obstacle for me involved figuring out how to get exactly two gallons of water out of one of them, leaving exactly half a gallon behind. This actually worried me. This is how bad I am at this kind of thing. But Fowler said we should just pour the water up to the two-gallon mark in the fermenting bucket (which we had just sanitized) and then dump it into our steel pot. So we did that, and my faith in Fowler's genius was affirmed.

Having filled our pot with water, I turned on the burner. Fowler filled the mesh sack with our grain (the Crystal and the Victory malt) and started to steep it per the recipe's instructions—which, unfortunately, were vague on a certain, possibly very important, point. The instructions said, "Place the grain-filled bag in the brewpot water and heat to approximately 160°–170° and steep 20 minutes." This might not seem vague. But I guarantee you that when you're standing there heating up a big pot of water with a bag of malt in it and you don't want to totally ruin this batch of delicious homemade beer you're making, it *is* vague. Here's the issue: You are waiting for the water to reach 160 degrees. With a pot this big, that takes a while. But while you're waiting, the bag of grain *is already steeping*. So does the pre-160-degrees steeping time count toward the twenty-minute total? Or not?

We just didn't know. So what did we do? We embraced not knowing and decided that it would be better to steep too long than not long enough, and so we left the bag of malt in the 160- to 170-degree water for almost twenty minutes. It was the very first step in the brewing process, and we already could be doing it wrong. Well, come to think of it, we could also have done the sanitizing

We embraced not knowing

wrong. But we didn't want to run to the Internet with every little question. That would have taken a lot of the fun out of it and been sort of an overall downer.

By the way, I should point out here that you really *don't* want the water to boil when you're steeping the grain, because that will apparently give a nasty taste to the brew, ruining it. But you don't want the temperature too low, either, because then the flavor and color won't come out as they should. It's a delicate balance, although I just can't say how precise you've got to be.

As Fowler and I waited for the grain to steep thoroughly, watching the floating thermometer carefully, we came up with some possible names for this piece:

The Grain-Filled Bag

To Steep or Not to Steep?

That Was a Boiling Sound

Was That a Boiling Sound?

This Is Never Going to Work

Can Children Buy Home-Brew Kits, or Do You Need ID?

Don't Drink Beer While You Make Beer

And then the timer went off and Fowler hoisted out the now-spent bag of grain and let it drip a little into the pot. The instructions explicitly say *not* to squeeze the bag into the wort (which is what the liquid is now called), and it's a good thing they do, because when you see that big, wet mesh bag full of grain, you want to squeeze the hell out of it, wringing every bit of moisture into the pot. There's a real visceral urge there, and we had to verify three times that we were not allowed to give the bag a good squeeze.

At this point, the instructions told us to dump the 6.6 pounds of liquid malt extract into the pot, and so we did. Once the extract hit the water and we added the hops (see below), we'd boil the wort for fifty-five minutes. (The home-brew books advise you to set the tins of malt extract in hot water before you crack them open, because this softens up the liquid inside, making it easier to pour. Frankly, though, when we brewed a second batch a few weeks later, we didn't warm the tins of liquid malt extract, and the extract seemed to pour out just as easily.)

We sniffed like a couple of fiends

What also goes into the boiling wort at this point is your bittering hops. At this stage, adding hops does just what their name states: it makes the beer bitter. (Later, you add more hops—hops of a different kind—for flavor and aroma.) Fowler and I are a little nuts about hops. The brew kit came with three ounces of hops, total, to be added in two stages, but at Smitty's I'd also bought six extra one-ounce packets (more Simcoe, plus some Argentinian Cascade). We were going to hop this batch to hell and back. (Fowler joked that if any went unused, we could chew it while drinking beer. I still think this sounds like a pretty good idea.) We opened two of the little bags of Cascade hops and two of the Simcoe hops and sniffed them like a couple of real fiends—inhaling deeply and making sounds that in another context would be obscene. (They were probably obscene in this context, too.)

"Can you actually add too much hops, though?" I asked.

"If adding too much hops is wrong . . . ," Fowler began, and then he dumped four ounces of hops (twice the amount of bittering hops that the recipe called for) into the pot, and we again sniffed insanely over the boiling wort. (As it turned out, I think we did add too much hops, or too much at the wrong times.) The whole room instantly smelled like hops, and I made a mental note to find an online retailer that sells hops-scented candles.

At this point, we had thirty minutes of boiling until we had to add the next infusion of bittering hops—an *extra* extra shot, and Fowler had read somewhere that this was the timetable to follow—but we had to get the water to boil in just the right way. We soon found out that this was not as easy as you might think, and I still don't know if we ever got it just right. You see, there are boils and then there are *boils*. When we first put the hops in, the water was boiling, but it was not a serious rolling boil. Fowler thought we needed to get it boiling harder, so he edged the heat up a little.

This adjustment started a cycle of micromanaging the heat that lasted for the next fifteen minutes, as Fowler became obsessed with achieving just the right boil. (He also took this time as an opportunity to explain to me how inferior my stove was to his, with its fancy gas and blue flame and whatnot.) The right boil is one where the wort is boiling in a rolling fashion but is not boiling over onto your stove. (As a guy in the bigger home-brew shop told me later, "If you let it boil over, you're going to have one hell of a mess that you wish you didn't have.") And the thing is, the wort will get to the point of boiling over in a split second, so you can't just click up the heat and then turn your back on the pot. (And turning your back on it, to us, was the reason for getting just the right boil. We didn't feel like watching that damn thing boil for an hour.) If the heat's just a tiny bit too high, the wort will get extremely foamy all of a sudden and start to rise very, very quickly—and you either get the pot off the burner right away or your stove gets flooded. We had a hell of a time with this (blame it on my stove), so Fowler was meticulous, like a man dismantling a bomb on a school bus.

So it went on this way—from the wort almost boiling over to almost not boiling at all—for about fifteen minutes. (Once again, we were probably ruining our delicious batch of home-brew beer, this time by constantly changing the temperature.) And then Fowler got it just right: a *perfect* rolling boil that had no intention of escaping from the pot. We watched it, willing this perfect boil to keep going. There was something Zen about watching that wort boil. It was foamy and brown and granular and lavalike, and it just rolled on itself in this endless cascade.

There was something Zen about it

To get some air and to get away from the stove for a minute, we went out into the yard while the wort boiled along toward the next hops addition. The vent over the stove was blowing steadily, and we were surprised to find that the outside of the house now smelled like beer, too. There was no escaping it. Which was a good thing.

When the wort had boiled for thirty minutes, we dumped in one more ounce of Simcoe hops. That left twenty-five minutes until we had to add the finishing hops, boil those for five minutes, and then finally get the pot off the heat—for a total of one hour of boiling. I had been cleaning up as we went, and we had nothing to do, so Fowler took my bike to his house to get more beer. While he was gone, I washed, resanitized, and then broke our floating thermometer. It slipped out of its protective sleeve and smashed on the floor. It was annoying, but I thought we were done with it for the night, so I didn't care that much.

ICE CUBES AND VODKA

Fowler came back with a couple more Torpedoes and we reread the instructions for what to do next. What was coming up next was adding the finishing hops: one ounce of Cascade and two ounces of Simcoe (only the one ounce of Cascade was listed for this step in the recipe, the ingredients for which we took as suggestions instead of scripture). So we waited until the timer told us to add them and we did and then we boiled the wort for five more minutes.

Then we turned off the stove, moved the pot off the hot burner, and turned our attention to cooling down the wort as quickly as possible. We had to get it down to 70 degrees so we could add the yeast and finish up this segment of the process. (The yeast likes it warm but not hot.) We were really getting down to it. And then Fowler asked where the thermometer was, and it occurred to me that we did in fact need the damn thing again. I told him what had happened. Fowler had started taking the whole thing very seriously, so when he looked nervous, it made me nervous.

"But wait," I said. "What about the stick-on thermometer—the one that came with the kit?"

So we dug that one out and gave it a look. It was just a tall sticker that adhered to the side of the pot. It had a vertical scale topping out at 90 degrees and going down to 32 degrees at the bottom.

"Well," was all Fowler said. He sort of wanted to kill me for breaking that thermometer.

We had planned ahead for cooling down the wort. We filled the sink half full with cold water and dumped in two trays' worth of ice cubes and what was left of a small bag of ice. Then I grabbed the pot and brought it over to the sink and sank it into the iced water. Of course, the pot was 160 degrees, so as soon as it hit the water, all the ice melted and the water in the sink heated up to room temperature. The little adhesive thermometer we'd stuck to the side of the pot just sat there, the temperature not even dropping low enough to register. Again, we thought we were on the verge of ruining our first batch of delicious home brew, so I opened up the freezer and improvised. I packed the following items into the sink around the wort pot:

6 freezer packs meant for my kids' lunchboxes

3 generic ice packs meant for the bottom of a cooler

2 frozen lids meant to keep plastic containers of fruit cold in my kids' lunches

1 bottle of freezer-chilled vodka

1 flask containing more freezer-chilled vodka

All that was left in the freezer that might have helped were some frozen pork chops and a strip steak, but I just couldn't do it. So we watched the thermometer and waited, feeling like we were watching our beer die a slow death.

But then the temperature did fall low enough to register at the top of the thermometer. (I had really been thinking—against all logic and laws of nature—that this would never happen.) And then it got a little lower, and then it dropped to the number we were waiting for: 70 degrees. This took maybe half an hour, which is a lot longer than what's called for, so we thought . . . well, you know what we thought. But there it was.

So here's what we did to finish it off:

1. Poured the wort from the brewpot into our sanitized 6.5-gallon fermenting bucket.

2. Left as much of the trub (sediment) behind in the pot as possible.

3. Added three gallons of purified water to the wort in the fermenting bucket, bringing the total to five gallons. More or less. The instructions said to add three gallons of water "until the level [in the plastic bucket] reaches the 5 gallon mark." In our case, it was one or the other: either add three gallons or add enough water to get it to the five-gallon mark. Obviously, some of the liquid boils off during the hour-long boil, so adding the three gallons of water the instructions call for will not get you up to the five gallons. So should you add just three gallons of water or should you add more? No idea. We added the three gallons, hoping that this was the right choice.

4. Sanitized the hydrometer, which looks like a bottom-weighted thermometer, and took the original-gravity (OG) reading. To do this, you float the hydrometer in the wort and see how far it sinks. The side of the instrument is calibrated, and the OG reading gives you your first glimpse of what your ABV is likely to be. Our reading was 1.030—right where it should be for an average ABV of 5 percent. But we wouldn't know for sure what this reading really meant until we could compare it to the final gravity (FG) reading, which we would take once the fermentation stopped. Together, the two tell you just how strong your beer is.

5. Opened the yeast packet and sprinkled the yeast powder into the wort. When doing this (as I might already have mentioned), Fowler thought it would be a good idea to cut the packet open right over the bucket, so when he clipped through it, the snipped triangle fell into the wort. This could have contaminated the whole batch, but by now we were used to the idea of ruining our beer, so I don't think either of us even cared.

6. Filled the sanitized airlock with water (you could use a sanitizer mix or vodka for this, instead), jammed it into the hole in the sanitized lid, and sealed the lid on the mouth of the bucket.

And then we were done with the whole first part of the home-brewing process. And as soon as we realized this, we noticed a packet of Argentinian Cascade hops that we'd forgotten to add sitting there on the counter.

We'd started brewing at nine o'clock, and I was in bed at one.

BOTTLING AND ITS SATISFACTIONS

After the beer had sat in the plastic fermenter for a couple of days, the airlock started to bubble as the yeast ate the sugars in the wort, releasing CO_2. This was immensely satisfying. We now knew that we were getting some fermentation and thought we probably hadn't ruined this part of it. It really started to go, so much so that the beer itself started to bubble out of the top of the airlock. And what came out really smelled like beer. (As usual, we started sniffing around the airlock like dogs at an overturned trash can.)

After a couple more days of mild bubbling (and our removing the airlock a couple of times to clean and sanitize it) the fermentation stopped, and we siphoned the beer, via the racking cane and hand pump, into a five-gallon glass carboy Fowler had bought. The initial kit I bought contained everything you need to make beer, but the carboy is one of those extras that is more necessity than extra. The big idea behind using the glass carboy, which is like a clear, five-gallon beer bottle, is to get the beer out of the plastic before it picks up any stale and nasty plastic-taste elements. Once it's in the glass, it enters the secondary fermentation phase. They call it this, but I can't say it ferments a hell of a lot more (the bubbling, anyhow, has stopped), and I swear no one has a good explanation for why this stage is called this. I'll file it under elements of brewing beer that we didn't get to in this first batch and probably just didn't understand. But this is when you would add various ingredients (coffee, vanilla, clove, or whatever) after the initial ferment—usually more hops, if you are dry-hopping the beer. (*Dry-hopping* means adding hops into the beer after the fermentation. Why is it called "dry" hopping when the whole thing is very wet? I don't know.*) Apparently adding anything extra during the initial fermentation itself just muddies the waters, and the intended taste gets lost in the mix.

If you look back at step 4 in the preceding section, you'll notice that we were supposed to take the final gravity reading before we put the beer into the carboy. Well, we forgot to do it. This meant that we had no accurate idea of the alcohol content of our beer. Since we had done nothing to make it have a higher alcohol content than the recipe called for (5 percent), and since we'd heard from endless sources that there was nothing you could do to get the ABV up after the fact, we just let it go. (Afterward, we figured out that we could have taken the FG reading *in* the carboy. Naturally.)

And then the beer spent two weeks in the carboy settling and fermenting some more (did it really, though?), and it was time to bottle it.

Bottling beer is very easy and is also oddly satisfying. (Any step we did correctly felt incredibly satisfying.) The dull clicking sound the bottler makes as it forces the cap onto the mouth of each bottle never gets old, and the sight of a freshly bottled beer is something you don't get tired of (unless you work in a brewery, maybe). We ended up with forty-two bottles. We were supposed to get fifty bottles, but our not filling the fermenting bucket up to the five-gallon mark stole that last eight-pack, apparently.

Our big recommendation on bottling is this: If you have bottles without labels, as we did (we got them from a friend of a friend who had given up home brewing), use the "sanitize" setting on your

---

* *Editor's note: Drinkology has the same question; see page 33.*

dishwasher to clean/sanitize them. It's that easy. And don't use detergent. Rinse the bottles with *hot* water beforehand—well enough so that they don't smell like beer—and put them in the dishwasher. The end. If you have to reuse bottles with labels, you'll have to either (1) mix up a gallon of sanitizer solution and use the bottle brush that comes with the kit or (2) use your dishwasher and risk having all the labels come unglued and mucking up the mechanical parts in your dishwasher. These are really the only choices.

This first time out, however, we didn't know whether to use detergent when cleaning our bottles in the dishwasher. We agonized over it for five minutes, with one of us thinking it was a good idea and the other not. Unfortunately, we used it. Less than fifteen minutes after starting the dishwasher, we happened to be looking something up in Palmer's book and right away came across his warning against using detergent. (Swearing ensued.) Since this was how just about everything had gone for us all the way through (as you've probably noticed), we took it in stride and waited out what I thought was the hour of my dishwasher's wash/sanitize cycle. And either the cycle always took longer than I thought or the sanitize setting added another hour, because it ended up taking two hours, naturally.

You can probably guess what we did while we waited, so I'll just list them:

Weyerbacher's Imperial Pumpkin Ale (8% ABV)

Dogfish Head 90 Minute IPA (9% ABV)

Stone Imperial Russian Stout (10.5% ABV)

Anderson Valley Hop Ottin' IPA (7% ABV)

Once the dishwasher was finally done cleaning the damned bottles, we did the following:

1. Siphoned the beer out of the carboy and into our bottling bucket. To do this, you hold the bottom of the hose in the carboy just above the trub (the hop/yeast/etc. residue) so you don't slurp that stuff into the bottling bucket. This is the last chance you'll have to leave behind all the trub that you haven't been able to get rid of previously. (On a related note, once we were done, I dumped the trub in the street in front of my house. The next time it rained, my car, parked right in the trub, smelled like hops more than you would believe.)

2. Dissolved our priming sugar in boiling water in a saucepan (five minutes) and dumped it into the beer in the bottling bucket. (This makes the bottled beer carbonate, for one, and they say it also gives you another 0.5 percent toward your ABV. If it does anything else, I don't know about it.)

3. Set the bottling bucket up on top of my washing machine (we were back in the basement).

4. Got all the bottles ready at the foot of the washing machine.

5. Attached one end of the siphoning hose to the spigot on the bottling bucket and put the bottle-filling attachment, at the other end of the hose, into the first bottle.

6. Flipped the lever on the spigot and let the beer make its way down the hose toward the first bottle. At the end of the hose, the bottle filler is designed so that if you touch the tip of it to the bottom of the bottle, the beer flows; when you lift it off the

bottom of the bottle, the beer stops flowing and you can move on to the next one.

As the beer flowed, I filled each bottle to about one inch from the top and then lifted the tip of the hose up and out and into the next bottle. As I did this, Fowler was on the floor with the bottle-capper, capping one bottle after another as soon as I filled them. He seemed to be enjoying it a little too much. But then he said I should do a couple, and I did, and I saw why he looked like he was enjoying himself so much. I can't say how right it all felt when things were going as they should. It really was a unique sensation, like the first time you have sex, or when you cut the umbilical cord of your first child. Okay, maybe not anything like either of those things, but it really is memorable.

And then we were done. All that was left was to put the bottles in case boxes and high-five each other like a couple of ten-year-olds.

FRONT VERSUS BACK END

Oh, and we still had to drink it, which happened a week later. A week is the minimum time the beer should spend in the bottles before you taste it, and two weeks is the minimum time to leave it alone before you start drinking it in earnest, apparently. At least for this kind of beer. But after a week, we had to try it.

First, the pop and hiss of the cap coming off—indicating that the beer did in fact get carbonated— was a massive relief. And this, too, was hugely satisfying. Fowler made some kind of noise that meant, "Did you hear that?" And I made a face with a slight eyebrow lift, which meant, "I did hear it, and I am massively relieved.

I'm starting to think that this might actually work out, despite all the stupid things we did along the way, despite our constant state of low-level drunkenness while brewing, despite dropping things into the wort and forgetting to add hops and take certain readings and breaking the thermometer and adding soap to the dishwasher. I'm feeling it!"

The beer poured foamy—we had to take it very slowly or our glasses would have been full of foam. I'm a big fan of having a head on my beer, but this bordered on the ridiculous. That said, I was happy that it didn't go the other way—flat. Nothing worse than flat beer. But it was foamy and had a great color (a glowing, dark, orangey amber) and smelled very hoppy.

So the foam settled a little, and we drank. This is when I became convinced that we had done something wrong. Or, to put it another way, that one of the many things we had done wrong actually came back and took its revenge on our beer.

It tasted okay at first. Maybe even better than I'd hoped it would. But the back end was not nice. It was bitter, and I don't mean bitter in a good way. It was thin and bitter and left a taste in my mouth that ruined the front end of it completely. (The front end, on its own, was good: hoppy, full of good ale flavor.) To me, it wasn't plagued by the "Oh, this tastes like you made it yourself" issue that you hear about. (That would have been much worse.) What it was, I think, is that we added too much hops at the wrong times and didn't have enough malt to balance it out. It was unbalanced, and there was no getting that balance back.

Everyone we knew—well, except one guy—said that they liked it, that they wouldn't change anything about it, that if they were served our beer in a bar they would think nothing of the bitterness and order a second round. These endorsements didn't ring false, like our friends were just being nice, but I think that had to enter into it. These were our friends, so they had to be kind of nice about it, right?

Fowler was an unrepentant fan of the beer from the start, and I'm not sure if it was because he really loved it or that he loved and took pride in it as he would a son who went on to lead a life of crime. Like he *had* to love it, because it was his, and he wasn't about to admit to anyone **It was like he *had* to love it** that he didn't. I just didn't like it. I tried to—I tried like hell—but I just couldn't convince myself that I wanted to drink it. I'd expected more. I had failed, and this product of my (sort of) hard work was something that I couldn't embrace.

Anyway, it was what it was. In the end, we got close enough to making a drinkable brew that we decided to do it again. I contacted Weyerbacher for our next ambitious attempt. We decided to try to clone their Double Simcoe IPA. Chris Wilson, the head brewer there, sent me the recipe and some words of advice and wisdom: "Remember, experimentation is half the fun. Of course, if the beer sucks, then it was all the fun." And I think that really sums it all up.

Index

Clipper City Brewing Co., 248
Clix Malt Liquor (brand), 168
clones, 62–63, 327
closed fermenter, 40–41
cloudiness: as fault, 264; of
    wheat beer, 204
CO₂. *See* carbon dioxide
CO₂ canisters, 266, 267, 307
Coca-Cola: and kvass, 164
cocktails, 275–83
cocoa: as beer additive, 192
Coedo Brewery, 131, 132
coffee: as beer additive, 95, 192
coffee stout, 192
coke (kiln fuel), 149
Colt 45 (brand), 170, 171, 232
commercials. *See* beer
    commercials
conditioning (stage in brewing),
    41–43; in bottle, 42, 196,
    264; in cask, 42, 98
conditioning tanks, 44
cone-top beer can, 52, 53
Consecrator (brand), 91
contamination of beer/wort, 25,
    262, 310; by *Brettanomyces*
    yeasts, 186
cooking tun, 38
cooling of wort, 39–40, 317–19
Coors (brand), 82
coriander: as beer additive, 115,
    207
corn: as adjunct grain, 69, 101,
    157, 168, 171; in chicha, 100;
    in whiskey, 182, 183
corn beer, 100
Corney (Cornelius) kegs, 266,
    267
corn whiskey, 183
Corona (brand), 279, 280, 281
Country Club Malt Liquor, 169
craft beer/brewing, 152;
    definition, 65–66; in Italy,
    217; in Japan, 130–32;
    movement, ix, 66, 167, 227;
    and pale ale, 150
craft breweries and art, 216
craft distillers, 183

cranberries: as beer additive,
    111
cream ale, 101, 168, 258
Crooked Tree IPA (brand), 128
Crown Cork & Seal Co., 52
Crowntainer beer can, 52
crystal malt, 17, 312
cultivated yeast, 20
Czech beer. *See* pilsner

DAB (Dortmunder Aktien
    Brauerei), 104
Danson, Ted, 229
dark ale, 65, 103. *See also*
    Belgian dark strong ale
Dark Horse Brewing Co., 128
dark lager, 24*n*, 129. *See also*
    amber lager, Dunkel,
    Rauchbier, Schwarzbier
dark malt, 16, 17, 94; in
    Weizenbock, 202; in wheat
    beer, 204–5
Days of Wine and Roses, 226
decoction mash, 37, 107
degrees Plato scale, 60
dextrins, 155
dextrose, 168
diacetyl, 26, 263
Dionysus, 217
distillation, 182, 183; freeze,
    202
Dogfish Head (brewer/brand),
    45, 46, 47, 100, 128, 176,
    244, 250, 252, 301
Dogfish Head IPA (brand): 90
    Minute, 252, 303, 323; 120
    Minute, 128
Doppelbock, 90–91, 92, 194,
    258, 259
Dortmunder ("Dort"), 103–4,
    258
Dortmunder Export, 103, 108
Dos Equis (brand), 279, 280,
    281; Amber, 199
double (descriptive term),
    104–5, 198
Double Chocolate Stout
    Chocolate Cake, 296–98

Double Daisy Cutter IPA
    (brand), 128
double decoction mash, 37
double India pale ale, 105, 122
double pale ale, 105
double red ale, 72
draft beer, 259–61, 265
dried hops, 31. *See also* aged
    dried hops
drinking games. *See* beer games
Dr. Klankenstein (brand), 189
drum roasting (of malt), 17
dry hopping, 33, 321–22
dry stout, 191, 192–93, 301
DUB (Dortmunder Union
    Brauerei), 104
dubbel ale, 67, 70, 78, 87, 95,
    103, 105–6, 197, 198
Duchesse de Bourgogne
    (brewer/brand), 110
Dunaway, Faye, 227
Dunkel, 106–7, 177, 199, 258
Dunkles Hefeweiss, 107
Dunkel Weissbier, 107
Dunkelweizen, 107, 201, 205,
    206, 258
Dutch beer, 151. *See also*
    Trappist ale/beer/breweries
Duvel (brewer/brand), 78

EBC (European Brewing
    Convention) scale, 61
Echigo (brewer/brand), 131,
    132; Stout, 132
Efes (brand), 151
Egyptian beer, 3, 4, 5, 6; and
    art, 214
Eisbock, 91–92, 258. *See also*
    Weizen Eisbock
Elizabeth I, 165
El Mole Ocho (brand), 250
The End of History (brand),
    81, 84
English beer. *See* British beer
English brown ale, 94
Enkidu, 7–9
entire butt, 166–67
Epic of Gilgamesh, 7–9

About the Authors

 JAMES WALLER is the author of the Drinkology series of books, which also includes *Drinkology: The Art and Science of the Cocktail*. He lives with his partner in Lawrenceville, New Jersey, and is thinking about maybe getting a cat.

TONY MOORE is from New York but now inexplicably lives in Central PA with his wife and three kids. He is an editor and writer and races home after work every day to have a cold beer.